TROPIC TEMPER

JAMES KIRKUP

Tropic Temper

A MEMOIR OF MALAYA

READERS UNION
COLLINS
London 1965

This RU edition was produced in 1965 for sale to its members only by Readers Union Ltd at Aldine House, 10-13 Bedford Street, London W.C.2 and at Letchworth Garden City, Herts. Full details of membership may be obtained from our London address. The book is set in 11 point Garamond type and has been reprinted at Collins Clear-Type Press, Glasgow. It was first published by William Collins Sons & Co. Ltd.

Acknowledgments

To David Stacton and Messrs. Faber and Faber for permission to use an extract from *Segaki*.

To Messrs. Collins and Miss Constance Babington Smith for permission to use extracts from Rose Macaulay's *The Towers of Trebizond*.

To Penguin Books, Ltd. for permission to use an extract from *The Travels of Marco Polo* translated by R. E. Latham.

To James Purdy and Messrs. Martin Secker & Warburg for permission to quote from *Colour of Darkness*.

"An' I'm learnin' 'ere in London what the ten-year soldier tells :
If you've 'eard the East a-callin', you won't never 'eed naught else . . ."

KIPLING : *Mandalay*

"I agree with those who have said that travel is the chief end of life."

ROSE MACAULAY : *The Towers of Trebizond*

Contents

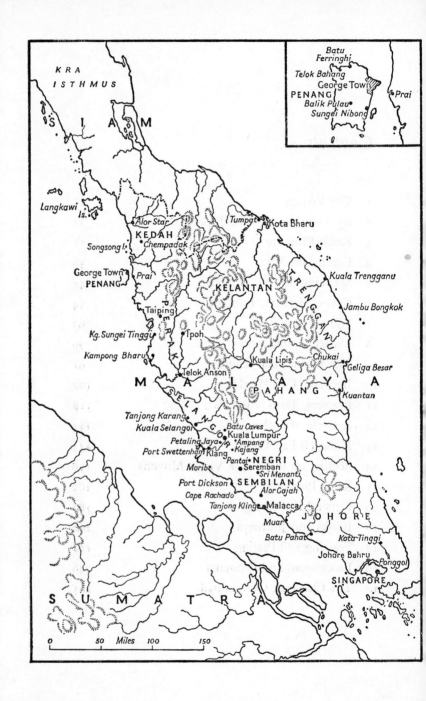

KRA
ISTHMUS

S I A M

Langkawi Is.

Alor Star

KEDAH
Chempadak

Songsong I.

George Town
PENANG

Prai

Taiping

PERAK

Kg. Sungei Tinggi

Kampong Bharu

Telok Anson

M A L

Tanjong Karang
Kuala Selangor

Petaling Jaya
Port Swettenham Klang

Moribe

Port Dickson

Cape Rachado

Tanjong Kling

Tumpat

Kota Bharu

KELANTAN

TRENGGANU

Kuala Trengganu

Jambu Bongkok

Ipoh

Kuala Lipis

Chukai

Geliga Besar

A Y A

PAHANG

Kuantan

SELANGOR

Batu Caves
Kuala Lumpur
Ampang
Kajang

Pantai

NEGRI
Seremban
Sri Menanti

SEMBILAN
Alor Gajah

Malacca

JOHORE

Muar

Batu Pahat

Kota Tinggi

Johore Bahru
Ponggol

SINGAPORE

S U M A T R A

0   50   Miles   100   150

Batu
Ferringhi

Telok Bahang
George Town
PENANG
Balik Pulau
Sungei Nibong

Prai

0

1. The Voyage

September in the pale-golden, tranquil, ever-beautiful city of Bath, where the avenues of lime in Lansdown are heavy with leaf.

Over the trim-gravelled drives of Georgian houses lean the expiring rockets of purple or yellow buddleia, bougainvillea, maroon and white valerian, the ballooning, soap-bubble clumps of hydrangeas, the massed glooms of laurel and blackish-green holly.

From Beechen Cliff or the road to Longleat the city's crescents, circuses and squares, laid out in arcaded and colonnaded and pedimented Bath stone, glow with that reduced " white glare " which Jane Austen's heroines found so febrile and exhausting : but now, in the cool light of early autumn, it looks like a landscape on the moon.

At the hospital, I am having an X-ray taken before my trip to Malaya. Fists behind back, elbows out, chin well up, I stand half-naked at the cold block of glass, in the tense attitude of one awaiting execution by a samurai sword. One chill tear of sweat and apprehension trickles from each armpit and slowly roller-coasts my racked ribs. There is suddenly a piercing light from behind : I am a helpless moth, a butterfly skewered by a blazing pin that seems to pierce the dead centre of my spine. It's over in a second. I dress and wait for the lifesize, translucent photograph, big as a 21-inch television screen. It shows me to be no more than an abstract pattern of bones and tartan hanks of muscle, sinews like twists of smoke, phantomesque and ambisexual. The report says : " The lung fields appear to be clear."

Back home, I undress and lie in bed holding the huge, cold photograph in my arms, trying to warm the dead bones into flesh. I stand it beside my bedside lamp and try to read into its curious negative my life's meaning or lack of it, gazing warily at the impersonal, elemental system that is myself, that screen through which experience flows, sometimes leaving marks and stains as if from illnesses, fractures, deformities, wounds. And there, between one beat and another, the heart in its grate of ribs burns like a lump of coal under the smouldering lung.

A fortnight later and I am aboard a middle-class, middle-aged liner that is to leave Southampton for Penang by way of Gibraltar, Port Said, Suez, Aden, Bombay.

With the utmost reluctance I have bought my first dinner-suit : in the first-class dining-room, the glittering brochures inform me, one is expected to dress for dinner. What would happen if I went in wearing my nice dark lounge-suit instead ? Would they refuse to serve me ? I must try it on.

A gale has been blowing all day and night in the Channel. It is cold in Southampton, whose modern centre is mercifully lit and blessed by swooping gulls.

The captain is ill, though apparently the passengers are not supposed to know this. A friendly bar steward gave me the information as, feeling already semi-colonial, I sipped a well-chilled lager and lime. Our sailing is delayed until the arrival of another captain.

After lunch, the passengers are treated to a free coach-tour to view the vintage cars at Beaulieu Abbey, a delightful jaunt. In Southampton Roads, as we bowl along in our hired coaches, we can see the great ocean liners lying high up in the water, like anchored clouds.

Already on the coaches the usual shipboard friendships and flirtations are beginning, peculiarly shallow, too shallow to be heartless. Behind my smoked glasses tinged with pink, I remain happily unmolested and anonymous. Is this a good thing ? I had determined that this time I would collect people as well as objects and places. I must try a little harder, but not just yet.

There are some bands of Chinese, vast families of them going to Singapore or Hong Kong : they too keep to themselves, steering away from the British. At tea-time in the Abbey Cafeteria the Chinese all sit at the same long table, chattering away animatedly in Cantonese with its complaining intonations that sometimes sound like cross, extra-rapid French.

The Voyage

A few of the British children have Chinese amahs who are unobtrusive, quiet, dutifully devoted to their spoilt, demanding charges. These amahs seem to have extinguished self: they wear black or white cotton jackets with high, stiff collars, wide black satin or lacquered silk trousers, hair severely cut and brushed straight back. One of them still has a long, sleek, black pigtail. The impersonal efficiency of these Chinese women is taken for granted by the children whose every whim they obey.

No one dresses for dinner on the first night. We sit anywhere we like; later we will be assigned to our tables, and also, I'm afraid, to our table-companions. A nondescript couple and an old lady with a rosary share my table to-night. They talk very little; I not at all. A few drinks at the swimming-pool bar after dinner. Not a word to anyone: the people all look awful so I go down to my cabin and read the only modern travel book I've been able to find about Malaya, and incidentally the best one: Donald Moore's *The Young Traveller in Malaya and the China Sea*.

We leave England in the middle of the night. I wake up about 4 a.m. The whole liner creaks and groans as we heave and battle our way down the stormy Channel.

Because of my Viking ancestry, I am never sick at sea. There are only half a dozen people for breakfast in the vast dining-room where the tablecloths are damped to prevent the plates and dishes from sliding about. I am alone at my table. The wooden frames or "fiddles" are in place round the edges of the tables, on which the shivering, slithering cutlery keeps up a constant, chiming chatter like the tintinnabulation of chilly wet elfin bells. The high, dismal waves keep lifting beyond the portholes that look like sick eyes opening and closing their lids in laboured winks as the racing ramparts of water drop and lift with head-aching regularity.

There are Indian, Italian and British stewards. I have a charming Indian table steward from Bombay; he is married, he tells me, to a beautiful Goanese girl, a Roman Catholic like himself, and they have three children, all boys, a fact of which he is very proud. My cabin steward, Ramsbottom—"call me John"—is from Lancashire. He is very efficient and friendly, and does not overburden me with "service": but after breakfast as I loll on my bunk doing nothing he looks in and says:

13

"You all right, sir? Not feeling sick?" He comes in for a chat and borrows my copy of *The Heart is a Lonely Hunter* which he enjoyed. "I never read a book like that before," he is to tell me later, shaking his northern bullet-head and smiling a canny smile at this memory of queer and unexpected pleasure.

Lunch. Only four people. The wine waiter is Italian, from Livorno. He deplores the lack of Italian wines on the wine-list of this very British ship. But I notice some of my favourite French and German dry sparkling hocks and burgundies. They are very cheap, too, less than half what one pays for them in England, and the best vintages.

Towards the end of lunch, as I toy with a *bombe surprise* tasting slightly of ether, the ship gives two particularly bad, lurching rolls: a whey-faced young woman at the next table suddenly claps her hand over her mouth and rushes to the door. Pity. Just too late.

Rounding Ushant it is very rough indeed, and the Bay of Biscay is severely agitated. I wander round a ghost liner, deserted except for the crew, the polite, smiling stewards and a few irrepressible children who are impervious to the storm.

I recline on deck, swathed in rugs, lashed by the flying foam, sleeping, reading, drinking iced hock that adds its scented mist to the salt spray on my rose-tinted sun-glasses.

A few days later. There is a tender twilight view of the Rock of Gibraltar spangled with lamps and gem-like neon. I long to walk those nightfall streets of a strange port, but we're not calling here after all.

The Mediterranean brings us calm seas and sunny weather and perfect, star-crusted nights. Unfortunately it also brings all the other passengers out of their cabins, and they all have tales to tell about their sea-sickness. The ship swarms with unpleasant people and their squalling kids. There is an extraordinary number of pregnant young matrons and O.K. hubbies. The only quiet retreat is my cabin. First boat-drill.

Three people appear at my table, and I prepare for "social contact." One of my table companions, a nurse going back to Hong Kong, is very sweet, and her lively chatter and friendly attentions turned out to be most welcome.

Port Said. Its low waterfront reminds one that it was built on the sand dredged up when the Suez Canal was dug. The "bum-boats," small craft manned by one or two Levantines, are loaded with tourist junk : they come out to meet the ship which will spend a few hours here. They fuss round the big liner in their dozens even before she is properly tied up to the gently-bucking pontoons. The Egyptian boys start bargaining and shouting to the passengers leaning over the rails, some of whom let down baskets on ropes which are hauled up again containing loathsome bits of junk. From a distance, the bum-boats look pretty, their brightly-coloured wares appear like masses of flowers. But as they draw nearer I notice the shifty, cunning look on the vendors' faces, often so much at variance with the beauty of their semi-naked brown bodies, and turn my gaze away from the piles of hideous merchandise—multi-coloured leatherware, poufs, writing-cases, wallets, slippers ; brass ashtrays, rugs, straw hats, neckties, cheap rings, watches, beads and bangles.

I walked in the afternoon town's sweltering heat for two hours, returning exhausted to the ship with impressions of filth, uncharm, roguery, poverty, disease, ignorance, nastiness, dirty postcards. Crowded, dilapidated slum houses round a few splendid new mosques. Fly-blown cafés and souvenir shops ; some odd names here—Simon Arzt and Harry Lauder. And always that horrid look of the calculating cheat behind the flash smiles on the shopkeepers' faces. At night, from the ship, the place looks a little better ; but nothing would tempt me back into that horrid little hell. We sail at midnight.

Next day is Sunday. The ship's service, which I do not attend, is crowded. "Onward, Christian Soldiers" rings out as the ship begins to manœuvre for position before entering the Suez Canal. Cargo-boats, troop-ships and liners are deployed like a war-time convoy, all white, orange and black under a hot sky of poisonous blue. The hubbies stream out of the service, making straight for the bar ; their wives in smart hats obviously enjoy it as a social occasion ; I have the feeling that even non-churchgoers attend, simply because it's something to do, somewhere to take the kiddies and keep them more or less quiet for an hour.

The Canal's dun-coloured banks run straight through the glum desert, with here and there a slight bend. Arab workmen are hacking dispiritedly at stone and cement fortifications placed at depressingly regular intervals along the otherwise featureless banks. In response to encouraging shouts from the lower decks two of the Arab labourers go through vaguely lubricous motions with one another. The heat is stunning, the humidity paralysing: one moves an arm and one is soaked in sweat. The pool is packed.

The brasswork, polished by red-capped Goanese in slow silence, has an evil glitter. In the dining-rooms the scuttles are out over the portholes in order to catch the slightest breath of a breeze.

Soon I am in a state of almost total collapse under the broiling sun of the Red Sea, an ocean of utter tedium. I sleep out in a deck-chair on the top deck all night. It is delightful to waken there after a gentle doze and blink at the gross, scrumptious stars, to watch the gently-rolling masthead lights describing their slow, small arcs among the constellations, to hear the swish and slap of the sea above the growling of engines and ventilator-shafts. It is lovely to walk alone in the warm, grey-pink dawn, with aching hair, in this great house on rollers, watching the leisurely Goanese swab great scarlet reflections of the sunrise across the faintly-swinging decks.

Breakfast : my first meal for several days. The white waves run past the dipping portholes like people waving and drowning. Then a light lunch on deck as we steam towards the Straits.

These last few evenings, at the hour when the crew use the swimming-pool by the bar, there have been full, dark-orange moon risings, hauntingly strange, intensely passionate. It is a dramatic moment when the great brownish-apricot moon hoists its monstrous bulk above the black sea-horizon ; sometimes the deep-golden disc is barred picturesquely with one long, thin black cloud. The stars are like sharp crystal studs loosely screwed into an old Venetian glass cloudy with age. The moon's face, seen looking over the horizon at such apparently close quarters, is more than ever like the face of a man. He looks like a Chinese good-luck god. The face is slightly tilted, which adds to the impression of good-natured jollity. At such moments, it is good to lean over the rail alone with a freezing-cold Dry Martini : I always spit the first mouthful into the ocean, as a libation to everything.

Awful competitive deck-games have been going on ever

since we passed Gibraltar. People play them even at the hottest time of the day. I absolutely refuse to take part in any, or to try my luck in the tote on the ship's daily run. Someone in the purser's office, breathing heavily, laboriously enunciates every morning over the public-address system, in a voice thick with adenoidal cockney : " The towt on the ship's dyly run is neow open at the swim-bin pull. The middle number fer t'dy's run is four 'unred an' twenty height. Four 'unred an' twenty height."

People seemed to enjoy the games less and less as the voyage proceeded. There is now often a good deal of crossness and bickering about who should play with whom. The jolly nurse at my table takes part in all the games and beats everyone at deck-tennis ; I feel proud of her when she tells me the captain played against her and complimented her on her game. She is a great sport, brings me all the ship's gossip and talks with enthusiasm about her Jaguar in the hold. She invites me to visit her in Hong Kong for a spin round the island : an invitation I was never to take advantage of on my trips to Hong Kong.

There are dances in the evenings, and I who thought my dancing days were over give the nurse an occasional whirl to the very stolid ship's band. One evening there was a fancy-dress party : we all had to go as characters from " Spartacus," or at least to go looking vaguely Roman. I devised a sort of pleated kirtle and swirling cape from a single bedsheet and constructed a "gold" laurel wreath and bangles from the outer covers of Benson and Hedges cigarette cartons. The smart thing, when dressing as an ancient Roman, is to wear one golden arm-band *above* the elbow : all the men seemed to know this. I made a large brooch and stuck a sucked raspberry-drop in the centre to make a very convincing and barbaric ruby. I covered a pair of rubber Japanese *geta* with golden paper and there I was, as depraved a Roman emperor as one could wish. Always when I put on fancy dress, whatever the period, I wear it to the manner born, which is to me a sure proof of reincarnation.

After the ball was over, I leaned for a long time on the rail, smoking, gradually undoing my bits of cardboard regalia and casting them upon the silvery wreaths of the ship's moonlit wake.

I also took part in a quiz, the other members of my team

tight-lipped with disapproval when I got anything wrong, though they never got anything right themselves. We won a second quiz, however, and received scribbling pads and metal propelling pencils as prizes. The scribbling pads had bits of metal inside their plastic covers, and the metal was magnetised so that when you put the propelling pencil on the cover it did not roll off. It was the first time I had seen such a useful and ingenious gift.

We reach Aden to-night, 26th September. Early this morning (6 a.m.) I woke from a dream in my top deck deck-chair and saw we were passing twin islets, one perfectly conical, named Abu Ail. A lighthouse, white and minaretted like a mosque, is perched on top of one of them. There are fantastic, wind-whipped clouds looking like a Topolski sketch of Bertrand Russell.

Aden. Surely one of the most hellish hells on earth. Heat, filth, obscurity lit by chill strips of white neon. The grim souvenir-shops gleam with tax-free watches, jewellery, tape-recorders, cameras, all kinds of " consumer goods," all slightly soiled, in an unspeakably sordid profusion. Sailors of all nations swinging the lead. Ragged Arab pimps scuttling side-ways along the dusty roads near the Prince of Wales's Pier in silent frenzies of greed and calculation, trying to interest the slowly-strolling liner passengers in various kinds of wares. Once they are at close quarters they mutter something about " special show," " clean ladies," " nice boys." Other harbour touts, swarthily-bristled, fulsomely-smiling, use one hand to bunch up in front their dubious-looking robes into unappetising cod-pieces, while the other hand makes gestures at once inviting and repulsive. Remarking my disinterest, they, too, make offers of " little sister," " big brother " and so on right through the family.

I stop a taxi, intending to take a quick trip round the port and the surrounding hills before returning to the ship. I have to bargain with the driver before we can start ; but after I've got in a lascivious young tout wedges himself in beside me in the back seat and refuses to get out. We are now spinning along some dark road. He is a smarmy, gum-chewing gent in smart Western clothes and I spend most of the drive trying to defend my modesty. Nevertheless I managed to enjoy the magnificent scenic views of the harbour at night from the winding, steep roads of the mysterious hills.

There is the sordid animation of the flare-lit, camel-haunted market up at Crater Town, where I pay off the taxi and manage to dodge my pursuer only to run into the arms of others. There is constant solicitation, even by respectable shopkeepers and old women and venerable greybeards. The atmosphere of crookedness, filth, stench, shiftiness, slyness and scorn and the bare-faced rooking and robbery is overpoweringly depressing : I wish I were back in clean, honest, courteous Japan.

Back to the oppressive domesticity of the liner : it is like living in suburbia on a perpetual Bank Holiday. I feel sorry for the adolescents on board, who, used to a life of caff, coffee-bar, rock-and-roll and teenage parties, are totally disorientated here, in a life typified by afternoon tea, polite cocktail-parties, evening stengahs in the lounge bar and the smug absurdity of ballroom dancing after a dress-up dinner.

We arrive in Bombay on Gandhi's birthday. Torrential rain all the time we are in port. The pullulating streets, despite their dirt and squalor, have a slightly gayer air than those of Port Said and Aden. There are many white, friendly smiles. At a pretty Jain temple high above the waterfront Indians interrupted their devotions to ask me interested questions, in their curiously Welsh voices : I liked their quiet, candid looks, their questions and gentle laughter.

Parsi towers of silence ; vultures cruising round them, languorously flapping disreputable wings. There is a great deal of Victorian Gothic architecture, solid and dependable, and much more interesting than the Palm-Beach-style concrete blocks of flats along the waterfront. Bombay is a veritable museum of Victoriana. Some of the names chime oddly still : Willingdon Sports Club, Crawford Market, Brabourne Stadium, Ritz Hotel, Prince of Wales Museum, Victoria Terminus. . . .

We pass a large open-air laundry where thousands of soaking Indians are bashing garments on stones. The teeming rain darkly drenches the hides of cattle wandering in the busy streets. Soaking, too, are the brown nags pulling hansom cabs that look like relics from the days of Sherlock Holmes : their drivers' dingy-white robes are soaking, clinging to brown, bony spines.

On this bus tour of the city I sense the utter apartness of the

British mums and dads accompanying me, their invincible dislike of all the foreignness, their refusal to make the most elementary effort of imagination, to identify themselves with what they see, to appreciate anything strange. A car with the bonnet raised and a perplexed Bania business gentleman bending over a small conflagration in the engine is the only thing that for a moment excites my fellow-passengers' interest.

We set sail again after twelve hours in Bombay. The rain is still pouring down over the Gateway to India, that monument to a vanished confidence. Reading Madame de Staël, I note that she says in *Corinne* that the historic landscape is the most beautiful of all.

The Indian Ocean merges somewhere into the Malacca Sea : this final stage of my voyage seems endless. I can't sleep. The thought of Malaya worries me : what is it going to be like ? I pace the decks all night while the Goanese scrub and polish and hoover the lounges, and I feel full of grim forebodings about the future. I'm sure Malaya is not going to be " me." The distant breakers here and there in the dark dawn sea are like suddenly upflung arms, revulsed faces of the drowning, uneasy, quickly-flashed smiles, clapping hands, waved programmes in a dim theatre. I sit at the grand piano on the open deck, draw off the tarpaulin and play some Chopin mazurkas, my face and hands lashed by cadenzas of spray and dying stars like flickering schools of flying fish.

The matt black face of a Goanese deck-hand, its blackness intensified as I look up from a lower deck and see it profiled against the dawn-lit white belly of a lifeboat. The Goanese are always silent, rather elderly but still boyish in their embroidered pill-box hats wrapped round with red or white-spotted green cloths, in their blue, embroidered denim overjackets and white, flapping trousers. I wish I could speak to them, but they are utterly remote.

The last boat-drill before Penang. Farewells to the nurse, the crew and stewards. I gave John what they call a " good drop " : I tipped him well because of his brisk friendliness and because, quite unasked, he had found me an empty cabin to do my typing in. On the whole, I liked the crew very much : they were so much nicer than the passengers.

Finally, the long approach to Penang, which the ship's

folders call " the most beautiful island in the tropics." As we approach, its green hills and palmy shores are overhung by great castles and cliffs of spectacular cloud. There is no one to meet me, and no message of greeting. Even before I disembark, I feel I am unwelcome in this land of clouds.

2. *By Train through the Jungle*

Shortly before we were allowed to leave the ship, it began to rain hard ; it was the late afternoon storm which is usual at this time of the year, from October to February. I had to spend the night in Penang, " the Pearl of the Orient." As I was the last off the ship there were no more taxis left on the quayside. I was taken in hand by an excitable Indian guide who commandeered two underlings to carry my luggage while he went to haggle with a trishaw driver. The latter agreed to transport me and my effects from Swettenham Pier to the E. & O. Hotel.

In Penang, as in Phnom Penh (though not as in the rest of Malaya), the passenger in a trishaw or three-wheeled bicycle carriage sits in a kind of bathchair, rather low-slung, in front of the pedalling driver. A generally very tattered hood or brown oiled-paper umbrella gives the passenger and driver a little protection from baking sun or pouring rain. Though I felt guilty reclining at my ease while a fellow being was used as a piece of sweating human machinery to propel me along, this brief journey was a pleasant one. My Indian guide, smelling of patchouli, squeezed himself in beside me, though there was hardly room for two, and after drawing up a black waterproof cover over our legs laid a bare brown arm along the back of the seat, dangling his incredibly slender hand over my left shoulder. We trundled leisurely through the rainy twilight, and despite the steamy heat I enjoyed this dream-like experience, watching the lights come on round the padang, the great open green space overlooking the sea and bordered by white colonial administrative buildings that were both dignified and pretty. I turned from time to time to watch the driver's wet brown knees rising and falling behind me in a slow, easy rhythm : he was an old man, wearing ragged shorts and a khaki shirt rotted into ribbons as well as a khaki solar topee stained black with oil and sweat.

Strong knees and wiry legs. A noble, lined, unsmiling face, eroded by sun and rain.

We passed a convent school and a Roman Catholic church, both glimmering ghostly-white in the dusk. Malays in sarong and in Western clothes, Chinese girls in samfu, a kind of flowered pyjama suit with short, flaring jacket and Indians in saris and (if they were men) long, grubby-looking white robes tucked up round their waists, wandered by under gleaming black or brightly-coloured, pagoda-shaped umbrellas. There were swarms of children everywhere, some of them Indians in their native dress ; a crocodile of Chinese schoolgirls running into church ; soft-eyed Malay boys gazing languorously from packed buses, their faces superbly sensuous, grave, unsmiling. This was my first deception : the Malays do not smile as readily as the Japanese, and the Chinese and Indians hardly smile at all.

The soft rubber tyres gently rumbled on over the cobbles while the rain drummed on the oiled-paper umbrella. We swept slowly round the forecourt of the E. & O. Hotel where my guide instructed me to pay the trishaw driver one Malayan dollar and asked for a dollar for himself and his hirelings. He told me he would call next morning to conduct me to the railway station.

The vast, domed hall of the hotel was full of bamboo and rotan furniture. I was shocked to hear a party of Englishmen drinking stengahs give repeated, angry shouts of " Boy ! Boy ! " until they were attended to by a bland, slow-moving, elderly Chinese waiter in floppy whites : no one would dream of addressing a servant in that way in England or Japan. The British-colonial arrogance obviously still hung on—though perhaps, I prayed, only in the last remaining Imperial strongholds like the E. & O.—in newly-independent Malaya.

The desk-clerk asked if I would like a " luxury air-conditioned suite " or " just a room in the Annexe." I instinctively chose the latter, and it was charming : a huge white room with two beds, massive, old-fashioned Edwardian furniture and two heavy, three-bladed ceiling-fans. No mosquito-nets, as there were no mosquitoes. There was a private bathroom with a huge " long bath " and a pelting shower. There was an outer sitting-room with desk, chairs and tables, open to the wide corridor which in its turn was open on the hotel garden's leaning palms and stone embankment beyond which rustled the rain-washed bay with a few small, lantern-lit fishing-boats. Scents of magnolia, frangipani and lush, wet greenery : I was glad I had chosen such simple, spacious accommodation, and in my happiness gave large tips to the three silent Chinese " boys " who had carried up my luggage. I was in Room No. 2, the only one occupied that night in the Annexe.

I spent over an hour bathing and changing, then went down to the hall for a drink before dinner—an excellent " Tiger " lager. I obtained immediate service from a Chinese waiter simply by looking at him and raising my eyebrows : it is quite unnecessary, as well as unmannerly, to shout " Boy ! "

There were a number of passengers there from my liner. They were going to take the express train to Kuala Lumpur, where they would spend a night and a day before taking the night express to Singapore, rejoining the liner there. I kept away from them : all that was now in the past for me, and I wanted a clean break with them immediately. I luxuriated in the feeling of being alone again : I enjoy no one's company as much as my own.

After a very British dinner of Brown Windsor soup, roast lamb and two veg. and chocolate pudding, I walked through the hall, under the slogging ceiling-fans, borrowed an oiled-paper umbrella from the porter, who tried to force a black silk one on me, and set off to spend a few hours rambling round the port— Farquhar Street, Transfer Road, Macalister Lane, Penang Road, Maxwell Road, Carnarvon Street, Buckingham Street, Beach Street, Weld Quay, Downing Street, Fort Road, the Esplanade, Light Street. The main thoroughfares were packed with people, trishaws, cars ; on either side crudely neon-lit Chinese shop-houses selling a bewildering variety of clothes, vegetables, fruit, fish. In some of the quieter roads I found myself walking through drifts of pink and white petals fallen from luxuriantly-leaved and blossomed trees : palms and casuarinas sighed in the moist night. There were narrow, dim-lit streets of old Chinese houses. Nearly every street and lane had deep monsoon drains by the sides of the road and running across the five-foot ways, which are raised, arcaded pavements found in the shopping districts of all Malayan towns, a relic of Portuguese influence on local architecture.

By Train through the Jungle

Before retiring for the night, I called at an air-conditioned ice-cream parlour for a milk shake. The place was glaringly lit, with no pretence at decoration and had none of the " atmosphere " found in almost any Japanese coffee-shop. The freezing blast of air-conditioning took my breath away as I came in from the hot and humid night, and soon I began to shiver with the chill. When I went out, it was like plunging into a hot bath.

I wandered back to my hotel. I had spoken to no one, encountered not a single smile. I was wary of the Chinese and Indian shopkeepers who, though not actually dishonest, were obviously on the make : one has to bargain with them in order to get a reasonable price for anything, and I wasn't interested in that hateful sort of commercialism.

It was a long time before I fell asleep. I lay sweating under the single sheet, listening to the boring thump-thump of a dance band downstairs, where Penang society was indulging in one of the favourite Malayan pastimes of choosing the Beauty Queen of something or other, presided over by an almost hysterical Indian " emcee." On the wall above my bedside lamp was a small lizard, known as a chichack, about three inches long, beady-eyed, and light fawn in colour. His little feet with their round sucker-toes were splayed out on the wall with passionate abandon and confidence. A twitch of his tail, and he had darted a few feet to devour a fly. He made a strange clucking sound ; I observed him carefully and noticed that he created the sound by beating his tail on the wall. I eventually fell asleep thinking of a shop I had seen in the main street of Penang selling pretty circular wreaths made of red pom-pom dahlias and the white, waxen flower snowing the grass under the garden trees : frangipani. The scent of the open wreath-shop was heavily sweet. In it, frames of bamboo were padded roughly with straw banded and whipped with raffia or rotan to make a light, neat, circular base for the flowers' pits of perfume. The perfume, piercingly fresh, that wafted through my window and to which I woke next morning : a perfume louder than the Sunday church bells, yet infinitely softer.

My guide, who I now see is wearing a label saying " baggage master," came while I was at breakfast. He hired a taxi to take me to the station : when I asked for a trishaw—it was a brilliantly fine morning—he shook his head disapprovingly. It is considered *infra dig* for Europeans to ride trishaws.

The railway station on Penang Island is the only one in the world from which trains do not run : one takes a boat instead, across to the mainland, to Prai, to get the train. My baggage master was full of gloomy foreboding when I told him I'd lost the keys to my suitcases : he said the customs would not let me through. But there was no examination of my baggage.

The ferry trip to the mainland lasted about twenty minutes and gave me a good view of the lovely Penang Hill with its funicular railway rising to nearly three thousand feet above sea-level. I was to get to know Penang quite well, and came to like it better than any other place in Malaya.

Seen from the ferry, it seemed the most islandy of islands. Again it appeared to be a land of clouds : great crenellated, leprous rain-clouds were already beginning to pile up over it, in all shades of white and grey, with some black wisps and white wisps of fluffy mist over the green-black, furry hillsides. The conical hills shone with bright green in the sun-patches which, when they struck the wind-greyed water, plated it with rough gold. Birds like martens skimming low, giving sudden quick, neat dips that flurried the tops of wavelets. Along the receding waterfront, a bare forest of junk masts, with here and there a brown, ribbed lateen sail raised, seeming to hang on precariously in the breeze like a last, withered leaf.

From time to time, crossing our blunt bows, the elementary, almost diagrammatic silhouette of a near-naked, brown, standing figure leaning strenuously forward as he rowed his thin, shallow craft with one long stern-fixed oar as thin as his arms.

Convoys of junks, squadrons of cargo-ships, swarms of small, one-manned skiffs, called "perahus". Moving water, birds, clouds, skeleton men in skeleton skiffs moving among forests of dead masts, an autumn graveyard of the sea.

A handsome Malay boy in pink singlet and faded blue shorts carried my luggage to my seat in the train's air-conditioned dining-car : again the freezing air strikes a chill, but I am thankful to get out of the heat, already intense, and the high humidity that has soaked my shirt. I ignore the other Europeans on the train. But after to-day I am determined to speak to at least one new person every day, or at least to smile at one.

By Train through the Jungle

Flags wave and the train draws out of the station, causing no emotion; it is so unlike a Japanese railway station—no one seems to care here. (But I must try to stop comparing Malaya and the rest of South-East Asia with Japan: even now I can see that any European whose first experience of the Orient has been in Japan is unfitted to live anywhere else in the Far East.)

The jungle takes over almost as soon as we have left the station; a virulent growth of strangling creepers kept at bay with difficulty along the lonely railroad track and round the few small kampongs or native villages. The jungle gives an overwhelming impression of brooding, lugubrious dullness, lit only very rarely by a patch of colour, stirred only very seldom by the wings of a bird. Greenness—many muted shades—and a sallow yellowness; the rotting brownness of the bedraggled lower leaves of palms.

Clusters of storm-bent, lay-about coconut palms round kampongs of small wooden houses with verandas, all built on stilts, thatched with attap, modestly decorated, standing in neat little gardens where there are big tubs of straggling orchids fixed on three-foot high wooden posts painted white and green. Good hard roads run near the railway from time to time. In clearings, white-cream cattle—oxen, humped and dewlapped water-buffalo. Banana-trees drooping their translucent green fans, the long, broad leaves splitting into fingers and fringes as they slowly coarsen and mature. Giant ferns, touched on the paler green undersides with rust-brown spores. Bushes swarmed over with a cobwebby creeper's lavender-white moon-flowers.

A kampong near a level-crossing whose black-and-white chequered barriers are down. Washing—chequered male sarongs—hanging out in the gardens. Some of the houses have roofs of battered and disintegrating corrugated iron. Some long, low concrete dwellings with rows of doors and windows wide open on a common veranda, workers' hovels occupied by very dark Indians, the women wearing cheap saris of a poisonous brilliance, the children skinny and half-naked. Behind, the lovely misty hump, as fleshy-looking as an ox's, of a densely-wooded hill. The train pauses for a few minutes. Outside my window stands a Malay boy, about fourteen, his swollen upper lids fat and smiling over slit-slant eyes, his broad white smile straight-lipped with vertical lines at the corners. His elegant, slim-hipped, dusky-gold body is clad in a blue and white sarong chequered like a tablecloth and loosely bunched in front, where it falls in easy, natural folds to his bare feet, that look surprisingly old.

Leggy rubber-trees now on both sides of the track, in rigidly geometrical plantations bewilder the eye with flickering vistas. Their very thin greyish trunks look top-heavy with dull-green foliage. They are scarred with slanted cuts like brown chevrons, long-service stripes dangling cups like lockets. A few Malay girls in trousers, shirts and shady straw hats are collecting the latex. Some of the trees have red crosses painted on their bark.

Beside the gravelled track, every blade of grass is bent and shining with dew and rain. Small fields of ripe, feathery barley. Bushes of white syringa. Tea plantations with hillside bushes in long, broad clumps. Scarlet hibiscus everywhere, the national flower. Rice in big flat flooded fields where women in bloomers and straw hats are fishing with very long poles. Herds of grey, mottled, pink-snouted, hairless water-buffalo with spreads of horn like the handlebars of Edwardian bicycles are rolling and wallowing in pits and pools of milky-grey mud. Others stand on the banks where the white sun quickly dries and cakes the slime on their hides. Despite their fierce horns, they are gentle-looking beasts.

Tin-mining. Huge triangular bamboo structures silhouetted against the sky holding up chutes down which cascades milky-reddish water. Red earth-scars, the colour of Cornish earth, on jungle mountainsides where tin is being mined. Red mud and pools and streams; one pool of milky pink at the bottom of a green-grassed, funnel-shaped depression: an old working.

Ghost sections of jungle : ash-grey tree-trunks under hanks of exhausted creeper. Patches of jungle where all leaves have turned brown. Leaves hanging from bare boughs like withered brown bats. The milkiness of rivers—from white to tomato-soupish. Here and there grey tree-stumps, charred and blackened, with sharp points, like jagged molars. Whole trees veiled over with dull creeper. Termite-riddled dead hulks.

Out in the open again : some of these more pastoral regions look almost like Berkshire, especially in the Slim River area. Pink fluffy flowers, clover-size, among coarse grass and moss. Herds of fine bullocks, flocks of ducks. Redrust butterflies.

Orange berries. Huge, elephant-like limestone boulders among tattered banana trees bearing bunches of tiny green bananas. The brilliance of sunlit palm-fronds, newly-sprouted, glittering against the dark tree-shadow of the jungle verges. Suddenly the startling clarity and neatness and primary colours of a railway-signal. An immense, almost cylindrical cliff, like a castle-cake, tree-covered except for vertical sides. Later come two-humped cliffs, (Padang Rengas) mysteriously marooned in the palm and bamboo plain. They have high stalagmitic caves, worn stone fringed and flanged at black entrances. These limestone outcrops becoming more frequent as the train bumbles along southwards at an average speed of 20 m.p.h.

Flashing colours of sarong and kebaya, chequered and batik robes and gaily-coloured signal-levers at pretty country stations with lovely flower-beds—bulbuls, lilies with white beards, magnolias, flame of the forest trees. Whitewashed brick flower-bed borders. " Laki " and " Perempuan "—Gents and Ladies. A little girl in her finery of blue and yellow batik sarong and gauzy vermilion scarf leans sideways out of the windows of an attap-roofed house on stilts, combing out a yard of long, glistening black hair. On the station platform, a rubber-estate worker, Malay woman, wears a green conical straw or reed hat with a patch of pale-blue cloth stitched on the top with black thread. The train moves off again among grasses of an almost lavender whiteness.

Golding coconuts. Gathering-stations for latex : men rolling it out flat between the iron rollers of a kind of mangle. Rough greyish-white sheets of latex hanging outside small houses in whose gardens there are a few rows of young rubber-trees, about six feet high, top-knotted with fresh green leaves that hang down in patterns as regular as a wallpaper's. Then a group of palms ; shaggy, blackish-green foliage, with one or two boys in sarongs leaning against their leaning trunks. A black, cast-iron telegraph pole whose wires swoop away into jungle, where creepers thick as a man's thigh are looped like pythons from tree to tree.

The train pauses outside another village, and I surprise a naked Malay boy, about eleven, walking calmly out of the jungle, his yin and yang nicely balanced. He immediately jumps into a pool of grey muddy water ; when his chest and shoulders emerge his brown skin is dulled with grey slime. I wink at him and he comes out with a long, slow smile. He picks up a large half-decayed banana-leaf lying by the side of the pool, wraps it round his middle, scrambles out of the water and dashes back into cover of a clump of bamboos that the wind gently articulates till they are like pale brown fountains blown over into plumes of fresh green, like spray, at the shimmering top. As the train draws away, the boy's blinding smile follows me like a searchlight. When the train draws in at the village station he suddenly appears wearing a hastily-knotted sarong, the grey slime on his chest and shoulders turning rapidly to fine dust that he rubs off with dark-lined hands. We say nothing, just smile. I get out for a brief stroll on the platform but the stink of rubber soon drives me back into the air-conditioned carriage.

Late afternoon. The train draws into the Edwardian-Moorish-Saracenic railway station at Kuala Lumpur. The name is printed black on vivid yellow boards, just as I had seen it, in a sort of vision, in a travelogue at a News Theatre in Lausanne a few months before. It was just after I had applied for my post at the University of Malaya, and at the time it had seemed a lucky omen.

But now I was not so sure. There was no one waiting to welcome me. I stood sweating in the colossal heat, surrounded by piles of luggage, trying to find a porter. When I did find one he brought along three others to help him carry my stuff to the taxi. I wanted it taken to the Majestic Hotel, just across the road from the station, but no taxi-driver would take me for that short distance. What on earth was I to do? Then one of the Indian porters grunted something, signalled to the other three and they each took up a piece of luggage and bore it on their heads through the subway under the tracks and across the road to my hotel. I followed along behind this khaki-clad train of bearers, feeling more colonial every minute. And very unhappy. And very hot.

3. Kuala l'Impure

Kuala Lumpur, the Muddy Estuary. Cocteau calls it—how wonderful that he even deigned to mention it—Kuala l'Impure. My own version, after one week here, is :

> Skuala Lumpur,
> Stuff it up your jumpur.

It is mid-October, and already the air-conditioned department store presiding heavily over Mountbatten Road displays a gargantuan, British-colonial Father Exmass, with the legend : " Come and visit Treasure Island " in fairy-lights.

The population of Malaya consists of over three million Malays, Indonesians and Aborigines ; over two million Chinese ; and over 800,000 Indians, Sinhalese, Eurasians and Europeans (including Canadians, Australians, New Zealanders, and Americans). The Malays are charming, sweet-tempered, lackadaisical, unbusinesslike, and work mainly as farmers, planters and fishermen. Their gentleness is continually exploited by the Chinese, who are prominent in industry and banking. The Indians generally do menial jobs and work as labourers, though some with superior education work in the professions. After a century of British rule, Malaya became an independent Federation in the British Commonwealth in 1957. This achievement of freedom, still only partial, is known as " Merdeka." There is a Paramount Ruler, the Yang di-Pertuan Agong. The constitution is mainly British, but in religious matters the Kathi or Muslim religious authority exercises magisterial powers.

Malaya is predominantly Muslim, each State having a State Mosque. Most of the Indians are Hindu, though there are a few Sikhs and a few Christians among them. The Chinese are Buddhists, Confucianists or Taoists.

English of some sort is spoken by most people, sometimes very well, but other European languages are practically unknown. The Chinese speak mainly Cantonese, Mandarin and Hokkien, with some Haka. The use of the Malay language is being encouraged, though not with much success among the large numbers of non-Malays who are reluctant to accept it as their national language. The Malays themselves find it difficult to understand the flowery, inflated, ceremonial forms of "pure" Malay which are being advocated. It is all rather a muddle.

I was warned, by a gipsy, not to eat salads or drink water in the tropics. But here I am doing these things and never giving a thought to scorpions, mosquitoes and snakes—pythons, cobras and the deadly krait.

The Federation of Malaya, over 50,600 square miles in area, occupies the southern part of the Kra Peninsula which hangs down from Thailand in the south-east corner of Asia. At its tip lies the island of Singapore. Across the Straits of Malacca lies the Indonesian island of Sumatra, which gives its name to a particularly plaguy wind.

First impression of Kuala Lumpur : Brighton Pavilion gone mad in a rather dull way, and with nothing like the exquisite treasures. The dumpy Edwardian-Moorish red-brick official buildings look as if they had been constructed from some rich child's bumper box of bricks. The Public Works Department has the temerity to floodlight them on ceremonial occasions, when they would better be left in decent darkness.

Originally a primitive Chinese trading centre, Kuala Lumpur has developed into a colonial city as suburban as Wimbledon.

The only beautiful building is the mosque, with its lemon-yellow domes and sighing palms. A decided smell of drains comes from the turbulent, muddy river that runs past it. In Victory Avenue is a statue to Sir Frank Swettenham, one of the founders of Malaya, represented here in cast-iron cocked-hat and sword. Port Swettenham, famed for baked crabs, is named after him.

There are a number of swish modern air-conditioned hotels with their own shopping-arcades, restaurants, bars and cabarets. Their pretentious luxury always bored me to extinction. I much preferred the very moderately-priced and charmingly old-fashioned Majestic Hotel, where I stayed for my first six months in Malaya. At first I had an immense double room with two beds cocooned in white oblong mosquito nets. Like my room in the E. & O. Annexe in Penang, it was comfortably furnished with massive Edwardian coat-racks, wardrobes, chairs and tables and desks. I also had a sitting-room and a tiled bathroom. My apartment was painted in white and lime-green which are almost the official colours of the old hotels and restaurants in Malaya. The rooms were all swinging doors, jalousies, vasistas and slogging three-bladed metal ceiling-fans which kept sweeping up all my papers into whirling snowstorms until I discovered that it was possible to regulate them to a gentler speed. The oblong mosquito nets looked oddly functional : the boy used to tuck them in well under the mattress and in one side of the net was the sort of aperture which is found in Y-front briefs. I had to crawl through this in order to get into bed.

The bed was delicious in many ways. It had a good firm mattress stuffed with locally-grown fresh kapok and I had a " Dutch wife," a long bolster for resting the legs on so that the air under the sheets had a chance to circulate and prevent night sweats, and day sweats too for that matter. The pillows were firm, and from them, as from the cupboards in the room, came a curious musky perfume—a mixture of dried poppy and verbena, a touch of mignonette, and something else quite primal, like dried human hair : the smell is musky-sharp and sleep-inducing. I found the same smell in many other Chinese hotels.

My Chinese boy gave me perfect service, running to my assistance immediately I rang the bell, attending to my laundry and other needs with silent, faintly-smiling good nature. In the mornings, when he came into my room with a chilled orange, a slice of chilled papaya, a pot of tea and *The Straits Times* he would waken me by gently rocking the edge of my mattress and spraying the air, on my instructions, with one of my favourite perfumes. It was delightful to wake up to his impassive smile and George Robey eyebrows and to lie for a few moments watching him pick my clothes off the floor, running the long bath to just the right temperature and using a pair of personal chopsticks, extracted from somewhere in his floppy whites, to place delicately a frail slice of lemon on my freshly-poured tea. The Malayan radio programmes were always frightful, so I would have a record of myself reading my own poems placed on my record-player, and to this I would do my callisthenics and face-twisting exercises. (*So* good for the jowls.)

Tropic Temper

I delayed for as long as possible the awful prospect of going to the University and telling people I'd arrived.

But on my first evening in K.L.—which is how everyone refers to Kuala Lumpur—the telephone, institutionally black, gave a series of merry trills and for a while I toyed with the idea of taking it up. When I did, there was nothing to be heard. Then it rang again and I raised it to my face like a slice of half-eaten water-melon. It was a very vivacious Welsh voice belonging to the wife of one of the English Department lecturers : they wanted me to go out for drinks with them after I'd had a feed. Remembering my resolution to speak to at least one new person every day, I accepted.

They were a charming and entertaining couple. They took me to The Spotted Dog which is the name given to the Anglo-Malayan Club, housed in a sprawling mock-Tudor building lying all along one side of the padang, right opposite the rose-brick minarets and Saracenic arches of the Secretariat building, which was decently shrouded in the faintly lurid green shadows cast by sodium-vapour lamps. We talked about the distant days when Soho was not yet suburban and about the sausages they used to serve at the Black Horse. (They still do.)

As midnight approached, I asked them if there was some other place we could move on to. They looked at each other doubtfully and suggested the Lake Gardens Restaurant, so we went there.

We sat in semi-darkness out of doors at rickety metal tables covered with rain-soaked tablecloths and ate Chinese food with Carlsberg lager. I was glad we were not sitting inside the restaurant itself, a miserable cement structure lit by the usual glaring white strips of neon that makes all food, and most faces, look like mud. It stayed open until about 2 a.m. Apart from the boring posh hotels, this place and the street-stalls in Campbell Road which I was to discover later are the only night-spots in town, unless one belongs to a club, of which there are two or three, all desperately dull. In the Batu Road there are some little, *louche* hotels with "girlie bars " and demented juke-boxes. The whole atmosphere at night is one of lugubriousness and dismal squalor.

After my companions had left me at my hotel, I wandered

round the empty streets.   But they were not entirely empty.
Here and there, on sagging camp-beds outside banks, shops and
offices, bearded Sikh and Gurkha watchmen huddled, watching
me walk past with eyes devoid of expression ; others were lying
asleep, completely covered by a single sheet, like corpses.   In
the five-foot ways along Batu Road whole families of beggars or
penniless country people lay pressed together, sleeping on the
bare pavements.

4. Feeling my Way

The heat was appalling. Even at night I never stopped sweating. I had no car, couldn't have driven it if I'd had one, and refused to take taxis. I travelled about the city for the first few days in buses—I only once saw another European on a bus—and on foot. As soon as I began to move I streamed with sweat, my clothes stuck to my skin, my hair was drenched and dripped on my collar and rained down off my brows over my rose-tinged smoked glasses.

After a few days I changed to an air-conditioned room at the hotel, and this gave me some measure of relief. It was heaven to come in after a stroll, to take a shower and relax in that artificially-cooled cube of a room. I think the boy must have used Cardinal Polish on the bare red tiles of the floor because I noticed the soles of my bare feet were bright red after I'd done my exercises. I invented and drew plans of an air-conditioned suit made of hundreds of perforated plastic tubes through which some sort of electricity would run coolingly while the body-moisture (as I called it in the prospectuses I drafted) drained off into a smart, scented tank which could be carried in a dorothy-bag and emptied at discreet intervals.

Despite the discomfort, I enjoyed walking about the town, poking my nose into unsavoury back lanes and visiting the native bath, a totally uninteresting and utilitarian place, costing only 10 cents, at the bottom of Pudu Road. It made me sad to see the looks of blank astonishment with which I was greeted there : no European had ever been known to enter such a place before. I felt I was an embarrassment and left without speaking to any new person.

I learnt to walk very slowly, but this did not help much because I wanted to practise the new " Slimming Stride " which I had devised to combat obesity, one of the great dangers awaiting all Europeans who live in Malaya and don't like games. This gait is very simple : you have to imagine that the centre of your body is a large ball-bearing on which the hips and the chest can swivel easily. With this in mind, you advance by thrusting out the left hip together with the right shoulder, giving the body a good twist round the waistline, then you thrust out the right hip (and foot too, of course) together with the left shoulder. This method of walking may look odd and feel unnatural at first, but with practice you soon get used to it and do it spontaneously. It certainly reduces the waist. But in hot countries, it does make you flushed and sticky in a very few moments. Still, better than cricket.

I liked the Chinese quarters of the city where all the tailors live and work in one part of a street, all the watch-menders in another. In one street, there were several locksmiths with hanks of old keys squatting at the pavement's edge. In High Street, not far from a Chinese temple, there were Indian hill tribesmen, Nepalese, selling polished stones like agates and cornelians, already shaped to fit coarse silver rings. They also had cheap trinkets spread out over part of the pavement in the five-foot way. In another street there were bird-dealers with piles of stinking cages full of agitated wild birds, and pet shops with monkeys, dogs and lizards in the windows. Then there were the rows of Indian shops selling materials for saris, cheap shirts, batik sarongs, gauzy head-scarves with mechanical patterns stamped on them in chopped velvet. I bought myself a lilac and rose-pink checked sarong, such as is worn by Malay males. It is simply a tube of cloth about four feet high and four feet wide : to put it on, you step inside it, fold over the top and fiddle it into a knot over your pelvic girdle. The Malay wears his sarong with unselfconscious elegance, and, if he is slim yet with a handsome *chute de reins*, he displays it with consummate grace.

In another street, piles of fruit and vegetables lay on the road outside the pullulating covered market, which I shall return to later. Old country women in loosely-wrapped turban head-scarves crouched beside squares of cloth on which lay their small stock of goods for the day—a little pile of chillies or red peppers, fresh pineapples or coconuts, dried fish, crabs, garlic, prawns.

Tropic Temper

At many street-corners were barrow-stalls selling sliced pine-apple, clutches of small, tough but very tasty bananas like monstrous mutation-hands, grinning slices of strawberry-fleshed, black-seeded melon. Some vendors had their fruit under steamy glass cloches : those who didn't provided a bowl of water in which one washed off the dust from the street.

The bridge near the Cold Storage is the haunt of the professional beggars, many of them Indian children. There are one or two cripples who squat on the pavement of the bridge, facing the mosque, displaying sun-tanned deformities. The Malays and Indians are generous and many as they walk across the bridge drop a small coin in each of the tendered enamel bowls, some of which are wearing out at the bottom. The Malays are particularly generous before or after visiting the Mosque at noon on Fridays, or on the feast days that are public holidays, when they wear their best national dress and the national head-dress, a sort of elliptical black velvet fez called a songkok.

Defeated by the heat, I once or twice entered the Cold Storage restaurant for a yoghourt shake, and found British matrons, released from household chores by the abundance of cheap native domestic labour, drinking coffee, smoking and gossiping. Later their hubbies would come in for lunches of baked beans on toast or fried egg and chips or a watery curry.

In Malay Street, near the bridge, are stalls where Indians fashion balls, chains and wreaths of flowers. Mostly white jasmine, of a heady fragrance. It is pleasant to walk through the hot, smelly streets with a ball of fresh jasmine flowers in one's hand, and to lift it occasionally to the nostrils like an Elizabethan pomander.

Just past the flower-stalls are the open-air barbers, mostly Indians, who set their chairs and small mirrors in the shade of the leafy banyan trees with their trailing brown root-branches. It is a charming, cooling sight to watch the white-shirted barbers at work, to see the silvery glitter of scissors and the tarnished glint of the mirror above a few bottles of Hearts of Love hair-dressing lotion and yellow and green flasks of jasmine and magnolia oils glowing softly as the smiles and the eyes and the brown-lined, pale palms of the " tonsorial artists " in the sun-flecked, scented gloom cast by the shadowy green rafts of foliage.

Farther along is the stonemason's shop, and from the room

above it comes the sound of a masseur tapping swollen limbs with little hammers.

After a few days spent thus strolling round the town I begin to think it really is time for me to betake myself to the University, about six miles out of town, and formally announce my arrival. But no one seems to care whether I am here or not, so I put it off for another day. Besides, the thought of " literature " makes me feel sick : merely to open a book brings on attacks of nausea. The idea of yet once more working through a syllabus—Wordsworth, Coleridge, Shelley; Matthew Arnold ; Dickens, George Eliot, Hardy ; Hopkins, Yeats, Eliot ; Joyce, Virginia Woolf, Graham Greene. . . . How sad and dead and overrated it all seems now, after years of too-intimate contact with it. As for actually teaching the stuff—heaven help us.

Some Indian street-vendors, white dhotis tucked up to reveal skinny, dark-brown legs glittering with black hair, walk along balancing small tables on their heads, the four legs hanging down. They hold the front legs with their hands. They sell things like grilled nuts and peas and chopped dates, roasted kernels, handed to customers in twists of English, Arabic, Hindu or Chinese newspaper. I bought some once : having no small change, I gave the vendor a dollar note, expecting him to give me fifty cents in return but he tucked the note away and walked off rapidly saying he had no change. Another day, caught in a thunderstorm, I had to take a taxi back to my hotel, and the taxi-driver, an enormously fat, elderly, white-bearded Sikh, insisted that he had no change. (Later I found out that taxi-drivers here are always trying this on. Of course, one never tips them.) This atmosphere of petty cheating and rapacity is so depressing.

Bread and cake boys ride on bicycles with large metal cylindrical containers on the carrier. A breadman delivering a batch of new-baked bread to the hotel holds the big, heavy tray at arm's length above his head.

The proud, bold, sabre-like characters sweeping majestically across the headlines of Arab newspapers. The Chinese newspapers with headline characters like little bunches of thorny flowerets. *The Straits Times* and *The Malay Mail* look so very staid beside these. The newspapers from England are at least a month old before they reach us here. Fortunately there are airmail editions of *The Daily Telegraph* and *The Times* and *The Guardian Weekly*. But the sweat from one's hands makes them begin to disintegrate very quickly and it is impossible to read them under a ceiling-fan. In a sense, it is very illuminating to receive newspapers when their news is one month old : one wonders what all that fuss was about in the headlines, now totally forgotten.

There are monumental palms, known as royal palms, outside the Government Offices and the Naafi and the Saracenic-style Railway Administration Building. They are straight as columns, with smooth, greenish-grey trunks. I prefer the ordinary palms : in streets and gardens, the bewitching bend of some of them, leaning forward like slender, dreamy, mop-headed boys in attitudes of impulsive yearning. Their rich, glittering dark-green foliage is feathery and almost black against the lemon-yellow, bulbous domes of the great Mosque, whose slim white minarets appear stiff and prim beside those dusky-green, languorous, noble and frivolous limbs of nature.

The Malays, like some of the southern Japanese, are great expectorators, hawking up gobbets and gouts of phlegm or wide, radiant stars of spit. In the Muslim fasting month, even to swallow one's saliva is to break the holy law. The roads outside the Indian lines are dotted with stars of crimson spit from the mouths of betel-chewers. The Malays always seem to spit just before, and after, the passage of a foreign devil, but perhaps I am mistaken.

The beauties, both male and female, walking and cycling in the streets ; Malay boys with full, soft lips like crushed flowers, figures like minor gods ; Chinese girls, their bones small and delicate as birds', taking neat little pecking high-heeled steps in their tight cheongsams slit to above the heart-shaped knee. I saw one Chinese girl, slim and tall, with the slit at the front, revealing the whole inner thigh as she tottered along. Most delightful of all are the Malay girls in batik sarong and kebaya, a short, diaphanous jacket worn over a modesty-vest or simply a brassière : their breasts are full but firm, and beside them the Chinese girls look flat-chested. Many Malay and Chinese men yearn for very full-breasted, blonde, big European women.

There is an extraordinary variety of costumes in the streets : rags, dhotis, saris, flowery Chinese samfu (the trousers half-mast and the little jacket seductively flared round the plump bottom), the white coat, tight white trousers, sash and turban of bearded Sikhs and Gurkhas ; the Europeans in their vast, wide-bottomed white or khaki shorts, the Australian and British soldiery, jovial, beery-faced, in bush hats and jungle green. Malay men in sweat-shirts and chequered sarongs ; boys with slick hair-do's in Singapore-style wide-bottomed slacks fitting snugly round the thighs and tightly round the hips. The Malays adore finery and smart clothes, and the boys nearly always have crisply-laundered white or flowered or striped shirts. They love new things, especially if they are brightly-coloured, and wear them with a fascinating, easy, natural elegance. Every Malay has a wrist-watch with an expanding metal strap ; and nearly every watch is one that tells the date as well as the time. It is possible to buy these quite cheaply, and really good Swiss makes are inexpensive in the free ports of Penang and Singapore.

The Malayan soldiery have dazzling white walking-out uniforms, coloured velvet songkoks and a silver-threaded purple or green or red ceremonial sarong wrapped round the hips and coming down as far as the knee. There are the khaki-shorted speed-cops in their white crash-helmets ; their short, brown, plump, hairless thighs are revealed in all their throbbing muscularity as they sit astride their broad-tanked motor-cycles.

On ceremonial occasions, Malays wear a sort of pyjama-suit of coloured silk with high collar, and sport a silver-embroidered sarong round their middle, though this is sometimes of the same colour and cloth as the pyjama-suit. Malays from the East Coast and Kedah wear loosely-knotted turbans with one end trailing over the left shoulder. This is called a pemuntal and is a modified form of the Indian turban. Some wear white cloth swathed round the black songkok. Another form of head-dress worn by Malays is the terendak, a sort of sun-hat made of conical cane-work or palm spathe.

There are also many ways of folding the big, starched kerchief in a form of head-dress known as desta, a Persian word. In Selangor, the state in which K.L. is situated, it is called a tanjak ; in Perak it is known as a tengkolok, and on the East Coast it is called kain satangan. This kerchief is usually about two feet by four and can be folded in many ways. The style of folding and the quality of the cloth—cotton, silk, batik or silver or gold-threaded brocade are some indication of the wearer's means and the state he comes from. High-ranking officers of State, royalty and chiefs are the only people allowed to wear the most splendid kerchiefs in the most complicated arrangements. (This is reminiscent of the ancient Japanese laws governing the colour, cloth and style of kimono.) Commoners in Malaya must wear the simple " style of the fowl with a broken wing "—the turban is wound and knotted very plainly, with one loose end thrown over the top of the head and sometimes hanging down to the shoulder.

All these varieties of costume and jewel-like gaiety of their colours do a great deal to enliven the rather dowdy streets of shop-houses and Western-style " contemporary " bank and office buildings.

At Edinburgh Circus, reclining on the grassy " roundabout," half a dozen creamy bullocks with swinging dewlaps like the deep fringe of a Spanish shawl and lovely, big, soft brown eyes are the most contented-looking animals I have ever seen. Their tranquillity and imperturbability are extraordinary. One sees them wandering freely in the streets and slowly sauntering along busy highroads, often unattended, sometimes followed by a little boy or girl with a switch who drives them to graze on the roadside's lush verges. One feels they are sacred animals, but there is a law now against letting them roam the streets. In the papers one constantly reads of farmers being fined for letting their cattle wander, but this does not seem to do much good, for they are frequently to be seen in the city streets, looking quite composed and charming, chewing the cud among rushing taxis, trishaws, lorries and cars. They are a delightful anachronism in modern town life when they move leisurely through the streets drawing slow, rumbling carts. They are heavenly bodies, belonging to the constellations of god-haunted zodiacs.

Unlike myself, they never seem to feel the heat, and always look enviably, superbly cool.

5. Speaking to New Persons

After a few more days putting off going to the palmy groves of tropic academe I got into a taxi one morning and set off for Pantai Valley, the site of the new University of Malaya, about six miles out of town.

My driver was an immaculately blow-waved, blue-chinned young Indian, his plump Indian-film-star visage dusted with a lavender talcum which seemed also to have strayed to his nose, under which was a thin, black, mascara-rich moustache accenting a tiny rosebud mouth.

Remembering my resolution to speak to at least one new person every day, I asked him if he liked driving a taxi. There was no reply so I said: " Which part of India do you come from ? " Still no reply, and I sank back into my seat feeling very discouraged. After ten minutes I felt I really must try again to make contact with the people and asked him : " Where did you get your hair done ? " With one manicured hand on the wheel, he used the other to draw from his shirt pocket a grubby card on which was printed, in English, Malay, Tamil and Chinese : " I am dumb." We smiled at each other and after that got along much better, without saying a word.

The breeze coming through the taxi's open window dries some of the sweat from my face. We are travelling along the new Federal Highway, famous for traffic accidents, and I notice groups of vultures squatting on the telegraph-poles as if waiting for gore to be spilt. Near the Central Electricity Board, the carcass of a dog, squashed flat, as in some horror cartoon film. In the distance, the pretentious modern tower of the Language Institute, a hive of cubicles and electronic equipment for learning languages the scientific way, the deadliest ever invented.

A turbaned Sikh guardian at the gate of the University precincts stops us : it is the first time he has seen me so I tell him my business and he waves us on. We skirt a long, muddy, weedy lake, passing on our left student hostels and the engineering department which has an incongruous entrance shaped like the memorial at Hiroshima. In the distance loom the science and arts faculty buildings and the library, all in severely modern style, quite impersonal. The colour-washed concrete walls are peeling scabrously. At the entrance to the Arts Concourse I pay the driver and arrange to go for a drive with him in the evening : it is wonderfully restful being with someone who can hear but not talk.

Inside the Arts building I meet various academics. I am ordered to start lecturing almost immediately on Henry James, an author I enjoy in small doses : after reading more than ten pages one realises what a womanish fusspot he is.

There is no way of getting back to my hotel : no buses, no taxis, and none of my new colleagues offers me a lift. So I telephone for a Yellow Top cab which takes nearly an hour to arrive : two dollars and sixty cents are already registered on the meter—in Malaya, unlike any other country I know, except Austria (Viennese taxis are the oldest, dearest and their drivers the unpleasantest in the world), one has to pay for the mileage from the taxi-rank if one telephones for a taxi. I refused to do this, and started to walk the two miles or so, in stunning noontide heat, to the main gate, pursued by the irate driver honking his horn. Near the main gate is a bus stop and I waited there for a bus : many Europeans drove past in cars but not one offered to give me a lift. In Malaya, it is almost unheard-of for a white man to walk and not to have a car.

I spent the rest of the day mugging up *Portrait of a Lady*, and was driven nearly off my head by its ponderous urbanity and heavy internationalism.

That evening, a meal of satay at the Gazebo Restaurant, a mournful drive-in lost somewhere in the sad wastes of Petaling Jaya, Malaya's first New Town, as the notices proudly announce. It is simply a blank huddle of concrete boxes : later, visiting academics, I saw that all their houses and all their furniture were identical. The new town, like so many of its counterparts in England, is a dead place—nothing to do, nowhere to go except the Majestic Cinema, a dull Chinese restaurant and the Jaya Bar where one can sit in a wooden cubicle, drink Anchor

Beer and listen to Chinese Opera on the juke-box. (Actually, this is very liberal : juke-boxes have been banned in Singapore.) And to think that the University expects me to live here, in a regulation University house with regulation furniture ! I smile and say I shall be delighted to do so, telling myself all the time, not on your nelly. More and more I feel I was born an Oriental.

The satay dinner was ghastly. Satay consists of bits of highly-spiced meat (not pork, of course) grilled on bamboo sticks over a charcoal fire and dipped in a piquant sauce made with chillies and peanuts. It is eaten with small packets of boiled rice wrapped in coconut leaves. The meat was greasy and the smell of rancid coconut oil which is poured over the grilling satay, sending out putrid clouds of blue smoke, was revolting. I have never liked peanuts, and the chilli sauce was agonisingly hot. But I ate up skewer after skewer of meat, washing it down with copious draughts of lager. We were the only diners in that open-air restaurant, and it was all very melancholy. After eating satay, the waiter tots up the bill by counting the number of bamboo skewers left on one's plate. It is an extremely cheap meal, if one is hard up. Then we were brought thick cups of weak coffee which were literally half full of condensed milk, so that it was impossible to stir it, let alone drink it. All coffee in Malaya is served in this disgusting fashion excepting at espresso bars, which are just beginning to come in, and in clubs and hotels offering Western cuisine.

My first lecture, on *The Portrait of a Lady*. The weather that morning : a slogging, wet heat and an almost blinding haze. I went into the super-modern, air-conditioned University library to cool off a little before the lecture and put on a few drops of Christian Dior Eau de Cologne Rafraîchissante. It wasn't very.

The lecture-theatre was large, air-conditioned, with a film projector in a glass cabin way high up at the back, nearly touching the ceiling. The seats were on such a steep rake and so close to the rostrum that I felt I was standing at the bottom of a well. Green blackboards, all scrawled over : I had to clean their vast expanses before I started ; it was like swimming the Channel in a snowstorm. So I was not in a very good mood when I turned to face my students for the first time. They were first-years—I had arrived in the middle of the second term of the academic year—about fifty of them, mainly females wearing saris, Chinese pyjamas, cheongsams, sarongs or Western-style clothes. Some of them were extremely pretty. Only five men; three of them, wearing glasses, were Chinese: there was one Indian and one Malay, a very good-looking and intelligent-eyed one sitting far apart from all the rest. Curiously enough, I never saw him again: he must have been a wild one.

They understand and speak English, and presumably write it too, with remarkable fluency and accuracy. They get my jokes with the same quick keenness as the Japanese. They also love to be given " outlines " and " projects " and lists of " themes " and " periods " and so on, which is very tiresome. After writing for five solid minutes on the blackboard my arm felt as if it was going to drop off, so I stopped. These students like their Eng. Lit. all neatly numbered and laid out neatly for conversion into exemplary essays. Though they are so bright and good, I feel they are much shallower than the Japanese students I had in Tohoku. They are light-weight, know less, and have none of the Japanese instinctive intelligence and powers of assimilation.

But one can say certain things to them which would not have been understood by many Japanese. I said that James's mature style reminded me of someone trying unsuccessfully to sneeze, and that his prefaces, so illuminatingly unrevealing, were like post-mortems after particularly savage and damaging games of bridge. They scribbled it all down very earnestly, barely giving themselves time to titter.

Afterwards, I was taken by a member of the department to the Jaya Bar, where, in a state of intense depression, I drank bottle after bottle of Anchor Beer. The place was, as usual, empty, though it is supposed to be the Eng. Lit. Dept.'s " local." A radiant Chinese, Mr. Tan, is the egregiously affable proprietor. We drank solidly from 1.30 to 3.30, without eating anything. Three pretty girls in various shades of lilac came in, played the jukebox (" Suku-suku ") and went out. A British soldier in jungle green came and went with a Malay girl. By 3.30 I was fairly aerated and took a taxi back to my hotel where I flung myself on the bed. To my amazement, when I woke up it was 10.30 on the next morning. I had slept soundly for 17 hours: talk about knock-out drops! My Chinese boy had come in and draped the mosquito net around the bed, tucking it well in under the mattress without my waking. My head felt terrible.

Speaking to New Persons

The boy came in carrying his long feather duster (similar to those seen in the back windows of Japanese big-businessmen's limousines), took one look at me and returned in three minutes with chilled oranges, which always restore me in the mornings, and a tall glass of ice-cold tomato-juice, lemon and Worcester Sauce. Then I realised I was not in the right room : I had somehow got into the non-air-conditioned room I had when I first arrived in K.L. I still don't know how it happened, but no one complained and there was no hint that I'd made a mistake.

Everyone here, at least among the Europeans, seems to be deeply in debt and living well beyond his means, which are usually considerable. Among the university staff I encounter people who tell me they are having a continual struggle to make ends meet : the education of children, the acquisition of cars, drink, refrigerators, air-conditioning plants, electrical gadgets (and soon, oh horror, the television) take up all their cash, and very few save anything. Europeans working in industry and those in government departments and commercial firms who have not yet been " Malayanised "—that is, replaced by a Malay— seem to come off best, living in palatial residences set in extensive grounds in the Lake Gardens area of Maxwell Road, where the residence of the Prime Minister, the Tengku Abdul Rahman, is also situated. Many of these posh houses have been only recently constructed in " contemp " styles both pretentious and banal. In the ambitiously-landscaped gardens Indian labourers, both men and women, are constantly seen at work weeding, bent double to cut grassy lawns with tiny sickles, keeping the always-encroaching jungle at bay.

In all the shops, even for the smallest purchase, Europeans are asked automatically if they want to pay cash or credit ; and there seems to be unlimited credit. For the first week after pay-day, bars and hotel restaurants are packed : for the rest of the month they are half-empty. It is a hire-purchase civilization where conversation consists almost entirely of chatter about cars, houses and servants. Most of the Europeans are vulgar without, unfortunately, being coarse, and their society is one of the most hag-ridden and commercially-minded in the East, besides being philistine, anti-intellectual, anti-creative, anti-egalitarian and plain snobbish. Behind the University's brash modern façade there is an almost total lack of intellectual and cultural life, a fact frequently referred to by bored and frustrated students. I felt at the time that besides having come to the world's most boring capital I had also been trapped in the world's dullest university, where most of the staff's free time is spent exhibiting feeble academic wit at endless committee meetings, staff association meetings, faculty meetings. There was no Common Room, no place where the members of the teaching staff could meet each other informally and sociably. I very soon gave up going to their gatherings where one simply sat and listened to people giving displays of academic and committee jargon, instead of meeting them. Stay here for *three years*?

Finding no fellow-spirits among the academics, I endeavoured to make contact with the people in my hotel, which I now rarely left excepting to take my after-dinner walk, when sometimes I was able to " waylay a Maylay " for a chat and a drink. The hotel had a pleasant lounge-dining-room-bar where I spent happy hours writing in my notebooks and observing the flora and fauna of the establishment.

Because the ceiling-fans made such a wind, the ash-trays on the rattan-framed, glass-topped tables were filled with a finger of water, to stop the ash blowing about. The willing and charming Chinese boys served delicious " highballs " made of Johnny Walker, dry ginger, crushed ice and a slice of fresh lime. The servants rarely smile freely and frankly at you as they do at first sight in Japan. A grave, impassive consideration comes first ; only after a few days do the smiles begin to come. The Malays smile a little more readily than the Chinese and Indians, but even they seem deeply suspicious, and this is very saddening, for they have such warm and easy-going natures. They love doing nothing : I sometimes think of them as Malayabouts. The Chinese bar-boys in their loose white cotton uniforms with floppy trousers and sleeves are reminiscent of oriental pierrots, especially when they lift a frail hand in a sleeve's overlong, full cuff. They pad around silently in white shoes, bringing drinks and chits and coasters.

They tell me their names when I ask them : but Chinese names all sound alike to me, and I can never remember them, whereas they always remember my name, though one of them calls me " Mr. Joke."

The food is good and very plentiful : four-course breakfasts, five-course tiffins and dinners. The chicken curry for Sunday tiffin is particularly good, with its rich, really hot sauce containing a curious, ribbed, tasteless vegetable called okras, paper-thin poppadums, crisp jambals or shrimp-flavoured rice-crackers and numerous sambals or side-dishes of chopped egg, flaked cucumber and melon, minced green and red chillies, grated coconut, diced pineapple and papaya, sliced banana and grilled nuts. It is invariably followed by a sago shape called Gula Malacca, with caramel sauce and coconut milk. Later I found that practically every hotel in Malaya serves curry and Gula Malacca for Sunday lunch : it must be an old colonial custom.

In the open, roof-top garden-room, protected from sun and rain by white-painted, split-bamboo blinds called chicks, there are often festive Malay, Chinese and Indian gatherings, and then the hotel is filled with gay, brightly-clad figures, hoarse oratory, Muslim prayers—these make the Chinese boys smile—chanting, dance music both native and Western, and drifting clouds of incense and perfume.

There is a strangely-mewing cat, ginger, with a docked tail, like nearly all cats in Malaya. Her voice is a long, squeaking croak like the sound of a slowly-deflating balloon whistle ; she is complaining over the capture and destruction of her day-old kittens. Her wailing, harsh, worried cry is in a foreign tongue : no Western cat could ever talk like that. She makes sudden, agitated runs and listening pauses, and sniffs not my fingertips but the back of my hand, as if she were a dog. Her fluffy white belly is still distended. The Malays, like the Burmese, reverence cats, but the Chinese apparently do not care for them so much, as it is the Chinese porters in this hotel who have drowned the kittens.

There are fawn-green chichaks on the ceiling above the french windows giving on the garden. One of them is beating his tail passionately as he clings, basking, to the ribbed plastic shade over the long, greenish-white tube of neon strip-lighting. He makes a sound like chinked dry pebbles.

There are orchids, though only the common pinky-blue ones, on all the tables. Orchids also in the lift, on the reception desk and in the vast washroom.

One evening there is a sudden plague of flying ants : they

are everywhere, shedding their scaly, tobacco-brown wings. Drifts of these are swept up by the boys. They are very unpleasant when they get into your hair; frantic swarms of them dance like demented, inverted-snowman snowstorms round all the street-lamps. I am covered with mosquito bites. And there are two flea-bites, circular, shading from a centre of deep, angry red to a pale rose corona; they are like targets, one on the inside of each ankle. The mosquitoes bite venomously through my fisherman-knit socks. Stick insects, praying mantises and giant green grasshoppers haunt the baths of warm light under the standard-lamp shades. And always there is the *cheep-cheep* of the chichak splayed on the wall.

The oppressiveness of the air for the last two days has been almost unbearable—a sweaty heat, with no sun. Such long periods of haze, I am told, are rare in K.L. People are, of course, blaming it on high-altitude H-bomb tests. Not the slightest breath of a breeze.

Last night, as I wandered with infinite slowness through the town's sweltering dark, occasional large lukewarm drops of rain fell gently every few paces, like great soft insects alighting on my hands and hair, as if the air itself had grown deliquescent. There were distant, slow flashes of dull-red sheet-lightning like reflections from a giant, dying conflagration. The stars were totally still, as if stunned into blank immobility round the moon's first quarter, that looked like a bruised, brown, decaying slice of melon.

Figures exhausted by the heat were strolling limply in pale robes under the brooding rain-trees, men and boys occasionally holding each other's hands, sometimes linking little fingers only, because of the heat. Some were lying on benches or in trishaws, crouching by walls or on the grass of the "roundabout" at the bottom of Mountbatten Road, or haunting the dim recesses of the semi-Moorish galleries outside the Post Office and other buildings round the padang.

A young tramp with a beautiful bare back and shoulder was lying on a bench under the over-curving cement arch of a small bus-shelter. I sat down beside him and said, in Malay, what at that time I thought meant "Good evening"—selamat tengah hari—which actually means "Good afternoon." He slowly raised his head with its long, dry, matted hair and gazed at me with dull eyes. " Saya tidak faham " or " I don't understand," he replied, understandably, then fell asleep again. He must have been either drunk or drugged.

But at least I had spoken to a new person. Now I felt free to spend the rest of the evening on my own. I went to the Cold Storage restaurant for a cool-down and a Seven-Up. Cheeky little Indian children officiously opened the doors for me and saluted as I went up the stairs ; they were still there when I came down : they opened the doors, saluted and extended their palms, dark-lined. But they did not have fine eyes so I gave them nothing.

I strolled down Malay Street to the Batu Road, only a few minutes' walk, but it drenched me with sweat so I entered the Oasis coffee-bar for a cream puff and the best cup of coffee in Malaya. From the window I watched the idling crowds of Indians pouring out of the Tamil-language cinema across the road where there were lurid posters of pussy-faced fat Indian film-stars leering smugly down on the car park. There the kreta jaga boys were at work : these are Indian thugs who haunt all the car parks in Malaya, extorting tips from motorists who leave their cars there. If the motorist refuses to pay up, he will find his car scratched or dented or the tyres deflated or slashed the next time he parks his car. The police keep sending the kreta jaga boys away, but they return as soon as the police have gone. They have a fantastic memory for car numbers.

I walked on down the Batu Road, past the Coliseum, Tivoli, Rex, Paramount and K.K. Bars, dim-lit dens with pounding juke-boxes and amiable hostesses continually haggling with the barmen and the proprietor over their cut on the customers' chits. I often used to call at the Paramount, which I liked because it was so pitch-dark : whenever the barman saw me at the bar he would switch off the shaded reading-lamp over the till, and then the whole establishment would be lit only by the glow from the jukebox.

Near the bottom of Campbell Road, outside the Odeon, a large open-air Chinese restaurant was crammed with white-shirted Chinese, and an enormous Chinese wedding-party was leaving in stately limousines, the boots loaded with bottles of beer—Anchor, Tiger and Dog's Head Guinness.

Tropic Temper

Again I was soaking wet, so I flopped into a taxi and returned to my hotel and my air-conditioned cube where, after doing my exercises, I forgot to wash the soles of my feet and left crimson footprints on the sheets when I got into bed.

Next day, the oppressiveness grew to a climax about 4.30 p.m. A tremendous tropical storm suddenly broke. Torrents of rain and downpours of lightning. Thunder abrupt as cartloads of coal being unloaded on the roof, tipped down metal hatches. It sounded like the dragging of heavy furniture through bare lofts by spasmodic giants. Dithering electric lights and wavering ceiling-fans as the current flinches. There is still a non-stop rush of traffic along the road outside the station : soon there come the wailing siren and panic bells of fire-engines. White-shirted cyclists, soaking wet, pedal persistently on through the rain that descends like rain in a film-set storm. Huge flocks of swallows or house-swifts flitter round the hotel's many-nested eaves, soundlessly flying, dipping, swerving, circling, bathing in the rain. A long, slow extinction of lights for at least twenty seconds. Thick, coarse, white, absolutely vertical rain, shrouding everything in its dense, knotted mesh. The flapping, three-bladed ceiling-fans growl and whir by stops and starts, seeming to flog my brain in this rending storm. The rain smashes the garden and the thunder drops on me like large, heavy objects thrown at me down flights of iron stairs. The lightning is wicked. I ring for my room-boy, receiving a thrilling electric shock when I press the button. This makes me more agitated than ever. The boy calms me down by taking out my dolls and puppets ; we play quietly with them until the storm passes, then I have a large vodka and comb my hair and I'm all right again. But it was a nasty turn.

Mr. K.'s 50-megaton bomb. He is like a grinning all-in wrestler with a half-nelson on the screaming world. It makes mere tropical thunderstorms seem very petty indeed.

In the dining-room, the flogging fan blows salt and pepper, sprinkled hopefully over my plate, into deep drifts on my napkined lap. An image of my desolation.

I made the acquaintance of a young Australian staying at my hotel. He has come to Malaya for a holiday. I liked his frank smile the moment he saw me sitting alone in the lounge, and the spontaneous way he immediately sat beside me and entered into easy conversation. I liked also his forthright, charmingly simple announcement of his very plain name, an appropriately manly one ; his warm, dry handshake, his modesty, his disgust with Singapore.

Suddenly, surprisingly, he tells me that he had just become engaged to a girl in Australia and decided at once to take three weeks' holiday, on his own, from his garage business at Woola-maroo near Sydney, as he felt it might be the last holiday he'd have for a long time. He couldn't afford to bring his girl, too, and I suspect didn't really want to. When I asked him what her reactions were to his sudden strange decision to visit Malaya alone, he replied: " She nearly strangled me."

He has a kind of boy's-paper maleness and an apparent lack of complexity. His accent : talking about " pounds " I thought he was saying " peons."

I introduced him to the Australian cinematographer who also lives at my hotel. At breakfast the next morning, Ted was all aglow with boyish wonder at the other Aussie's camera and equipment—" cost over a the-ousand pe-ounds," he gasped. They're off together this morning to film the new harbour works at Port Swettenham.

Ted and I never had much to say to one another after that, though he stayed about a fortnight at the hotel. His very lack of romantic imagination about his girl made him, I thought, extremely romantic. His feelings were like those of a noble savage, obviously honest and uncomplicated by any ideas of " love " or all that slop. An admirable basis for a good, sensible, successful marriage, I should have thought. He was a good ambassador for Australia : he made me want to go there.

6. Caves, Markets, Temples

Ever since I was a little boy in South Shields, excitedly exploring the rocks, fissures, crevices and caverns in the cliffs at Frenchman's Bay, Trow Rocks and Marsden Grotto, caves have had a peculiar fascination for me. As I grew older, rock-climbing scared me deliciously and horribly, but in caves I felt utterly secure and happy, and could scramble about the highest galleries without fear. I loved being enclosed in complete darkness in under-ground passages and going down mines. It made me feel at one with life again, a revivifying return to the tomb.

Before I left England I had read about the famous Batu Caves outside Kuala Lumpur, and soon after I got there I went to visit those remarkable formations, a visit that was to be the first of many more exhilarating ones.

This first visit was made towards the end of October, late on a Sunday afternoon, after a blow-out curry lunch and many bottles of Anchor beer, so I was not exactly in the best condition for energetic exploration. I therefore confined myself to the outer caves ; in any case, exploration of the inner caves and of the subterranean streams can only be done by a stranger if he is in the company of an experienced guide.

Batu Village, over which the fantastic, cathedral-like cliff-caves tower, often wrapped in scarves of mist like a classic Chinese scroll-painting, is about seven miles from Kuala Lumpur. One can go by bus, then walk to the foot of the cliffs, which are part of a massive, tree-crowned limestone outcrop rising very impressively and almost vertically from the plain round K.L.

The entrance to the caves is through iron gates decorated with gaudy peacocks, the birds of Lord Subrahmanya. A short path flanked by small booths selling iced coconut-water, flaked ice with artificial colourings, fresh lime-juice, sickeningly sweet-ened, and the usual brands of belly-busting pop, leads to the foot of a flight of hundreds of steep cement steps that rise and rise dizzily until near the top they turn slightly right to enter the main cave. The unmistakable stink of bats greets me as I begin the climb, with many pauses for eructation, to the top of the steps, where can be seen, yawning ever wider, the vast, stone-draped, stalactite-hung arch, at least two hundred feet high and decorated with pretty weeds and wild flowers, that leads into the main cave.

Two adolescent priests in saffron robes and wearing huge sun-glasses that almost obliterated their faces were sitting on a bench near a little whitewashed shrine in a tiny grotto on the platform at the top of the steps. Have they been paying their devotions to the shrine and to the tinselled, much-eroded image —of what?—that is hung with wreaths of sweet-smelling jasmine buds and flowers? Can the image be some sort of Buddha?

The interior of the main cave, with its lofty, dome-like roof, is filled with the yawps and screeches of Chinese Opera coming from a transistor radio carried by a bevy of little Chinese teen-agers, the girls in crisp Western frocks, the boys in drainpipes and cool white shirts, their thick, jet-black hair slicked and glittering with pomade. How cool they contrive to look! They snap each other incessantly with miniature cameras, in coy poses, all the time chattering away with immaterial twitterings—I feel they have the bone-structures of birds or bats.

There are other caves scattered over the flanks of the cliffs, and most of them are unapproachable without rock-climbing equipment. But I manage to reach one : the stench of bat dung in it is overwhelming : the cheeping creatures are hung in dark semicircles high in the domed roof. There are said to be some albino bats in this cave. One or two raven-like birds and a brilliantly indolent vulture flap round the entrance, waiting for me to fall and break my neck.

I crawl back to the main cave, where there is an Indian temple, neatly enclosed in low brick walls, with two white-washed shrine-grottoes containing tinselled figures. A youthful Indian priest or acolyte, indicibly slim and graceful in a white sarong-like robe falling from his thin hips, comes towards me with burning eyes, bearing before him a dish piled with frangipani and jasmine flowers, powerfully scented. His just-divined buttocks glow duskily like " moons that never wane " through the diaphanous robe. He presents me with a flower and I place a few small coins in his startlingly chilly hand. He has a vermilion caste-mark over a spot of silver on his noble forehead.

Later I hear him intoning a prayer and return to the shrine to see a small, still young Indian woman's figure, clad in red and gold sari, standing with mysteriously withdrawn immobility beside the image in one of the grottoes. At one point in the boy's chanting she joins the palms of her hands and bows her head. The acolyte waves a lamp with a loosely-burning flame in front of the tinselled image then brings the lamp to the young woman. She strokes the flame twice with her fingers, then the youthful celebrant brings her a dish containing something which she raises to her forehead and pops into her mouth. Her hand flutters to her throat as if blessing the object she swallows. The priest then detaches what looks like a string of plucked flowers from the image and lays them in her outstretched hands. She brings her palms together, bows again and moves away, her perfect, reverent gravity queerly contrasting with the young priest's abstracted, almost mechanical ritual movements. They reminded me, in their measured impersonality and carefulness, of those performed by the Bishop over the communicants in the Stefanskirche in Vienna on Whit Sunday.

Back at the bottom of the steps, I stopped to watch a small boy extracting the juice from lengths of sugar-cane by passing them through a mangle. He shoved them through, time and time again, until the very last drop had been expelled and the sugar-cane was cast aside like a bit of broken cardboard. At another of the stalls I saw a boy taking blocks of ice which had been preserved—in this 90 degree heat !—by being covered with fine orange-red sawdust. This sawdust I had often seen piled outside coffin-makers' yards : it comes from the great trunks of reddish wood they saw up to make cheap, primitive caskets for poor people. At another of the stalls, which was ambitiously displaying for sale Cadbury's Chocolate and tubes of Smarties, there was a wooden block holding a slanted blade, like an inverted carpenter's plane. A boy drew a small block of ice towards him over the blade, causing ice shavings to fall into a glass beneath which was then filled with lemonade or coconut juice or the sugar-cane drink.

In the car park, three little white-clad Chinese boys and one irl were playing " giant steps," just as I used to do on Tyneside.

It must be one of those universal games, like hopscotch, (which I have never yet, however, seen played here).

I passed through the Lake Gardens on the way back to my hotel. The well-tended lawns, the English-looking trees, the Anglo-Saxon nameplates on the gates of houses all reminded me of Wimbledon, of Surrey homesteads. Then hedges of flaming hibiscus and screens of pink and blue orchids growing as thickly as an English garden's giant sweet-peas would suddenly bring me back to the tropics.

I stop to inspect the National Museum, housed in little more than a Nissen hut, which was the inspiration of General Templer. After the Emergency, he declared that the Malays must have a " tradition " they could respect, and so this museum was set up. (It is now being replaced by a much bigger and worthier building, in which the contents will be displayed in accordance with the advice given by an expert from the Victoria and Albert Museum.)

There is still not much to display. A couple of cannon (I suspect they are Portuguese) stand outside. Within, some fragments of Chinese pottery, a few bronze figures, a stone ithyphallic lingam. The nicest exhibits are four handsome male attendants in gleaming white tunics, blue ceremonial sarongs round their slim hips, black velvet songkoks on neat brown heads.

Just as I am about to leave, a tremendous rainstorm unleashes itself over the Lake Gardens. After dashing a few hundred yards through the downpour along Damansara Road, the rain mysteriously stops and I am walking on tarmacadam quite untouched by the wet.

At night, the Lake Gardens café again : there's nowhere else to go. Sweating heavily, I try to cool myself by resting my bare arms on the damp tablecloths covering the small tables. Wickerwork chairs, made for dwarfs and very uncomfortable and ancient, are tilted against the table-edges so that they do not collect pools of monsoon rain. Everyone is sitting inside, under cover. To be out there all alone, in the streaming rain, as I was to-night, is to experience vastation.

Some Chinese males, both young and elderly, sport on their beardless faces a few long, carefully-cultivated, silky hairs that sprout monstrously from moles, usually on the chin. Old men's mole-hairs are long, grey and bent or crinkled. Young men's are long, black and silken. One sees them from time to time gently stroking those few straggling hairs. They are very precious to the gamble-loving Chinese, because they are considered to be very lucky, and so they caress them with reverence. But I find my fingers itching to tweak them out.

The top-knotted young Sikh boys, with their straggling tendrils of back hair, make me feel creepy. They sometimes wear a little muslin bag over their precious bun : later, a pre-folded, ready-made turban gives their faces great dignity and nobility.

People here are still talking about Patrick Anderson's lively and amusing book on his life at the University of Singapore, *Snake Wine*. The ones who are most enraged are those who were left out : those who appear in the book still express indignation and display the usual put-on fury, but it is obvious that they are secretly delighted, in a boring, suburban way, at not having been left out.

To-day I saw a trishaw completely covered with reed brooms, bamboo rakes, feather dusters, mops, sink-scrubs, dusting implements made of soft yellow brush-grass and all kinds of native-made brushes and sweeping utensils. The driver, his sweat-rotted shirt in ribbons, sat pedalling at the front wearing faded blue shorts, rubber Japanese sandals—how universal these have become during the last year !—and an ancient, stained pith-helmet. He was very old. He looked like a working god enshrined among the implements of the trade he patronises and blesses. He looked glorious with that sunburst of golden brooms behind him. I stopped him and bought a bamboo rake : it was ludicrously cheap, for something so perfectly made. I practised a few Malay phrases on him, but he did not seem to understand. We stood and smiled at each other for a few minutes, mopping the sweat from our brows in the shade of a rain-tree in Jalan Victory. He was a lovely old man.

Most of the trishaw-drivers in Malaya are old men. They are a dying race, because the government considers that they hold up the traffic of posh cars and stinking diesel lorries and rackety motor-bikes, and so is refusing to issue any new licences for trishaws. Another bit of beastly bureaucracy. It will be a sad day when there are no more trishaws left in the streets of K.L.

They provide a much-needed note of leisurely simplicity and old-fashioned individuality. It is delightful to see a trishaw trundling slowly among the heavy traffic, laden with a flowery bevy of Chinese children or an elegant Malay grandmother in all her finery.

At breakfast, minute flying ants, like very tiny "money spiders" swarming over my table. I put a few crumbs of palest-amber cane-sugar on the tablecloth but they ignore them. The sugar here comes in large crystals, like square glass beads. Finally, one of the ants, instead of just bumping into a crystal and running past it, embraces it, crawls all over it and then rivets itself to the sweetness. A reflex makes it detach itself from the crystal and rush away to tell the others, but before it has gone an inch it is back again, sucking up the precious sweetness. A slightly larger ant comes busily running backwards and forwards through the sprinkling of crystals, but although it keeps bumping into them it does not acknowledge the sweetness and fusses away over the tablecloth's dull white desert to investigate a burnt-out match and a pipe-cleaner. But eventually it cottons on : anti-joy conquered by life's underlying, essential sweetness. It *is* so, or why do we go on living : it is not simply being glibly optimistic to suck life's quintessence whenever we can, to put oneself in shafts of sunlight whenever possible. But like those flying ants we sometimes have to be almost hit over the head with them before we realise the treasures at hand each day. And we are so conditioned to the bitterness and hardness and hopelessness of life that goodnesss and beauty, when they present themselves (for they are always there), go unrecognised, or are mocked because of their shining difference.

The "Sunday Market" in K.L. is actually held every Saturday night. This is because for the Muslims Sunday begins at sunset on Saturday. The market consists of a long lane with shanty shops and cafés on either side. Here are sold all kinds of local cakes and sweetmeats, pewter ware, kitchen utensils (marvellous cake-shapers), funny white woolly hens with broods of woolly chicks underneath, steamed corn-on-the-cob, Malay and Javanese batik sarongs, models of temples and ancient, sway-back-roofed Malay houses, velvet songkoks, embroidered stoles, gauzy veils stamped with velvet patterns, men's checked-tablecloth sarongs, collections of wavy-bladed knives (called keris). Piles of fruit and vegetables, fresh coconuts, their tops trimmed and sliced by a sharp chopper, full of cool juice. Bottles of ice-cold Pepsi-Cola and an orangeade called Green Spot. No beer or spirits available here.

There are hosts of young and older boys, mostly wearing nothing but a sarong tightly knotted round the hips, serving in shops, sweeping, cooking satay, tending charcoal fires and boiling pans of sweet-corn.

After midnight, there are three- and four-year-old boys and girls tucking into bowls of spicy noodles, plates of sliced cucumber; Chinese children eating grilled fish and bowls of rice with quick-flickering chopsticks that shovel the food into their little mouths with terrific speed and agility. They hold the bowls right up to their lips in order not to lose one grain of rice.

One handsome young blade is wearing his sarong draped loosely from his shoulders, where he holds it safely from inside with both hands, presumably to cool his hot waist; most of the boys are naked inside their wide cylinder of checked or striped cotton.

Near the Batu Road entrance to the market there are dense crowds of people watching the antics and listening to the witty patter of Chinese quacks selling rejuvenating potions and body-building " hormone and vitamin " tablets and pink pills to promote " sexual efficiency." They display pictures of muscle-bound, copiously-codpieced body-builders and big-busted American girls as well as pseudo-clinical drawings of the stomach and sexual organs, all in lurid colour.

A narrow wooden bridge over a stream can take only two single files, moving in opposite directions. A notice says that the city council will not be responsible if the bridge collapses. The packed crowd moves very slowly across the bridge, giving rise to opportunities for discreet *attouchements*. This is one of the haunts of the " billy-boys," the name given to young male prostitutes, and of one or two elderly female touts. But for the most part it is the scene of happy family outings, where groups of modest, gentle, friendly country people in gay sarongs can stroll and eat before catching the last bus home to their country kampong.

All along one side of the Campbell Road, another favourite

Saturday-night haunt, are cafés selling Green Spot and Anchor beer. On the pavements in front of the cafés are small open-air kitchens where adolescent boys cook noodles, chop cucumber and grill satay for the customers. The stalls are open to a late hour and always provide an animated and interesting spectacle.

British colonialism, officially frowned on, still remains in street-names like Campbell Road, Mountbatten Road, Treacher Road, Travers Road, Brockman Road, Swettenham Road, Seven Dials ; St. Mary's Church, too, strikes an odd note.

The moon like a half-dissolved Alka-Seltzer tablet.

One day at sunset I visited the great mosque with its three lovely lemon-yellow domes. It is surprisingly small inside. Shoes off at the entrance to the outer courtyard, where there is a notice saying : " No footwear to be worn on any cemented part." A pair of child's rubber Japanese *geta* and a pair of dusty " two-tone " shoes beside my own split and grimy casuals. Inside, a cool dimness, the western windows open to admit the dying sky over the Moorish Central Post Office and the yearning palms of the padang. Long strips of reed matting are laid on the tiled floor.

An elderly attendant in a sarong greets me with a gap-toothed smile and says " Good morning." I thought at first he was making a mistake in English, but I realised later that as the evening is the time when the new Muslim day begins it is logical and natural for a believer to say " Good morning " instead of " Good evening " or " Good night."

There were only a few worshippers on this Tuesday night, old, middle-aged and young men who were standing, kneeling, bowing to the west and Mecca with profound deliberation. Most of them were wearing the black velvet Malay songkok : one does not remove one's hat in a mosque. No women are allowed to be present. One or two worshippers, having presumably made their orisons, were lying flat on their backs on the cool stone floor in postures of elegant ease. One was sleeping soundly. Two little boys were playing pat-a-cake. I watched a stout, prosperous-looking gentleman kneel down with some of the clumsy deliberation of a camel and bow his forehead to the ground : it was not so much a bowing of the forehead to the ground as an elevation of the behind.

As I left, the attendant came with a blunt pencil and asked

me to write my name in the visitors' book. I did so, noticing that the previous visitors that day had been a Canadian doctor and his wife.

Do thieves ever steal shoes from outside mosques? Surely it would be the greatest possible misdemeanour for a Muslim?

I read somewhere later that infidels are not supposed to enter mosques unless invited and accompanied by one of the faithful. But I was always entering mosques alone, and was always welcomed kindly.

Children have been setting off fire-crackers all morning—once right inside the Jaya Bar! They are getting into the mood for Deepavali, the Hindu Festival of Lights which is held to-morrow, 7th November. It is a public holiday.

The day starts for devout Hindus with an oil-bath at dawn. Then all members of the family put on the new garments which have been specially made for the festival and gather before the shrine of Lakshmi, Goddess of Prosperity, Love and Beauty, who they believe comes down to visit the earth on this day. After parents and children have offered up prayers to her, they have a feast of sweets and cakes before setting out to visit friends and relatives or to visit the Hindu temples where special services are held. At night, Hindu homes are bright with oil lamps and fairy-lights are strung outside among softly-flickering candles. Temples, too, are illuminated all night to symbolise the victory of good over evil. It is a time of deep devotion and family rejoicing.

On the morning of the 7th I went to visit the Hindu temple in High Street. The streets were almost deserted, even at ten o'clock in the morning, but a number of shops were open, including Robinson's Department Store, the Cold Storage and Ubaidulla's newspaper and stationery shop.

I was soon running with sweat. I took a few photographs —one of the open-air row of hairdressers in Malay Street, doing steady business, and some of the Mosque. There was a very large number of hideously deformed cripples and mutilated children squatting on the bridge, hoping for generous alms on this festival day.

In the end, it was not the Hindu temple but a Chinese one which I visited. A very obsequious Sikh saluted me as I went in.

Under the main gate was a children's hairdresser with his mirror and bowl, shaving the pate of a two-year-old Chinese boy swathed in rainbow towels. He was sitting absolutely still, transfixed with the importance of the occasion, while his young mother in garishly-flowered pyjamas looked proudly on. An old granny was collecting bits of hair as they fell.

Many small children were playing in the large yard outside the temple. Some old women in black and a few decrepit beggars were squatting on the ground beside the door, eating rice and small scraps of vegetable from bowls brought to them from inside the temple.

Two huge, gaudily-hued lanterns of paper and bamboo were hanging on either side of the main door, whose uprights were of black-painted wood inscribed with massive golden Chinese characters. Two heavy, gilded carvings representing figures fighting or dancing in a landscape of trees, mountains and temples hung within the door before the main shrine, which was all gilded and decked with paper and devout offerings of fruit and rice-cakes and fistfuls of incense-sticks and forests of crimson candles stuck on skewers of bamboo fixed into tubs of sand. Figures of two Chinese sages with long, silky beards were set behind glass in the centre of the shrine.

Everywhere there were Chinese characters of black or gold or vermilion, lanterns, scrolls, billowing clouds of incense from inch-thick incense-sticks. There were several minor shrines, one in a sort of backyard with washing hanging out. Two stalls were selling incense-sticks, imitation paper money, paper kites, lanterns, boats, hats. People were sleeping in the shade; there were groups of friends eating, drinking and talking at bare trestle tables. Two khaki-clad policemen, Malays, were sitting chatting and smoking at another table. Worshippers kept coming and going with burning paper money, clutches of incense-sticks, bits of paper scrawled with characters.

There were various pictures in Chinese style, not very good, and one large, garish, indecipherable oil-painting almost in very bad Ecole de Paris style. A ping-pong table in a side room where two old men were playing mah-jong.

A little girl comes in, takes up two drumsticks, one in either hand, and beats once, simultaneously, a large brass gong and a vast drum like a vat. The combination of the two sounds is curiously thrilling. Before the notes have died away she has dashed out into the sunshine again to play with her friends.

I used to think Japanese Shinto shrines were confusing, but this Chinese temple is simply inscrutably odd; it is much dirtier than any Japanese temple could be, more casual, and, despite all the visual excitement, strangely drab, lustreless, lifeless. How I missed the Japanese gaiety and openness! In a Japanese temple I would have been greeted by smiles and offered sweet rice-cakes and green tea by the priests. Perhaps some student eager to practise his English would have explained things to me. But here, never a word or a smile, despite all my endeavours, only old women's rather forbidding stares, the impassive faces of beggars and children, a feeling that I was an intruder, unwelcome and unwanted. It was very sad. But I shall go back: perhaps it was a bad day. It felt heavy with fall-out.

After that I went to the Green Room air-conditioned café for a cup of tea and a Marie biscuit: it was empty except for the nice Malay boys behind the counter. They accepted cigarettes and put on for me a record of a Malay pop-song, lightly sexy, hoarse and haunting.

One of the boys took me to the great covered market nearby. We entered it by the tall doorway where the stalls of live chickens and ducks and geese stand: the fowls are kept in wire cages or in broad, cylindrical wickerwork baskets, about a foot high, plaited to form a hole at the centre, through which the birds are thrust or hauled squawking out by the unceremonious vendors. The cement floor was slippery with droppings; feathers were flying in a shaft of sun as yet another victim was selected. A shriek and a snap as its neck was twisted. There was an all-pervading, powerful stench, an atmosphere of perpetual, terror-ised suspense among the birds.

It was a relief to move to the fish and sea-food section, where all was comparatively calm, each stall displaying only a small quantity of fish, perhaps just two or three or even just one of a few varieties, all small, together with a few handfuls of parsley-sprigged crayfish, rosy posies.

I hastily averted my eyes from the sight of raw meat hanging in clouds of flies in the butchery section: the meat deep red, in places almost purple, with big gobbets of dark yellow fat.

Vegetables and fruit : a sumptuous display. Great mounds of fresh coconuts. Melons, papayas, thousands of dwarf bananas and some combs of the larger kind. The small ones are much less floury in texture, and are packed with a darker, sweeter flesh. Baskets overflowing with green, golden and black plums, damsons, oranges (green Chinese ones and pale-yellow ones), apples, nuts and grapes. Little boys of five or six are kept constantly sorting the fruit, examining each one swiftly and carefully, putting aside in a special basket any which showed signs of going bad. There was every kind of vegetable : sweet potatoes, cucumbers, gourds, pumpkins, egg-plant, chillies, peppers green and red, sweet-corn, onions, garlic, lettuces, cauliflowers, cabbages and tomatoes—all looking fresh and clean and neatly arranged.

All the assistants in the market were boys and men. Not one of them tried to persuade me to buy. The only things I brought away with me were two savage bites on my right ankle from chicken-fleas. Oh, those pecked, cowed, miserable, anxiety-ridden, silent fowls !

Chinese names over shop fronts : Bang On, Hang On, See Fun, Fun Fatt Kok.

I bought, after some tedious bickering with the Chinese shopkeeper who wanted to charge me five dollars for it, a large bamboo and oiled-paper umbrella for ninety cents, which was still too much, but I couldn't be bothered to go on bargaining. It is lighter in weight than the Japanese ones but not so well made nor so pretty. The bamboo ribs are a house-painter's green, tipped with cheap red paint like rat-poison at the outer ends ; the oiled paper is an opaque yellow-brown, like seaweed. A square of black waterproof canvas is fixed under the metal cap on the top. It opens with much crackling, creaking and rustling.

My girl students, as they slowly slink across the campus, carry vividly pretty silk umbrellas to protect them from the heat. Striped or ringed, the roof of the umbrella is not flat but rises to a sharp point, giving the effect of the top of a pagoda.

On the first rainy night I walk out under my oiled-paper umbrella. Boys riding bikes are wearing plastic macs back to front to protect them from the driving downpour. The sound of the raindrops rattling on my ribbed brolly is like the continuous tapping of a hundred tiny drums. Its shadow, cast sideways on wall or pavement by the street lamps, is purely elliptic. I gaze up at the complex rigging of the interior, with its light, delicate bowl of bamboo struts that is mysteriously illuminated and obscured as I stand at a zebra crossing with the light of the orange Belisha Beacon pulsing off and on, shining through the translucent circular ceiling of golden-brown paper. The satisfying *snunk* of the wooden catch as I push the fat bobbin of wood up the shaft to open the umbrella reminds me of the snunky sound made by the hood of my pram when I was a baby. This umbrella gives me the same feeling of security, in rain or sun, that the hood of my pram did then. Oddly enough, when I have this umbrella up, no one looks twice at me, astonished to see a white man walking the streets at night. No one looks at me at all : the umbrella makes me accepted. So I always go out on rainy nights : at such times I no longer feel I am a foreigner.

7. Some People

Faded oriflammes, tatty old flags and banners, coarse strips of red and yellow bunting have been hung out along Victory Avenue for the Colombo Plan meeting at the end of the month. Immense, vulgar, scarlet plastic hibiscus flowers hang on lamp-standards. They have five small electric bulbs representing stamens. The Town Hall and Federal buildings are all swathed in bunting. Someone has draped a bit of dirty old rag over the head of Edward VII, whose bronze bust stands outside the Secretariat, glowering across the padang at the olde-worlde beams of the Selangor Club. How crude a flower the hibiscus is ! And its giant artificial reproductions hung all over the town are even cruder. But it is the national flower of the Federation of Malaya.

That dim Peninsula Hotel, all tricked out with fairy-lights, looked faintly inviting ; I pushed through the languid swing-doors and found the interior in almost total darkness, which was a blessing. It contained the standard rotan furniture and low, glass-topped tables. In the distance, through an archway, there was a white, fluorescent fizz of light over the blanched cloths on the dining-room's vacant tables. On the wall behind these were three indistinguishable hanging scrolls and two scrolls covered with black Chinese calligraphy.

The hostesses were blowsy Chinese girls in flowery pyjama suits or samfu, Malay girls in wide-swinging dresses with stiff petticoats : with their basilisk-glare of blue eye-shadow they looked like Spaniards. A large, chattering party of Indians was being served with drinks : they were discussing business matters and had no time for the hostesses' genteel attentions. Two of the hostesses, beautiful Eurasian girls in smart frocks, were dancing together to the music of the juke-box.

A stout Chinese hostess with a face like a suet pudding

comes very slowly to take my order: a glass of orange juice, and I have to repeat the order twice. She slops away. The vapulatory ceiling-fans slog overhead. Everyone is moving at half-speed in the tank-like gloom. Discontented fish-faces stare glumly at me as they moon past. It's like being in a haunted aquarium.

The jukebox is like a bottle of highly-coloured boiled sweets; it slams out "It ain't what you do it's the way that you do it." A few potted plants, bamboos, palms droop in corners of the bare, tiled floor.

Only after I've been sitting sweating for five minutes does the Malay bartender languorously switch on a standing fan at my elbow. The overhead fan always makes me feel I'm going to be decapitated by its three whirling blades.

The girl slops back with the orange juice and a chit. She looks as if she's about to sit beside me so I at once put on my dark glasses and turn away to look through the wide-open window at the Shell station, the Selangor Club and the sodium-vapour-lit padang beyond. The window is unglazed: it is simply a deep, open arch. Above it is a tiny lizard, a chichak, well displayed on the wall: he is only about an inch long. He has an almost transparent, pale-brown body, elegantly, almost heraldically contorted; two dark, unwinking, beady eyes, a long, slender tail and five splayed, round-ended "fingers" on each paw. His little angled limbs are spread around his twisted body like those of a baby abandoned in sleep.

A hopeless melancholy and a sense of desperate boredom waft lifelessly over me with every swish of the ceiling-fan. God! why have I come here? Why have I landed myself in this benighted hole? The chichak answers my silent groans with a cheerful, cheeky cheep-cheep.

I consume my drink as if it were slow poison; the straw is bruised, squashed and battered by raw, jagged hunks of ice until I can no longer draw on it. Puddingface unloads her floral backside into the chair next to me. "Another dlink more?" Averting my eyes, I fling down a dollar bill and grope my way out quickly into the damp-hot dark.

I wander to the Lake Gardens, where I can be sure of being alone, and gradually relax with the cool beer, the bloomy dusk of the foliage, the leaning palms like slender schoolboys standing with all their weight on one foot, giving them a slim-hipped, *déhanché* look. The palms look as if they ought, with their tilted mop-heads, to be playing flutes. Some Malay boys are playing the bare-foot Malay football game called sepak raga, using a ball of plaited rotan. Though the Malays are a languid race, they can be extremely nimble at games like sepak raga, badminton and table-tennis.

Some Malayanised English words can be seen everywhere on notices and signboards. They are slightly comical—" talipon " for " telephone," " steshun " for " station," " lif " for " lift," " bas sekolah " for " school bus," " pos " for " Post," " buk " for " book," " kelas " for " class." The plural of words is formed by adding a number 2 : for example, " tickets " is " ticket2." " Man " is " laki " and " the Gents " is " laki2."

There is a lot of talk about the possible merger of Malaya, Singapore, North Borneo, and Sarawak. The Prime Minister is going to London to discuss plans with Mr. Macmillan. Already I have heard one person referring to himself as " a pre-Mergerised Malay." People don't seem to feel very strongly about it : most simply don't care whether they're mergerised or not, and a recent article by John Strachey on the subject in the *New Statesman* was I thought unnecessarily alarmist. Personally, I hope that in this life of take-over bids there will be no more mergers of anything, especially countries. (Therefore no Common Market, please !) I prefer the individualist who insists on remaining himself ; likewise I prefer countries which remain small and keep to themselves. Once they begin uniting, look out for trouble. All these big, united nations are dangerous— Russia, America, Germany before 1945. I wish Malaya would remain unmergerised, but her leaders have very grand political notions, and I fear that merger will come.

In K.L., cyclists and trishaw drivers use the pavements to ride on with impunity. There is a ceaseless stream of bicycles down the pavements of Jalan Victory : pedestrians have to jump for it, because usually the cyclists have no bell and give no warning of their silent approach.

The British Council, I am told, is situated in the very appropriately-named Bluff Road.

The plump Chinese girl attendant was deep in her *True Romance* magazine. She was sitting outside her open-air tea-shop, a small booth in which were massive metal tea-urns scrolled with large gilded Chinese metal characters. Cups of about twenty different brews of tea were displayed on the counter, each cup covered with a steamy circle of glass. I took up a stance with my camera, and the boy in the next booth shouted a warning to the girl; but she was so deep in her romances, she heard neither him nor the cluck of my camera.

At night in the Batu Road, a small Chinese boy frying noodles and vegetables in a large black circular metal pan like a vast, shallow sandbath, outside a restaurant. He added some oil and stirred the lot expertly with chopsticks, in a true cook's slap-dash manner. Another little boy was frying sweet-corn. It smelt delicious.

Again I encountered that middle-aged procuress—or is she simply a poor crazed woman?—who wears very flowery samfu and sits at the front table of the " kedah kopi " or coffee-shop in Batu Road. Whenever she sees me coming, she always jumps up and runs a few steps after me crying: " Tuan! Tuan! Come on, boy, come on then, boy," as if I were a dog. She pronounces " tuan " (sir) like the third syllable of " Widow Twankey." One night I suddenly turned on her and said, quietly but violently, " Frig off." I shall never forget the look of shock on her rather nice face as she stopped dead in her tracks. It was the first time I had ever said a word to her, and I think the shock came from hearing my voice rather than from what I said. She never pursued me again.

Bevies of " billy-boys " parade and undulate arm-in-arm along the road to the station and Jalan Mountbatten, which they refer to as " the street for meeting foreigners." Inviting smiles, a murmured " Hallo." They turn to look back, and not in anger. They are said to be very good-natured; but very mercenary; they're harmless, and I always give them a gentle brush-off.

Around the edge of the padang, the green sodium-vapour lights stain the rich green turf a greener green, making the dark areas between the modern cement lamp-standards seem almost blue. On fine nights, there are always figures lying asleep on the grass, and couples of all sexes, lying on a blanket or a newspaper. If one walks there at dawn, one stumbles over a few beggars wrapped in rags. Boys and girls and old men sit on the

Some People

tiered benches next to the Selangor Club, gazing at the moonfaced Maidenhead dial in the clocktower of the Secretariat, at the ceaseless traffic hurtling down Market Street and turning into Jalan Raja. Boys sit chatting on the rim of the Victorian public drinking-fountain opposite the Chartered Bank.

There is a lovely feeling of ease and leisure here at night among the dim, light-clad figures, the dark-dropping casuarinas, palms, banyans. The brilliant vermilion flowers of the shady flame of the forest; the bright yellow blooms of the angansana tree; the heavy, leathery red blossoms of the tulip tree shelter, at dusk, the cooings of spotted dove and striped ground-dove, the twitterings of innumerable swifts and swallows.

I met an Indian from Madras with a really striking face : big, dark, burning yet gentle eyes with immensely thick black eyebrows over them; very full, dry, well-modelled, dark-red lips parting on a generous smile of perfectly white teeth that sometimes open to reveal glimpses of a tongue whose colour is sheer raspberry-pink. Rather gaunt cheekbones, high-set, a noble hawk-nose, narrow brow, thick, gleaming, tumbled hair and hollow cheeks, each pitted with a cluster of smallpox marks. His tiny ears, his slightness, his hands like—twigs, matchsticks, elegant claws. A fuzz of black hair just peeps over the top pearl button of his open-neck sports shirt. I like his quietness, his silent smiler's soundless laugh, his face unmoving, void of any attempt at expression, except for the eyes and mouth, which tell, and yet conceal so much.

We visited the airport restaurant about 10 p.m. for an excellent meal which we prepared on our own table in a cooking-contraption known as a " steamboat." There was an agreeable tropical darkness over the small tables, each with its own dim lamp. We watched the Malayan Airways mail-plane depart about 11.15. Here where the prevailing winds always blow in the same direction, only one runway is needed instead of the three required in more erratic climates. It was pleasantly cool sitting behind the double white-wire fences bordering the tarmac. It is a very modern airport, soon to be extended, but disfigured by a gigantic, dull mural in the passenger lounge. (There are these huge, flat-looking murals everywhere in K.L. Only a few are worth looking at.) One good thing, at the airport one can weigh oneself, entirely free of charge, on one of the two large luggage-weighing machines. I am 180 lb., fully clothed, which is said to be the ideal weight for a person of my inches. On our way back into town, we were stopped on the road by a police check-point : some Chinese thugs had kidnapped a Chinese millionaire. It's always happening. The police were carrying pistols and rifles ; they were very polite and cheery.

Every day except Sunday, there are professional letter-writers and form-fillers outside the Post Office and Government offices. They sit at small tables with portable Olivettis while the client, usually a Malay or an Indian, sits on a camp-stool and dictates his letter or gives information to be entered on some long, dun-coloured official form.

I had to spend a whole day at various offices of the Immigration Authorities getting my passport and papers in order. On my first visit to the Immigration Office in the dingy-white Suleiman Building just opposite my hotel I had to queue for an hour to get a form. Every time I pass this office there are long queues of people of all races ; there are always trishaws and a taxi or two in the forecourt.

The form required stamps to the value of five dollars. I also had to " obtain " two small photographs smaller than passport size. On the hot, moist morning I dreaded a queue at the Post Office so I asked the desk-clerk at the hotel for five one-dollar stamps, as he did not have a five-dollar one. The form distinctly says, in two places, " affix *stamps* to the value of 5 dollars " (my italics). However, the desk-clerk assured me that a single five-dollar stamp is necessary, that he had seen an " information film " in the Lake Gardens in which people were shown how wrong it was to affix more than one stamp. Such a film seems pretty pointless when one is told, on the form itself, to affix " stamps."

I walked down to the Post Office as slowly as possible—it's only about half a mile—but long before I reached there I was bathed in sweat. It trickled all over my face, swung like tiny brilliants from my ear-lobes, soaked my neck, throat, chest and back. And I'd forgotten to bring a handkerchief.

After queueing for fifteen minutes to buy the stamp I went a little farther, to Robinson's Department Store, at that hour full of mems choosing Christmas cards while a revolting children's angelic choir sang " The Twelve Days of Christmas "—on and on, all twelve of them. I bought a hanky to mop myself with : as usual there was an excruciatingly long wait as the assistant wrote out the details of my purchase in triplicate and then went to get my change from the cashier's desk.

I was already exhausted by the morning's efforts and took a taxi to the Immigration Office—after the driver had first taken me to the wrong place (I was too whacked to notice where we were going). There I joined a queue of about fifty people that was slowly inching forward to the counter. A nice young policeman in khaki shorts was on duty and as soon as I joined the end of the queue he motioned me to go to the front. Whereupon a young Indian standing nearby exclaimed passionately : " No ! He must wait in the queue and take his turn ! " The policeman, a Malay, smiled wearily and did not insist, and the Indian stood there in grumbling triumph watching me with bloodshot eyes full of hatred and suspicion. It wasn't as if I'd tried to jump the queue : I was quite ready to wait my turn ; but I followed the Malay policeman's example and did and said nothing.

In fact, it soon became evident that the policeman was correct, and that he had done right in asking me to go to the front of the queue, which was one for obtaining official forms. As I had already obtained mine and filled it in, I had to go to the counter and have the details checked against my passport and have my fingerprints taken.

One of the officials therefore beckoned me to the counter. He was very quiet and friendly, something which has to be appreciated when one considers that all the clerks here were bored, weary, overworked : under such conditions I should have gone raving mad within a few hours. Yet the clerks worked patiently, slowly away, day after day, at this, their life's work.

Immigration offices, like " gay " bars, are the same everywhere—depressing, melancholy places. But how different it was in Japan ! There my professor accompanied me in the staff car, so as to get the business over as comfortably and speedily as possible. Here, no one from the University gave me any help or advice. It was the ordinary Malays themselves who helped me ; I was surprised and grateful to be treated so well by them.

I have to go back yet again, in a month's time, and queue for my identity card.

Tropic Temper

The street-sweepers here are low-caste Indian women, dark as bitter chocolate, thin as the brooms they wield. They go barefooted; their grey hair is the colour of pewter. Despite their dirty and dusty occupation they wear the most brilliant, though obviously cheap clothes. The colours: poisonous, ochreous orange, raging magenta, virulent purples and peacock blue-greens, biliously bright yellows and almost fluorescent scarlets. All the colours of a traffic-signal. Is this in order to make themselves more easily visible in the harum-scarum Malayan traffic where they wander, carelessly, ceaselessly sweeping?

Mr. Krushchev set off his 50-megaton bomb yesterday, and to-day's press is full of outraged world opinion. Mr. K. may after all be an extremely clever and far-sighted man: surely, after all this uproar of shocked protest, America must now be shamed into abandoning her own tests of these devastating weapons, the unimaginably inhuman inventions of human—or are they?—scientists. In a way, Mr. K. may even be a kind of saint, taking upon himself and his people the ignominy and the guilt of this really diabolical act in order that the rest of us may be saved. Better a Russian 50-megaton bomb in the Arctic wastes than an American one on Berlin or Peking or Moscow. And the fall-out is drifting southwards, over Russia.

America and Britain now have a great opportunity to re-instate themselves spiritually and morally in the eyes of the world by publicly announcing their abandonment of all further nuclear tests and by giving an immediate assurance that, with the co-operation of Russia, they intend to carry out gradual multi-lateral disarmament.

Malay mothers do not carry their children on their backs but on the side, the child's legs straddling and gripping the out-thrust hip. This prevents bow legs.

The great fat black and greasy-looking counters of a Chinese shopkeeper's abacus. Some have counters of polished red-brown wood, like chestnuts.

I have a new Chinese room-boy, unobtrusively kind and attentive. He has a radiant yet mischievous gold-lit smile on his witty, plumpish face with the long, full mouth of a born laugher. His twinkly look, his youthful baldness at the temples with the big tuft of black hair in the middle of the forehead give him the appearance of a seventeenth-century Chinese page-boy at an Oriental court. He is married, with three charming children who are both gay and polite : I give them kaleidoscopes and Smarties, which they adore.

A visit to the Malayan National Film Unit, " Filem Negaru." I was shown brilliant colour films of top-spinning, kite-flying, Malay dancing, mock-fighting (bersilat, the Malay art of self-defence), shadow-puppets (wayang kulit) and native crafts. I am to write a script, in pantuns, the national verse-form, on the Mandi Safar festival at Tanjong Kling, near Malacca.

I met the Chinese friend of a colleague. He was incredibly thin, small, not very good-looking but charming, like a grown-up little boy. His silences were enchanting ; his false air of innocence made me feel very protective, though quite unnecessarily. Slightly bandy legs and simian walk, quite untamed, go well with his curiously thin and compressed lips, his broken teeth and retreating smile, the eyes like shining dark-brown abacus counters, the wildish brush of hair, the pretty eyebrows of a very still and quiet monkey. His totally hairless hands, arms, face. He understands some English, though he doesn't speak more than a few words. One imagines him to be both restful and passionate, devoted and indifferent, like a cat. His thin, gold-ringed fingers are like a bird's claws. He drinks only fresh lime-juice.

Colombo Plan headlines : " Provision for a Special Song, Receptionists, Street Decorations and Relays of Umbrella Men."

The delicious pinks and greens and yellows of turbans—sharp pastel shades, sherbet tints so clear and pure, they make the mouth water. To-day I followed for a long way the most exquisite lime-green turban I've ever seen.

Though the Selangor Club now admits non-whites—which is why it is known as " The Spotted Dog "—it still has, for me, a heavy atmosphere of colonial privilege. I would rather not belong to it for that reason. Yesterday afternoon, I walked down past the padang where the club was crowded with mems tea-ing and smoking and nattering, watching their menfolk, in long white baggy shorts, punting a football about. There were also some Indians playing hockey, in vivid turbans. And some Malays, looking bird-frail beside the elephantine whites.

Outside a restaurant from which floated an overpowering

smell of garlic and asafœtida, I was stopped by a middle-aged, bearded Indian in fresh white shirt and well-laundered white drill trousers held up by a thin gold plastic belt. After a long, excessively polite and smarmy preamble, he came to what I was incredulously beginning to feel was, after all, his point : could I spare a few dollars for a poor jobless man ? No. If he'd been better-looking and less ingratiating I would perhaps have given him something. As it was, everything militated against it.

There are always beggars crouched in corners, outside the mosques and temples, outside the post office, sitting hunched-up on the ground amid their rags and sticks, extending their palms and wailing. There is an awful old woman, grey haired, grey faced, with the dreadfully baleful countenance of that unhealthily-plump creature in Blake's picture of Nebuchadnezzar. She is always crouching under one of the Town Hall's arches, mumbling bits of dirty rice, bread, bruised fruit. Her pale, distended eyes follow me like a complaint while she munches away with bloated, greasy lips. This is no country for a sensitive person.

There are hundreds of women labourers on roads and building-sites, wearing pyjama-suits, round, pointed, plaited-bamboo hats and, to shield their faces from the sun, a green cloth stretched on a light bamboo framework projecting from beneath the "terendak" hat and covering almost the entire face. The effect is of a very protuberant, roughly-made nun's coif.

A woman carries two loads of earth in square wooden trays balanced from either end of a bamboo pole laid across her shoulders. I watched how the women pick up these loads. First they lay the pole across both shoulders ; then they bend to the left to hook up the first load and raise this as they bend to the right to hook up the other load—in bucket, basket or box—and then with one or both hands holding the pole they walk away with short, quick, almost dancing steps, in a rhythm exactly following the springing movements of the bamboo pole.

Deep-red dragon-flies hovering over the green-red borders of the hotel flower-beds : the deep, dusky magenta of their wings.

A Chinese gentleman at the Malayan Travel Advice Bureau gives me his advice on how to get to Malacca and Singapore—go by bus. It is about ninety miles to Malacca and the trip costs only three dollars and fifty cents (it actually turned out to be only three dollars). Stay there at the Government Rest House. (I felt instinctively that this would be no good.) Next day take bus to Singapore, stay at the Cathay or Orchard hotels. He insisted that no reservations were necessary either for buses or hotels. So I did not bother to make any.

He told me an amusing Chinese proverb : eat in Canton, dress in Hankow, live in Suchow and die in Luchow. These cities were noted respectively for good food, beautiful silks, lovely girls and fine wooden coffins. (And besides, those who are buried at Luchow are preserved for ever in the well-drained, sandy earth of the region.) He made everything sound wonder-fully easy ; in fact, he gave me the wrong advice about every-thing, But he was so nice, I never went back to complain. I never went near the Malayan Travel Advice Bureau again : it is hopelessly inefficient.

This evening, persistent questioning by that rather clumsy, thick-set young Chinese waiter, about twenty, with the two large upper front teeth encased in gold and set in a broad white grin —when he's feeling amiable—in his broad brown peasant's face. I had just had a visit from an Indian schoolteacher and the waiter had seen me sitting with him in the lounge discussing his teaching problems : how to teach sexual matters to boys and girls who already knew all about them.

After the teacher had left I had dinner alone, and before I'd finished my soup this waiter came up to me and said, in an abrupt and almost bullying way—caused I think by his limited and stilted English—" Who was that you were talking to ? " His voice had an almost jealous note and was slightly trembling with suppressed excitement. I looked at him, trying to contain my astonishment, and for a moment thought of refusing to answer him. However, I swallowed my irritation and said, as calmly as possible : " He is a teacher." " How did you get to know him ? " " I was introduced to him by someone at the University." " Why did he come here ? " (At this, I could hardly believe my ears. I decided it was not deliberate rudeness, but simply ignorance and naïve inquisitiveness prompting the questions, though he had never questioned me like this before.) I answered : " To discuss his school work with me." " Oh." (This rather suspiciously.)

His interrogation temporarily suspended by the arrival of

another waiter bearing the next course, he strolled ponderously away. But in a few minutes he was back, announcing, to my even greater astonishment : " You are right, sir. He is my teacher. He teaches me in Form 4."

It is true. Quite a lot of Chinese continue to attend school even up to the age of twenty-four, in order to make up for time lost during the Emergency.

The manner of questioning was very unfortunate. I felt that most Europeans, interrogated in this way, would have expressed their annoyance or snubbed him. But I think the tone of the questioning reflected the tone of the speaker's native tongue which was Hokkien. He spoke gravely, rather energetically, in strong, clipped phrases, wearing a solemn but penetrating expression on his peasant face that was by no means lacking in craft and guile. His questioning me about my own guest offended me, but I felt there was no offence intended. He just lacked subtlety, English, and the Western code of good manners.

The day before I leave for Malacca and Singapore, I meet a Malay boy who says to me : " You are my brother." How sweet those words from a total stranger. Round his waist, on a piece of string, he wears a small linen bag containing a magic talisman to ward off evil spirits from the stomach and loins. He gives it to me, to protect me on my journey.

8. *Malacca—Singapore*

It was a Saturday lunch-time and I wanted to catch the 1 p.m. bus to Malacca from the Pudu Road Omnibus Station. At 12.45 I was standing outside my hotel trying to find a taxi but they were all full. Families of dozens of Indians from new-born babies to great-great-grandmothers were jammed into tiny cars; the Indians seemed to gaze out at me pityingly and with fatuous condescension as I stood there with my brown-paper carrier-bag containing all my necessaries. Finally I stopped a trishaw and trundled off slowly to the station. The Kuala Lumpur–Malacca Express, silver-painted, was still waiting in the crowded station yard when we arrived. I rushed to the ticket window to buy a ticket, but they had all been sold. I would have to wait for the three o'clock bus. I took the precaution of booking my seat then and there: lucky I did so because it was the last one.

In the jungle, distance is reckoned in chews of tobacco. My ticket says: " Valid for oen [*sic*] journey."

The bus is packed when I arrived, just before departure. I sit in my seat, in the baking heat, waiting for the thing to start; I am the only European on the bus and I am sitting next to a young Malay, who looks like an estate worker, holding a silent baby on his lap. We smile and I say a few words in Malay. The young man answers but I can see that he feels embarrassed when other people on the bus turn at the sound of my Malay, so we pass the rest of the journey in silence.

A delightful cool breeze comes through the unglazed windows as the bus moves through the city outskirts into the country, past the Lady Templer TB Hospital out into semi-jungle and mile after mile of rigidly-planted, gloom-casting rubber estates broken only here and there by kampongs and the shimmer of padi and palm. In the kampongs there are pretty houses raised on stilts; they have attap and corrugated-iron roofs which, when new, blaze and flash in the sunlight. There is washing hanging out everywhere—shirts, shorts, sarongs. Swarms of semi-naked children, men working half-naked in the fields and plantations. We pass over a bridge; below is a stream in which boys are bathing naked; their black hair and brown bodies glisten most beautifully. They wave to the bus; I wave back, and they jump up and down in the water, waving and laughing.

The bus rattles very noisily along, giving a frightfully loud blast on the horn each time it passes another vehicle. The roads leading through the rubber estates are very well kept. It is a fairly comfortable ride, and my fellow-passengers are good to look at, but there is not much room for one's legs and the seats are hard.

Kampongs on some estates have small temples and mosques with miniature, harlequin-painted onion-domes. Here and there one sees among the rubber trees small Chinese temples with broad, three-tier, red-and-brown-tiled roofs. On hillsides there are the horseshoe shapes of Chinese graves in burial grounds.

Sometimes in a clearing there is a badminton court, always weedy, as if it wasn't used much, with a decrepit referee's high chair, rickety posts and rusted neon arc-lamps or strip lighting.

Water-buffaloes and gentle, heavy oxen, soft-eyed, their huge dewlaps like silky fringes hanging and swinging as they plod along with small boys astride.

Everywhere there are signboards saying " Site for proposed new building " or giving the name of a rubber-estate's owner.

The sweet smell of Malays on the bus, their reserve broken occasionally by brief sentences and smiles. The children are quiet, exemplary in their polite behaviour. They are all in their best clothes, and all the men have crisply-laundered shirts. The Chinese, too, are immaculate. A few Indians look grubby and unshaven.

We stop for about twenty minutes at the market town of Seremban, a gay, swarming, muddy place. It has a rather pleasant Rest House, and lovely gardens in a picturesque valley with two artificial lakes starred with water-lilies. At one end of the lake gardens is a model Malay house built in the Minangkabau style of architecture from the East Coast, that is, rather like a long-house, on stilts, with fine double-roof up-sweeping at the gable-ends. One of the most interesting facts about this building is that it is built entirely without nails.

Housed in an old royal palace which was moved here from Ampang Tinggi is the State Museum containing many fascinating exhibits including aboriginal weapons and old Kelantan silver-ware.

To the south-east of Seremban is Sri Menanti, the seat of the ruler of the state of Negri Sembilan. There are two palaces, one is the modern style and one in the old Minangkabau style. The modern one, the Istana Besar or Grand Palace is an imposing building set in beautiful grounds ; the other, the Istana Lama, built in 1905, is one of the most graceful examples of old-style Malay architecture in this region.

From Seremban, a road branches off to the popular coastal resort of Port Dickson, known to everyone in Malaya as P.D. It has soft, sandy beaches shaded by tall, feathery casuarinas and palms. Excursions can be made from P.D. to Lukut, where there is an old Portuguese fort, or to Cape Rochado, a place where there is a lighthouse commanding magnificent coastline views. On clear days, the island of Sumatra can be seen from here.

We have a change of bus-drivers at Seremban. Nearly all the passengers have been stretching their legs and wandering round the market stalls buying nuts and fruit, tasting slices of peeled apple and pineapple and melon from vendors' carts. In the public lavatory, I notice that elderly Indians squat down to piss. A Chinese gentleman, fortunately with very wide pants, for some reason can only do it after rolling up his trouser-leg.

When we enter the State of Malacca, many humble kampong houses have finely-turned balustrades and wooden balconies ; fretted wood-work, especially above doors and on window-shutters. Indigo-blue curtains blowing at the open windows. Most houses in this region have, leading up to the outer room, an open veranda, flights of prettily-tiled stone steps with curving, stone balustrades painted pink or lime-green. This is the Portuguese influence on Malay architecture. In some places where the houses have fallen into ruins beneath the encroaching jungle, all the wooden parts have rotted away or been eaten by white ants, leaving only a flight of brilliantly-tiled stone steps leading upwards into a void.

Across a bridge, and we are in the market and bus station of Malacca. I take a taxi to the Rest House; the taxi has no meter—I am obviously going to be rooked. But when I get to the Rest House, contrary to what the gentleman at the Malayan Travel Advice Bureau told me, I find it is not possible to get a room without reserving it a week beforehand. The Rest House is full, and so are all the other larger hotels. I drove round in a taxi from one hotel to another for at least half an hour. Finally I got fixed up at the Sun Wah (Chinese) Hotel: a very noisy room. The top of the walls was just wire mesh, and previous occupants had poked peep-holes in the partitions. There was the constant racket of mah-jong players, cocks crowing, bells ringing, couples having sex. On the wall was a notice saying: " No Gambling. No Opium Smoking," to which a wag had added the words " in Bed." The furniture consisted of a large double bed and an old wash-stand with bowl and ewer. When I returned from my evening walk, I found the double bed occupied by a young Chinese; I had to share it with him, as the hotels were all packed and there were no more beds to be had. I suppose I couldn't expect much more for three dollars a night. Necessity does indeed acquaint us with strange bedfellows. We were plagued all night by mosquitoes.

But before returning to my hotel I had wandered round the town, casing the joint, as is my habit. It was not a very interesting place at night, though the streets of shop-houses and coffee stalls and restaurants were lively and crowded. It was nice just to walk round looking at faces. (I have become a people-watcher.) I had some nice fried mee at a Chinese stall in the open-air market, followed by the strangely-sweet durian whose fetid smell is so off-putting. But Malayans love this curious fruit, and I, too, soon acquired a passion for it.

The names of streets were Portuguese, Dutch, English, Malay and Chinese: Texeira Road, Eredia Road, Heeren Street, Jonker Street, Newcome Road, Egerton Road, Lorong Bukit China, Gaja Berang Road, Chan Koon Cheng Road, Kee Ann Road. From Bona Vista Road, Tranquerah Road and Wisdom Drive, the latter running right along the sea-front near the Rest House, there were superb views of the moonlit off-shore islands, black and palm-fringed in the glittering water: they were like bits of cut-out scenery, with lighted ships lying at anchor behind.

These small, low islands are uninhabited, but are visited by Malays, Malayan Chinese (called " babas " if they have lived more than a hundred years in Malaya) and Hindus on pilgrimages. They have fine beaches and ancient tombs, which it is possible to visit in hired boats.

Other good vantage points at night—and by day also—are the Old Fort on St. John's Hill and the Church of St. Paul. This church is said to be the oldest building erected by Europeans in South-East Asia. It was here that the body of St. Francis Xavier was enshrined before being taken for entombment in the cathedral at Goa. By day, from these two points, one can enjoy splendid views of the Malacca Straits scattered with small fishing-boats sailing back and forth between their fishing stakes and the small green islands.

I saw some of the Malacca bullock-carts, with their curving roofs of woven palm-leaf, near the lovely beach at Tanjong Kling, just out of town.

All the shops were open, of course, until very late at night. There were some stalls selling Malaccan handicrafts—the famous Malacca Canes, stout walking-sticks with carved and decorated handles, and baskets and boxes called ketumba and rombong, woven from mengkuang or padanus leaves. These leaves are dyed and are woven into pretty star and flower designs ; they are quite cheap ; the larger ones are sometimes used as suitcases by the Malays from the kampongs. Malacca is noted for a particularly complicated " mad " weave. I also paid a brief visit to the amusement park—every large Malayan town has its " World," as these parks are generally called— where I watched some graceful Malay ronggeng dancing to cha-cha-cha, samba, rumba and quick-step tunes. The lithe-hipped Malays are wonderful dancers and some months after I arrived in Malaya they took to the Twist with ease and zest. They were the best Twisters I ever saw.

Sunday morning in Malacca : old ladies in their batik finery and dull-gold jewellery, going to church or mosque ; they wear gold combs, tortoise-shell pins and sprigs of fresh jasmine or bunga raya (hibiscus) in their sleek black hair. Some of them are smoking Portuguese cigars (with the band on).

I walked past the Town Hall, called by the Dutch name " Stadhuys," and Christchurch with its big Dutch gables, its great curving gallery and massive pulpit. Both were built by the Dutch in the colonial style late in the eighteenth century. They used salmon-pink bricks shipped from Middleburg in Zeeland and covered with red laterite. To-day Christchurch is an Anglican church.

A little farther on was the Porta di Santiago, also known as the Dutch Gate, symbol of the State of Malacca and all that now remains of the great Dutch fortifications. Beside it is a row of very elegant colonial-style houses. Some house-fronts still have balustraded gables and there are pargetted façades bearing old Dutch or Portuguese coats of arms ; houses are painted white, cream, pink, green, blue, one colour next to another, never two the same. This variety of colour can also be seen in Penang, in the Market Square in K.L. and in many of the smaller towns of Central Malaya.

Another interesting place is the Cheng Hoon Chinese Temple, the oldest and most striking in Malaya. Its main gate has a remarkable double roof. This " Abode of the Merciful Clouds " is in Temple Street. Founded in the seventeenth century by Kapitan Li Kup, it was dedicated by Malacca's pioneer Chinese to Kwan Yin, Goddess of Mercy.

Before catching the bus to Singapore, I just had time to visit the Perigi Raja or Sam Poh's Well in Bukit China Road. As is the case with so many wells and fountains in the world, legend has it that the traveller who tastes its water will never forget his visit to Malacca and that he will one day return. The well is supposed to date as far back as the founding of Malacca by Raja Iskandar Shah in the thirteenth century. I did sip some of the water—for in Malaya all water is perfectly safe to drink— though I knew that even without its magic aid I should certainly be returning to Malacca, and many times, for I had taken a great liking to the leisurely charm of this historic place.

On our way out of Malacca the bus passed Bukit China, one of the largest Chinese cemeteries outside China. It contains graves dating from the Ming Dynasty. The horseshoe-shaped tombs are displayed all over a wide hillside. On top of the hill are the remains of a Franciscan chapel and convent. Most Chinese graves are constructed high on hillsides, facing west, for the Chinese believe that the spirits of the ancestors become angry if they do not have an unimpeded view.

The bus journey from Malacca to Singapore takes six hours, with a stop for lunch. This time I was sitting next to a Malay gentleman of about thirty who spoke very good English and very kindly pointed out places of interest on the road. When I groped in my brown-paper bag for a clean handkerchief he said something that puzzled me : " Is that your treasure-chest? " He poked his head forward and took a peep inside, eyeing my flagons of scent and brandy. Later on, he explained, laughing, that he was a Customs inspector at Johore Bahru. He assured me that he would see to it I passed through unmolested. We crossed pontoon ferries at Muar and Batu Pahat, where the river marks the boundary between the States of Malacca and Johore. After Batu Pahat, my travelling companion fell asleep for a few minutes and as he slept his head slowly descended on my right shoulder : for some reason this made me feel very proud and happy. It must have been my paternal instinct coming out.

He woke up and showed me where fighting had been very bad during the Emergency. The rubber-estate owners had been ordered to cut back their trees from the roads so as not to afford cover for bandits. Many soldiers had left their names scrawled on the reddish cliff-sides of cuttings through which the road was built. We passed endless rubber plantations, palm-oil estates, pineapple fields. As we drew near Johore Bahru we began to see palms whose leaves were spread out stiffly like giant fans. Traveller's palms. My friend pointed out the Istana Bukit Serene standing on a hilltop, and the towers of the mosque Abu Bakar as well as the dominating square tower of the Government Offices. He told me that in the Istana Gardens there was a replica of a Japanese tea-garden. I was sorry to see him leave the bus at Johore Bahru. We exchanged names and addresses but unfortunately never met again.

After a short stop in Johore Bahru, the Singapore Express crossed the famous Johore Causeway linking Malaya and the island of Singapore. It is 3,465 feet long and reaches a depth of seventy-six feet below water level; it carries a double railway line and a twenty-six feet wide road. Singapore's entire water supply is borne through a huge pipe running alongside the railway lines; electric, telegraphic and telephone cables are also accommodated along it.

Tropic Temper

There is still a journey of about seventeen miles to the city of Singapore after crossing the Causeway. Malays are in a minority here, for the population of over a million is mainly Chinese ; but Malay is the common language of the community, though English is widely spoken. The island lies only eighty-five miles north of the Equator, but I always found it cooler than Kuala Lumpur : in the early evenings, particularly, there is generally a cooling breeze from the sea, and the mornings are fresh and pleasant.

Again in Singapore I found it terribly difficult to obtain a hotel room. I wanted to stay at the Orchard Hotel, which has such a good bar, and went straight there from the bus station, but there was nothing available. Perhaps they didn't like the look of my brown-paper bag. I spent about an hour driving in a taxi from one hotel to another and finally got in at the Cockpit —very " classy," and very expensive. All they had was a double room without bath, air-conditioned. The service was poor : I had to ring for towels and soap, and when I got to the bathroom I found the water had been cut. There was a drought or something. I had to bathe in cold water ladled from a tub.

By this time I discovered I had a raging cold and decided that I would return to K.L. the very next day, by train. On my return to my room I saw there were no bedside tables and no bedside lamps. A notice saying : " Gentlemen are requested to wear jackets after 8 p.m." finally put the seal on my discontent. I hadn't brought any jacket with me.

Singapore : the beauty and excitement of the waterfront at night, ships and cruisers lit overall with strings of white electric bulbs. The Chinese section : a lively muddle of streets and markets and shop-houses. The squalid huddle of sampans on the river. The Raffles Hotel, a dream of whiteness, like a big wedding-cake set among traveller's palms on " gracious lawns," ludicrously opposite the Naafi's " Britannia Club " where the taxi and trishaw drivers wait in a shifty and dissolute rout to rook tourists, servicemen and their families. The Singapore taxi-driver's leading gambit is : " Where you going, Jack ? I take you for two dollars." To a newcomer, this sounds pretty cheap, but the taxi-driver doesn't switch on his meter : if he did, the unwary passenger would see he was paying two dollars (with tip) for a forty-cent ride. Never tip a Singapore taxi-driver, and never get into his taxi before he has switched on the meter.

The Singapore Chinese are surely not real Chinese, I mean not truly representative of that wonderful race. I found them loud-mouthed, mercenary, mean. (In fact, I discovered later, it is not until one gets to Formosa that one begins to meet the true Chinese : the Straits Chinese and those in Hong Kong and Macao are not very good examples.)

I used to think Japan's street architecture was commonplace and squalid, but it is nothing compared with the filth and disorder and drabness of the Chinese quarter in Singapore. The attitude of Chinese in shops and restaurants : a mixture of disdain and impertinence.

A brief visit to the Criterion bar in Orchard Road, a bar so excitingly described by Patrick Anderson in *Snake Wine*. It had obviously declined : at eleven o'clock on a Sunday night it was almost empty. There were only two hopelessly drunk British sailors in soiled whites and two elderly Chinese gentlemen sitting at the bar. The gramophone was deafening. Rubber Santa Clauses with idiot eyes and Blimpish moustaches seated astride gin bottles. A sparse display of fairy-lights : amateurish murals of sailors with girls. I fled.

Outside, across the road, was something infinitely more interesting—an interminable Chinese opera being performed by glove-puppets to a vast audience, mostly children, stretching out from the pavement into the busy road.

The brilliantly-painted and illuminated stage was set up in front of a furniture shop ; people were leaning out of upper windows on either side of the street, and passing motorists would often slow down to get a quick look at what was going on.

Most puppet shows in Singapore were introduced from Formosa and are of Hokkien origin. Penang was the first place in Malaya to show Chinese puppets : they can also be seen sometimes in Malacca, but only very rarely in other Malayan towns.

There were about twenty people behind the vermilion, green and blue proscenium, which was really terribly pretty, covered with pictures and hundreds of dazzling little electric light bulbs that kept winking off and on.

A red velvet draw-up curtain was embroidered with bold

silver characters. There were only two puppet operators, a young man and a boy of about twelve. There were three young women, one of them carrying her baby, who did the female voices and sang songs or recitatives. One middle-aged man in dark, horn-rimmed glasses was playing the main male parts and two younger men played smaller roles, taking part also in the male singing recitations. As he intoned, chanted and sang his part the chief actor, sitting at the back of the stage on a stool, kept gesturing with his hand-mike. He was trying out his lines behind the shattering row of a lengthy overture, performed mostly by percussion instruments. When the overture suddenly stopped, the roaring traffic along the road was heard again, and the ringing of the ice-cream vendor's bell.

Although they must have performed the play hundreds of times, the actors seemed to be enjoying the dialogue which was barely audible above the traffic noises and the clashing, banging, drumming, fifing and one-string-fiddling. These instruments were performed by about a dozen musicians, all men. The cymbal player sent a little boy squatting on the boards beside him for a stick-ice, and sucked it diligently while keeping up the complex and inscrutable rhythm on his dashing, hissing cymbals. At several points in the action the actors seemed to be improvising replies which provoked smiles and laughter, not among the audience, but among the rest of the company.

I wondered how the audience could follow the story: it was all so confusing and so difficult to hear. Apart from the children, the audience was composed mainly of old people who presumably knew the story by heart.

There were three drop-scenes on clumsy rollers: one canvas was painted to represent a palace interior, another a formal garden, the third the inside of a temple. At the bottom of each drop-cloth was a strip of semi-translucent paper through which the puppet-manipulator watched the movements of his glove-puppets.

These were exquisitely and brilliantly dressed and had many changes of costume and accoutrements. The finely-made heads are imported from the Chang Chow district in the Province of Fukkien where they are manufactured, but the costumes are made in Singapore.

The figures were only about six inches tall, yet their move-

ments " carried " extremely well, helped by the formal clothes
and the extravagant gestures. They performed sword-fights—
reminiscent of Punch and Judy bludgeonings—courtships,
quarrels, love-songs ; they took part in discussions, arguments
and duets.

It all seemed very static and wordy, yet the children and
adults were enthralled and amused : despite all the distractions,
the noise and the dangers of passing traffic, their attention was
held throughout. I felt that at last I was seeing the true character
of the Chinese, seeing them as themselves, not as immigrants or
refugees degraded by poverty and debased by contact with the
colonial West. I liked what I saw that night.

A little girl, running to watch the puppets and not looking
where she was going, fell sideways into a deep monsoon drain.
She was given no sympathy, help or comfort ; the spectators
just smiled and gently laughed at her. She wasn't much hurt
and soon picked herself up and hobbled away. She didn't cry ;
she laughed, too. I thought the attitude of the bystanders
admirable. Perhaps Westerners comfort and cosset their
children unnecessarily, so that they are conditioned to bawl at
every slightest hurt, every deprivation, every loss of ease and
privilege. That is not how Orientals bring up their children.
It seems to me the Oriental method is a better preparation for life.

Next morning, with a high temperature and a blinding cold,
I took the express train back to K.L. On the way we passed
a diesel locomotive with a pretty name : Bunga Mata Hari,
No. 20115. "Mata hari" means "sun" in Malay, and as "bunga"
means flower I gathered that the train was called " Sunflower."

When the train arrives at Seremban, free copies of the excellent *Malay Mail* are distributed to passengers, " with the compli-
ments of the Malayan Railway Administration." An excellent
service. The food on these trains is quite good.

Back in Kuala Lumpur. Sir Frank Swettenham, in his
admiral's uniform and cocked hat, was taken down from his
public pedestal in Jalan Raja by the Japanese during their
occupation of Malaya, and later restored. It says on the tablet
that the statue was "put up by public subscription," as was the
bust of a moodily benevolent Edward VII (not, apparently,
removed by the Japanese). One wonders what kind of "public"
subscribed, and whether it was merely the " clublic."

Tropic Temper

There is no statue of Queen Victoria to be seen, though our present Queen's photograph or the reproduction of one of the Academy portraits is often hung in bars and offices and other public places. But simply everywhere one sees the bespectacled, amiably-beaming, Rotarian face of Malaya's Prime Minister, the Tengku Abdul Rahman.

It's a relief to be back. I even felt a kind of fondness for K.L. as the train drew into its Saracenic station. I didn't care for my first visit to Singapore. But I shall go again for the Chinese New Year and hope I shall receive a better impression.

9. The White Man's Burden

Many Malays feel the iron rule of Federal authority weighing heavily upon them. They were, in fact, though one hesitates to say this, freer under the colonial-imperialist British.

There are some disturbing features in this shining new independent state. It was rather distressing to read, for example, in *The Straits Times* of 10th November, 1961, that several people's homes had been visited and searched by police early on the morning of the 9th, and that the occupants, one of them a student—which here might mean a school-child—had been taken off to the police station without explanation. "Certain papers were seized," says the report. Again on 18th November pre-dawn police raids on private houses were reported.

A very sinister atmosphere surrounds the school strikes which frequently take place. In Malaya, it is the children who strike, and they always seem to be very well-organised. Who organises them ? At the end of November they had struck in Singapore and had set up picket lines over an examination dispute. There were many pictures in the newspapers of school children linking arms and forming long chains to prevent " blacklegs " from entering the examination halls. Most of the strikers wore handkerchiefs tied round the lower part of their faces, giving these thirteen- and fourteen-year-old children the air of bandits. What would happen in England if children went on strike over the 11-plus ?

Again, the distinguished literary magazine, *Eastern Horizons*, published in Hong Kong, is banned by the Malayan government. So much for the vaunted " democratic freedom of the press " in the Federation. It is free, but only up to a point. The same goes for " free " speech.

The cases of wrongful imprisonment reported in the newspapers are also frightening. I quote here a verbatim account taken from *The Straits Times* of 9th January, 1962 :

" Measures 'beyond the control' of the authorities are holding up the banishment of 104 people in a Seremban prison.

The House of Representatives was told this today by the Minister of Internal Security, Dato (Dr.) Ismail bin Dato Abdul Rahman in reply to Opposition queries.

He said the 104 prisoners were held under banishment orders and were awaiting shipment.

Mr. Karam Singh said the detainees had suffered great hardship, with the result that some of them had had to be admitted to mental homes.

Mr. D. R. Seenivasagam (PPP-Ipoh): ' When is it likely that these people will be banished ? '

Dato Ismail : ' I will banish them as soon as possible but the matter is beyond our control.'

Mr. S. P. Seenivasagam (PPP-Menglembu) : ' What are the difficulties ? '

Dato Ismail : ' Honourable Members can study the banishment orders.'

In reply to another question from Mr. Lim Kean Siew (S.F.—Dato Kramat) on the number of persons detained under the Emergency Regulations and the Internal Security Act, Dato Ismail gave the following figures :

711 enemy personnel; 52 persons who had assisted the terrorists and 222 subversives—a total of 985 persons detained since Aug. 31, 1957.

Persons released since Merdeka Day total 911, of which 92 were released with conditions limiting their political activities and 819 released with no conditions."

No Europeans appeared to show any concern at this shocking and inhuman state of affairs. There was very little I could do about it apart from laying the case before Peter Benenson and the " Amnesty " movement of which I am a member.

On 16th January, 1962, there was this report in *The Straits Times:*

" . . . the Government had refused to permit the Bookshops, Publications and Printing Presses Workers' Union to stage the play ' Serenade in a Coconut Plantation ' because it encouraged student participation in industrial disputes . . ."

The White Man's Burden

The Government had issued a statement explaining why it had refused permission to schools in Singapore to perform certain items :

> " The Government had good reason for refusing the schools to perform some of the items. Not only did they emanate from Communist China but ' they are questionable by themselves.'

The original words of the ' Embroidery Dance,' for instance, were :

> " *Oh, beautiful scenery*
> *A new atmosphere appears everywhere.*
> *Embroidery to be presented to Chairman Mao.*
> *Wishing our leader a long life."*

This partly explained the Government's warning on agitators in schools, a report of which appeared in *The Straits Times* on 23rd November, 1961 :

> "The Government tonight revealed that ' irresponsible agitators ' were instigating students in some Chinese secondary schools to hold meetings and openly defy the authority of principals and teachers in their campaign for the cancellation of the forthcoming government secondary four examination.
> . . . The Government warning tonight followed three separate mass student meetings held last Friday at the Chung Cheng High School in Goodman Road, the Chinese High School in Bukit Timah Road, and the Nan Chiau Girls School in Kim Yam Road."

On New Year's Day, 1962, this report from Alor Star, the capital of Kedah province, appeared in *The Straits Times* :

> " There are still about 480 Communist bandits, including 70 women, operating in the 100-mile-long Malayan—Thai border jungle . . .
> . . . there was evidence that the people's support for the terrorists was ' gradually diminishing.' "

Such items of news appear regularly in the English-language newspapers : it is something, of course, that they are allowed to appear, but at the same time one wonders how much of the truth is printed, and how many items are suppressed by the Government. The only European or American I ever met who showed any kind of concern about such matters was a woman, the vital, dedicated Shirle Gordon, editor of a small broadsheet called *Seed* which is published in English, Malay and Chinese. No one I knew at the University showed any interest : in fact, university people gave me the impression that they were afraid to become involved in political, economic and social matters.

Pictures in *The Straits Times* of round-the-world passengers on the luxury liner *Kungsholm* when it called at Penang, at Swettenham Pier. They were being entertained by charming Malay ronggeng dancers and bersilat self-defence masters. Among the be-pearled, be-diamonded, be-sun-glassed, be-sandalled, fat, elderly passengers, not the trace of a smile, not a sign of imaginative appreciation. I was reminded of the words of Noël Coward's song from " Sail Away " :

> *Why do the wrong people travel?*
> *Please do not think that I criticise or cavil*
> *At a genuine urge to roam,*
> *But why, oh why, do the wrong people travel*
> *When the right people stay at home?*

At every corner, I seem to bump into a pregnant European woman. Of course, Malay and Indian and Chinese women became pregnant also, but they seem to conceal their uninteresting state better : in this respect saris and sarongs are superior to the sack-like Western maternity garments which actually seem to make things look much worse than they really are. People say that it's the climate and the hot, spicy food that make Westerners breed so unrestrainedly. And of course, apart from sex, there's nothing much to occupy one's time here. The baggy-bottomed British menfolk, pushing prams, wander along beside their teeming wives, turning everywhere into a Saturday morning on Ealing Broadway. I did not think Independence had undone so many.

Fortunately not all white people are horrible, though even the best-looking suffer by contrast with the neat and elegant Malays. The other day in the lounge of my hotel I watched two really sweet, plump, elderly Australian ladies in flowered hats and dresses, floating in dollars and traveller's cheques, who were quite rightly delighted with themselves and with everything. They were escorted by two extremely attentive and handsome young couriers from a local travel agency.

I saw a young Australian soldier to-day, the seat of whose jungle-green trousers was black with sweat. He had obviously been driving a jeep for some distance through the noontide heat. One often sees Westerners with damp behinds. A broad black patch of sweat stained the back of the soldier's deep-green bush-shirt, and there were huge crescents of dark wetness under his arms. His long, thin lips were beaded with moisture that was dripping regularly from his long, thin nose. It was a relief to see someone who looked hotter and wetter than I was. The Malay women were only just looking at him, in admiring horror; European women gazed at him with maternal sympathy, and with the gentility that makes things so much worse.

Touching, the damp backs of Malay boys and labourers cycling home from work, the faded batik patterns of brown and blue and green—usually such ugly and feeble patterns—dismally stained. Touching, their rough, brown, delicately barbaric faces with the full lips, the hinted moustache, the bright and sleepy dark eyes, the brilliant bush of pomaded black hair they are always so lovingly combing and re-combing.

Yet how neat, how composed, how cool most of the Malays, Indians and Chinese look in the slogging wet heat: a kind of matt bloom on their faces, a crisp calm in their simple, spotlessly-clean dress and in their leisurely walk. The Malay, they say, is " nature's gentleman." He certainly belongs to a lovely race.

Once in Penang I was astonished to find in my hotel a lobbyful of Italian gentlemen all in the most sober clerical grey lounge-suits, stiff white collars and dark, " safe " ties. Some semi-apostolic, semi-commercial delegation. Behind their pious, pouched, pallid faces was that Italian look reserved by men for passing women. Their conformist eyes kept roaming after the luxurious forms of sarong-clad Malay girls and Chinese ladies in samfu or cheongsam with a hungry anguish: I felt their pious repressions would end in chronic dyspepsia. Some of them already had pinched, red noses in their sallow faces.

A French journalist, making boring jokes about the word

" Merdeka," which he insisted on pronouncing as " Merde-caca."

· Last night, one of K.L.'s rare, fashionably cultural evenings at the Abdul Rahman Hall: a piano recital by . . . It was a social evening, so perhaps the playing didn't matter. There had been masses of advance publicity about his precious Gaveau, which he had brought with him. Had the severe air-conditioning tautened the wires ? He might as well have brought a sewing-machine, and not a Singer. It was a display of vulgar technique : I have never heard so many wrong right notes. " The Bad-tempered Clavier."

After the show I went on to an odious night-club where I ate some Foo Yong Hai—a mixture of scrambled egg, prawns and spring onions. Afterwards went to look for a coffee-shop about 2 a.m. but everything was shut, even the dreary Lake Gardens. I passed three times through a police road-block. The car had to slow down, but as soon as the police saw a white man inside I was smilingly waved on. I, too, waved out of the window, at practically everyone. Later I discovered that yet another " towkay " or Chinese businessman had been captured by Chinese thugs, and held for ransom.

When I started writing poetry seriously, about twenty years ago, I often thought how wonderful it would be to know other poets. We would read each other's work, discuss it and criticise it, give each other help and encouragement and appreciation.

I had to learn, by painful experience, that poets hate each other's guts. They will stoop to anything to do each other down, an attitude derided amusingly in Rose Macaulay's *Towers of Trebizond*. (I may add here that after twenty years as a poet I have now stopped writing poetry : I no longer wish to be known as a poet. " Writer " is more honourable nowadays, and less pretentious.)

So when I returned to K.L. from Singapore and found a telephone message from a poet, D. J. Enright, who is Professor of English Literature at the University of Singapore, I wanted to run away and hide.

He came to see me the next day and we met in the lounge of my hotel. He was much nicer than I had expected : tall, with brown curly hair, a pale, Shelleyan face (good) with very

Shelleyan eyes and mouth. A gap between his front teeth, a gap even larger than my own, shows in his infrequent smiles, and makes a bond between us more than anything else could have done. Abrupt, curt manner of speaking : he is unsure of himself and is feeling his way. I can sense behind his attitude the weight of prejudice which people who have never met me always seem to have. A faint Midlands accent. His ploy with a large pipe at the outset soon gives way to cigarette and holder. Massive silver or pewter rings, set with curious stones, on his slender white fingers. On the whole, for two strangers temperamentally very far apart we got on quite well. He regretfully shook his head when I asked him if he was going to see any other members of the English Department. He took me in his large car, through a blinding thunderstorm, to a dinner at a lush and phoney Chinese Restaurant, the Mandarin Room. He is returning to K.L. from Alor Star in a week's time. We arrange to meet again then. Perhaps poets aren't so awful, after all.

Anthony Powell describes Blore-Smith thus : ". . . big brown eyes and shapeless face still suggested an undergraduate." This reminded me of the appearance of a University lecturer in his early twenties who told me, with pleased dismay : " My students call me *sir* ! " I replied : " As long as they don't call me madame, I don't mind."

I paid my first, and only, visit to a Staff Association meeting at the University one Saturday afternoon; they were discussing whether they should be a trade union or not. Two hours of jaw-racking, eye-watering tedium, after which there was announced, with jocular academic heartiness, " a break for light relief." For this relief much thanks. I am definitely not a committee man. But it was amusing to observe one white speaker, like a local Lady Bountiful presiding over a charity committee meeting or opening a bazaar, with a good deal of manner, studied inflections and little " interesting " gestures like touching his lower lip, rubbing the side of his nose, seeming suddenly to notice something on the back of his right hand, brushing it away.

Some very ponderous laugh-raisers like : " Although not much of our secretarial labour appears on the surface, I can assure members that a good deal of burrowing goes on underground." (Chortles.)

Tropic Temper

The almost Victorian earnestness of the Malay speakers : though they, too, are not free from self-importance, they are the kindest people at the University.

After sloping off in the rain under my oiled-paper brolly, I was lucky to get a lift from an American zoologist with a new, spiky beard on a very round face who had come to Malaya for a few months to study tree-shrews. I told him about a little monkey from the trees outside my hotel window who had stolen a lighted cigarette from my room and sat in the tree blowing smoke down his nose and sharing the fag with a companion. " Gee, I wish I'd had my movie-camera to that," the zoologist cried. He seemed, like most Americans, to be wonderfully easy to entertain and to talk to ; everything one said, however commonplace, filled him with almost incredulous amazement. I told him the rain had been coming through a hole in my shoe and he replied at once, turning his round, bearded face full upon me and gasping a little : " You don't say so ! Gee, that's terrible." Like most " experts," he was disappointing and unconvincing, not nearly as expert as one expects an expert to be. He hadn't heard of the giant monitor lizards that inhabit Songsong Island off the north-west coast of Malaya. We were discussing the appearance of the University architecture and I threw out the remark that Pantai Valley was a British Brazilia. " Gee, that's brilliant ! " my companion gasped, and stopped his car to write it down. The entire drive back to my hotel was like that, preposterous.

I went to a screening of " Felix Krull " at the German Embassy. Very weak highballs for hosts of German businessmen and their wives, for those brawny blond engineers from Fraser's Hill hydro-electric power scheme, which apparently the Germans are doing : the Ambassador urged me most strongly to go : " they are only too glad to show one round." Dry-haired blondes, simpering over all those " küss die Hand " courtesies performed by the men with such arch gravity. On being introduced to a gentleman as " a student of our language and literature," he immediately broke into an interminable passage from the " Nibelungenlied " which he recited with military precision, as if he were shouting across a parade-ground.

A reception and dinner at the French Embassy were surprisingly provincial ; poor drinks, one glass of champagne each at dinner which was only very moderate in quality, provided by the Merlin Hotel kitchens and served by boys from the hotel staff who lined up as we left to smile, bow and say : " Please come again." One of them was a friend of mine and I winked at him as I walked out but he did not wink back because Malays cannot wink : their epicanthic fold prevents it.

A theatrical party given by the local amateurs to celebrate their production of " White Horse Inn." I was taken by the nice Welsh couple from the English Department. We had all been asked to go as anarchists, but I hadn't a thing to wear as I'd left my capes in Japan and my bombs in Britain. I had to make do with my very snug-fitting black toreador pants, high-heeled boots, dark glasses and a few dabs of " Perfect Disgrace," a new scent I had concocted myself. (Another, " Flagrant Délit," I used to spray my students with during their finals.) When the Welsh pair arrived at the hotel to pick me up in their car, the lady found she had no cigarettes so I escorted her into the hotel lounge to buy some. She was wearing a slinky black dress and dangling ear-rings and a yard-long cigarette holder and she was made up to the eyes as Rosa Luxembourg. I shall never forget the startled look on the faces of the nice Chinese bar-boys as we slunk up to the bar together.

There were many flaming red shirts at the party, one Joe Stalin (someone had got his Russian history mixed up) and any number of Olga Pullovsky spies.

" All these people here," a very vivacious young lady informed me, squinting through harlequin glasses, " spend all their time on drama, think of nothing else, live for our quarterly productions." I looked round at the joyless, desperate, odd-looking bunch and thought : poor souls. They all, of course, had " party pieces." It was terribly difficult to find someone to take me home. I only went to one other party, a " queer " one which was even more desperately dull, though all the so-called " gay society " of K.L. was there.

Christmas Eve in K.L. I had a fairly good time with the Geordie boys, soldiers from the A.A.C. stationed in Seremban, at the Paramount Bar. They were all wearing grotesque masks and paper hats which they had been given at a party in the Kowloon cabaret-bar upstairs. They were waving rattles shaped like small Chinese drums, and blowing whistles. The bar hostesses and taxi-girls looked on with bored indulgence while the bar-boy whose name is apparently Mr. Boum gazed at them in frank wonder, as if at some absorbing theatrical spectacle. The dangling, twisty metallic decorations were obsessionally drilling and screwing the sweaty air of festival. The Eve of Xmas began with a torrential monsoon shower lasting forty minutes.

My hotel is almost deserted. Many people have left the capital for cooler localities at Fraser's Hill, Penang Hill, the Cameron Highlands and Maxwell's Hill at Taiping. The newspapers, however, as always, announce that hotels in the capital are " packed with gaiety-seeking crowds."

There are great preparations at the Majestic for Christmas Eve dinner—turkey, plum pudding and all—and the dining-room has been sumptuously adorned with chains, lanterns and a huge, shapeless Xmas tree : this is not a real pine, but something like a loose-foliaged yew, and it is so lopsided, it looks as if it will topple over at any moment. There are crossed pairs of crackers and paper hats on all the tables. But there is only one diner, an elderly, plump Sikh in a strawberry-pink turban who seems to be the only resident left in the hotel besides myself. All the waiters and boys are in freshly-pressed and starched whites, looking smart and pretty and terribly expectant, as if they were hoping to behold all kinds of foreign fun and incomprehensible red-devilish abandon.

I sat in my room until nine o'clock, when I heard one distant cracker being pulled, a faint blast on a toy whistle, and once again total silence. I went out and ate some mahmee and meehoon at a Chinese street-stall.

New Year's Eve is on a Sunday. As on an English Sunday, I woke up feeling something had happened overnight, like a fall of snow or a stopped clock or some disaster that has muted all life on earth. I go out for a morning walk under a hot, heavy, clouded sky in almost deserted streets. Church bells.

As I sauntered back to my hotel for lunch, I visited the English Cemetery behind the Railway Administration Building. The high, grassy bank outside my hotel window must be a part of the cemetery. The very English tombs, crosses, angels, headstone inscriptions with " Nearer my God to Thee " and " Fell Asleep in Jesus " in the midst of palms, bamboos, lush grasses, magnolia, oleander and hibiscus, under the sweltering, clouded sky. The place is well-kept and rather pleasant. It will be overlooked by the new mosque which is being built beside it. Little stone pegs mark out grave-sites still unoccupied. Nowadays most white people are flown back to Europe when they die out here. Graves of the von Langenbergs prominent near the entrance. On the whole it is a happy place. The old gravestones cannot dull the vibrant green of the grass in which small plants with violently-variegated leaves are growing wild. Lizards and long-legged frogs and grasshoppers are all in movement, displaying sudden long jets of energy. The songs of the cicada and the bulbul, the tree-starling and the black-headed finch are stunned by the silent heat. A wild black dog that has been loping about among the graves follows at my side like a shadow as I wander back to the hotel for my makan. (Cold turkey.)

Race prejudice? I am the only European at the University who uses the daily afternoon bus which comes to convey members of the lowlier administrative staff back to town. (All the rest of the staff have cars.) As the bus fills up, I notice that the seat next to me is always the last one to be taken. This would seem to indicate a certain reluctance to sit beside me. I have noticed the same sort of thing happening in England, in reverse: the seat next to a black man or woman is always the last to be occupied in a full bus: but coloured people can be as guilty of race-prejudice as white people. Perhaps it is not actually race-prejudice, but simply shyness: but shyness is so often a form of raging pride. It is all very difficult to understand. One must simply not mind, and not bother if one appears to be discriminated against, then there might be an end to discrimination, and to the white man's burden.

I used to think the Americans were awful in Japan, and that what they had done to Japan (in a cultural sense) was appalling. But perhaps if it had been the British it would have been a good deal worse, in a less obvious way. There is, after all, something in the American brashness and forthrightness. When I see the British in Malaya, I shudder, and am thankful that they're not in Japan. Certainly in the East the American way of life seems less hidebound and class conscious, the lesser of two not very distinguished evils.

10. Between Two Worlds

Here, as in Japan, it's nearly always the plain, bespectacled, eager but boring boys who stop me in public, anxious to have a chat and practise their English. In Japan, it was often to satisfy a raging curiosity. But the Malays have not the very endearing, kittenish inquisitiveness of the Japanese. Even if they do manage to work up a lively interest in anything, they keep it quiet, unsmiling.

On the whole not many Malays will stop one in the street to practise their English : they're all too familiar with English and the British (and the Australians) and so the need and the urge are less strong, though sometimes I feel the curiosity is still there, undiminished.

When I smile at a nice face in the street, I very rarely get a smile in return : what I usually get is a puzzled and suspicious stare. The Malays are simply not used to being smiled at by the British. It is very saddening.

The name given to Communist guerrillas during the Emergency was " the people inside." I feel that this name, invented by the Malays themselves, applies to the Malays as a race : they do not try to make one feel shut-out : one simply is shut-out.

Soft-mouthed Malay boys with lips like faded, bruised carnations.

I like the look of that brown-faced, venerable Haji (one who has made the pilgrimage to Mecca) with the long blue shirt-tails hanging outside his white sarong ; sometimes he wears a rolled white turban, sometimes a white cap. He carries a tall stick. I feel his saintly remoteness as he trudges along on his old sandals every evening at sundown to the almost-deserted mosque.

Streams of little girls in violet sarongs covered with a sort of long white cotton kebaya or jacket-smock trotting gaily out of a building near the mosque.

A Malay labourer, wearing an emerald-green shirt slightly faded to an original and lovely tone.

A giggle with a Malay girl in the Federal Dispensary. I was buying a new bottle of scent and the pretty girl assistant smeared some on my wrist. It smelt really revolting, and I said : " It smells like cough syrup." She at once pouffed with mirth and astonishment. Was it the first time she'd heard a Britisher make a joke ?

Malay girls never sit side-saddle on the pillions of their boy-friends' motor-bikes or scooters, as they do in Spain and Italy and Japan. Even when wearing a sheath-like sarong the girl will be seen hauling up the bottom before straddling the pillion ; an ugly, graceless sight. A girl in sarong or cheongsam would look so pretty sitting side-saddle.

How dull and dismal most batik designs are ! The designs are quite mechanical, the colours—brown, purple, green, yellow —not very attractive.

A Malay friend : his dark hands with pale palms that have deeply-etched, dull-red lines. The tiny pink nails. Coming in from his night-classes he has ink-stains on his little, wrinkled, monkey fingers. Perfect, white teeth set in purplish gums : the purple colour is skin pigmentation. That thin roll of coarse cloth knotted round his middle—what is it for ? Is it magic ? Has it some religious significance ? There is some sort of medal wrapped in it. He wouldn't remove it. He said it was to keep up his underpants.

Riding along a country road in a bus, I glimpsed an albino Malay girl, about sixteen, with straw-coloured hair and eyebrows, white skin. She was an extraordinary sight as she walked along the country road with her dark-skinned, black-haired companions. There appeared to be complete understanding and friendliness between them : none of the Japanese distrust of the albino.

In Malaya, the foot is a part of the body that must not be touched or played with by a stranger ; he may not approach it, whether to stroke or slap; whether booted, sandalled, stockinged or naked. And to touch someone with one's foot is the worst insult. But in Thailand, it is the head which must not be touched, and this reminded me that my Negro landlady, Madam Sheba, didn't like anyone to touch her head, and was so very sensitive about it that she wore, day and night, sleeping and waking, a resplendent turban, always beautifully wound in a style of which she alone knew the secret. She told me that Peter Jones's store had offered her a thousand pounds if she would give public demonstrations of how she tied her turban, but she refused, because the head is sacred and she could not allow it to be exposed, never mind touched, in public.

These vetoes on feet and heads are abandoned in the more intimate context of love-making, where everything is permitted.

The difference between Malaya and Japan is this : in Japan, a foreigner can live a pleasant life on his own, on the streets, where he sees so much that is interesting and delightful. Here in Malaya, street life is not so nice, nor so rewarding æsthetically and socially for a foreigner, though the Malays form an outdoor, night society. But the foreigner is not admitted to it, and it is always thought terribly strange if a foreigner tries to enter it. It is comparatively rare to see a foreigner walking the streets at night (or even by day). So in Malaya one must build up one's own private little world, and live in private rather than in public, if one is a foreigner. But while I have no wish to become a Malay, I do want to get to know them on their own ground and on their own terms. This is what is so difficult, when one is a white man : the Malays regard me with suspicion, and with stony hearts.

A lunch of two curry puffs, a mangosteen and a glass of coconut milk. But it doesn't bring me any nearer. The only approach is love ; and then the Malays unseal their secrets. But one can't be making love all the time.

Getting to know a foreign nation through one's sexual relationships with its members is no mean way of coming to an understanding : it's one way of keeping one's finger on the pulse of the public. Sex is a kind of love that can be almost intellectual in its inquiries. But love is love, with nothing intellectual about it. One's whole life should be an act of love, occasionally illuminated, and even explained, by acts of sex. And people aren't everything. They're only a small part of life : one must approach also with equal love all places and animals, plants and objects, touching them, speaking to them, listening to them and entering into them as if they were persons, and letting oneself be entered and penetrated by them too. This inter-penetration of the world and oneself is my idea of living and learning. And he who learns in this way can also teach.

The shaman outside the gates of the Jame' Mosque in Kuala Lumpur. He was dressed in a filthy old green shirt, with cheap cuff-links, and frowsty dhoti. He had long, matted hanks of dull black hair that had been twined and rolled until it resembled rusty black wool.

Almost the whole of his face was covered with a luxuriant black beard, also rather rusty. There were whitish-blue horizontal streaks of what looked like ash on his low forehead.

Before him was spread—he was sitting cross-legged on the ground—a large piece of blue plastic material on which there were various brass ornaments, one of them an oil-lamp in the shape of a cobra poised to strike, with a small flame burning from its fangs : round the lamp were cast some small yellowish flowers, very faded, perhaps jasmine. Near the wall stood several large framed photographs of the shaman and two pictures of northern Indian women, perhaps minor deities, executed in crude colours, garlanded with white flower-buds. One of the photographs showed the shaman sitting somewhere in the jungle, wreathed in snakes.

There was a large tray with joss-sticks burning in it and some lumps of white stuff, like camphor, about the size of small cubes of sugar.

A young Indian in Western clothes joined the crowd of crouching spectators, of which I was one, and gave the shaman a fifty-cent piece, which the shaman shoved into a small brass vase already crammed with coins and one-dollar notes.

Then he cast a necklace of large, carved brown beads on the ground in front of the young man, who picked up the necklace by taking only one bead between two fingers of his right hand.

The shaman took the necklace from him and began pronouncing the young man's fortune, speaking in Hindi.

Then he took a silver stick with a flat silver spear-shaped end and pointed it at the picture of one of the women. He then gave the silver spear to the young man who held it very tightly in his right hand, and the same time bowing his head, shutting his eyes hard and moving his lips in some fervent but silent wish or prayer.

Meanwhile the shaman took one of the white cubes and lit it

at the lamp. It immediately caught fire and the holy or wise man held it in his bare hands, letting it burn brightly on his fingertips while he intoned a sombre chant. He extinguished the flame by rolling the white stuff in the palms of his hands. After placing what was left of it in the ashes he stroked his beard. Perhaps it was anointed with some sort of essence that enabled him to hold the fire in his hands. The young Indian bowed to him and walked away with a broad grin on his handsome face. I jumped up and ran after him to ask him what it was all about, but when I asked him the smile disappeared, he looked about him uneasily and would say nothing. We walked a few steps together, and I offered him a cigarette, which he refused. Perhaps he was in a state of grace. After a few more steps in silence, he stopped, bowed slightly to me and made off rapidly in the opposite direction.

The Nepalese have a Mongoloid look. They are the most inscrutable of all the Indians in Malaya, and more " apart " even than the Boyanese Malays, who have their own language and refuse to speak real Malay. (They correspond to the " *eta* " class in Japan.) The Nepalese spread their stalls out on the pavements : beads, rings, lighters, polished pebbles for rings, large carved cowrie shells bearing legends like " Be Happy " and " Lucky Goodness." Silver bracelets, trinkets, heart-shaped medallions. A group of young Malays up from the country : they are helping one of their mates to choose a stone that looks like a well-polished pebble, almost an agate. They hold about half a dozen of the brownish stones in a piece of crimson paper, supplied by the vendor, in order to evaluate better their colours and shapes, which are mostly oval. These Malays from some kampong in a remote rural area are also very distant ; they do not seem able to integrate with other Malays. Theirs is still a life of kapa-kichi—the little axe with which offending outsiders are attacked—and of magic and superstition. They believe still in werewolves, in men with tails who change into tigers. It is in these rural areas mostly that men become possessed by devils and run " amok." These country people are exclusive : in their speech they frequently invert words and syllables, to keep what they are saying to each other a secret. In the ulu or deep jungle country, no Chinese would ever dare to look at a Malay girl : if he did, he would be in danger of mutilation or death from the " little axe." There is some of the arrogance of Islam in their proud apartness. It is curious to see them bargaining with the Nepalese : one wonders how two such self-contained races ever reach agreement on anything. For such as these, Merger will not mean a coming-together.

Malays think you must be out of your mind if you smile at them in the street. They have most of them long ago forgotten that a smile is a token of affection and friendship.

The self-consciousness of the Indians : a very important lady, bespectacled, huge, swathed in gorgeous scarlet and gold sari, is approached by a little Malay flag-vendor, a shy schoolboy. The Indian dame makes it a very ladylike event, dropping her ten-cent coin in the box with studied graciousness and slowly pondering the message on her purchase as she moves majestically on. She is very much the " social student " type of Indian, probably with a pass degree in economics, English and social science. One should admire the Indian determination to be smarter than the smart and as up-to-the-minute as possible, as if to be even slightly behind the times were a social disgrace : but it is repellent in Indians as in Europeans. The Japanese intellectuals often have this " progressive " itch, too. It is good to keep abreast of the times, but not *all* the time, for then one is taken in by the merely fashionable.

Indian shopkeepers are among the most tiresome in the world. They won't let you just stand for a moment looking at what they have to offer. As soon as you stop and show the slightest interest in their wares they are upon you with smiles of fulsome politeness, high-pressuring you immediately with : " What can I interest you in, sir ? " The " sir " is always the last straw. It always drives me away. Followed by the smiling, hopeful cry, with its Welsh inflection : " Something else more ? " The Indians' guttural booming of Welsh-accented English is both comic and irritating : it makes them sound so smug.

I fight against the depression always induced in me by most Indians, by their gloomy faces, the dingy whiteness of their long, trolloping, sheet-like robes, gracelessly worn, their stick-like limbs ; by their poverty, the reclining misery of beggars, as well as by the awful stodginess of more prosperous Indian families—the plump, sleek parents and their stout, cheeky children. Oh, the unutterably smug look of those great fat heavy black pigtails, almost obscenely rich and silkily-plaited, of Indian schoolgirls and women. Young matrons sometimes wear their pigtails tied in a gross chignon at the nape, like a great coiled turd.

The stout, pompous, full-bearded Sikh taxi-driver looked, with his great bun of grey hair swathed in a toque-like turban —from which yellow-grey curls straggled down the back of his neck—like a Victorian granny.

Elderly Sikhs make efficient watchmen ; they are so officious and self-important, always hoping to catch someone at fault. Others, minor businessmen, venerably yellow-grey-bearded, their once-noble eyes now lost in brown pouches and bristling yellowish eyebrows, their mouths invisible in rich white moustache and beard, trundle their massive corpulences along on ancient bicycles too small for their big fat knees in baggy khaki shorts.

The young, modern Sikh, smartly lounge-suited, with a pre-fabricated turban on his head, his beard neatly oiled and combed and rolled closely under his jaw-line, knotted under his chin and full cupid's-bow mouth. Big, luminous brown eyes, almost bovine in their thyroid, visionary stare, shaded by long, thick, sweeping black lashes. He is carrying *The Guardian Weekly* as a symbol of his emancipation.

The duskier-skinned Tamils, their foot-soles so pale ; the wet insides of their mouths full of flashing teeth, their tongues the raspberry-pink colour of a fresh, ripe fig's succulent interior.

The long loops of flesh formed by the distended lobes of a fat old Tamil woman on the bus ; the tops and edges of her ears are curiously decorated with cheap-looking, dull-gold chains and low-carat leaf ornaments. The wagging of the long, darkish loops of flesh that had once, presumably, been distended by huge ear-studs. Her dress was a sizzling, violent green colour swathed with mustard-yellow and magenta-purple draperies, cheap and rough-looking. Gold studs in her nostrils ; on her fingers a couple of thin gold bands : on her wrists, innumerable bangles of thin coloured metal. Round her plump, stolid neck were several gold or goldish chains. These, rubbing against her lavender-talcumed nape, had left a floury sweat-mark below her smooth, fat bun spiked with gold pins and adorned also with one gold—or brass—safety-pin. She occupied two seats, and was monumentally impressive. I couldn't help wondering what she wore underneath.

Waiting at the bus-station in Ampang Road I saw a dhoti-clad Indian bearing before him a big brass platter with some sort of floral offering on it. Occasional passers-by dropped money, a small coin or two, in the plate. As he drew nearer I noticed that his pale pink tongue was protruding, sticking or rather hanging right out, vividly contrasting with his mahogany lips and face. I was just thinking how wet and pink the tongue looked in the sun when suddenly—the impact took over a second—I realised that he had a silver spear stuck right through it. It was impossible for him to draw in his tongue. A mystical beggar: what absolute faith he witnessed to! There was no wound, none of the blood that Christ would have shed in similar circumstances. I was too impressed to tender him any of my unworthy money. All I could do was kneel before him. But that was not what he wanted, and he passed on.

Three strange, silent Nepalese: their incredibly filthy clothes, their brown, Tibetan-like faces, their long, black, braided hair, plaited with thin red cloth, wound like a greasy crown round their heads. Utterly expressionless faces. I followed them a long way, admiring their sturdy walk: suddenly they vanished round a corner and I couldn't find them again.

In the Muslim fasting month, there are many old Malays, wearing white skull-caps and dressed mainly in white, squatting on the five-foot ways and on the bridge beside the beggar cripples. These old men have small bags of rice open beside them, part of the tithes of rice offered to the Mosque by Malay padi farmers. The cripples, illegally begging with children, some of whom are barely three years old, also have bags of rice beside them at this time of the year. The chill little touch, slightly clammy, of the thin hands of child beggars at night, touching my bare arm in a clinging, timid plea, is heart-breaking: their light hands are like weary, dying insects alighting with weak feet on my big, hairy hams.

The Malay kiss: they sniff and snuffle at one's skin; like the Japanese, they find the smell of a white person's skin exotic and exciting. They sniff the nose first, then the cheeks and eyes, ears, neck and hair. With the right person, it can be delightful. One must, of course, sniff back. But many Malays have also been educated in Western-style kissing, and in what they call for some reason the " French " kiss. Some Malays have gold, silver or pewter teeth—usually only one, as an ornament. Sometimes teeth are surrounded by little gold frames, giving a kind of *cloisonné* effect, the white and apparently perfectly sound teeth peeping through golden, square or heart-shaped or circular rims. The effect is oddly cheering. When you kiss a person with gold teeth, the kiss is warm.

Each slim Malay office-boy, cycling dreamily home from work in the fretful afternoon heat of a gathering thunderstorm, has a comb, often with several broken teeth, protruding from the back pocket of his trousers.

Eating round the cleverly-cut cog-wheel of a slice of chilled pineapple, eating it down to the fibrous hub—but don't eat any of this, as it's an emetic—what nicer way, sometimes, to spend an otiose quarter of an hour ?

A Chinese bar-boy : he has a very self-assertive, self-important manner, but despite his cheeky bossiness he is charming, with his squint eyes, squinting upwards and away from each other in the tilting lids. Dark down on his upper lip ; a well-formed mouth : but he has the disconcerting habit of pushing out with the tip of his tongue a small denture holding three top front teeth.

The British soldiers call him John or Charlie : they usually call Malayans by those names. He is constantly on the move, switching lights, air-conditioners, fans, off and on, getting ice-cubes, making drinks, squeezing oranges, answering the telephone for the girls. He loves making out chits and adding up bills and is obviously jealous if anyone else takes on these tasks : like all Chinese, he is fascinated by business, by account books and money. When the proprietor comes in and does a little clerking, the bar-boy stands beside him watching, mute with admiration but itching to do it himself, rattling the abacus and pushing out his dentures in excited absorption as the night's takings are totted up.

An official from the Malayan Film Unit comes to my hotel to talk about a script I am doing. Oh, the official sentiments, ladled out with the unctuous, breathy sententiousness of a third-rate travelogue . . . " We are all brothers here in Malaysia, fighting, working, playing—and loving—side by side—Indians, Chinese, Sinhalese, Malays, British, Americans—Muslims, Buddhists, Christians, Hindus—all in the common bond of suffering but progressive humanity, etc." Trying hard not to puke, I contemplate his broad, flat, bespectacled face, shiny, pitted with great pores, like some big, glistening bun. Then he smiles, with white, perfect teeth, and his face is transformed : he is, after all, a human being, pleasant and charming.

Then he starts the travelogue sentiments again when he asks me if I will write a commentary on the film that is to be made of a state visit to India : the King and Queen of Malaya, the Yang di-Pertuan Agong and Raja Permaisuri Agong are already there. He suggests a beginning : " We arrive in Bombay, Gateway to India, land joined by many ties, cultural, spiritual, and economic, with our beloved motherland of Malaya and so on and so on. . . ." I express my doubts: not my sort of thing at all. " But, Mr. James, when we get to Agra, just think, to the Taj Mahal, that poem in marble, when we consider the swarming business-centres of Calcutta, the administrative glories of New Delhi, then what we need is a poet's touch, Mr. James, *your* touch. . . ." He hauls out of his brief-case a copy of *Life* magazine and reads out to me, in full, with awe-struck admiration, the " poetic commentary " written to accompany some colorpics of Chartres. " Something from your pen, Mr. James, in that line. . . ." No bloody fear.

We can destroy God by being good without him.

One thing I do like in Malaya : no one is surprised if one rides beside the driver in the front seat of a taxi. I only do this when the driver has an interesting face or seems disposed to talk. Some of the Chinese drivers have very tiny lanterns, unfortunately of plastic, dangling in their windscreens for the New Year. One Chinese driver gave me a rather peculiar sensation when I saw him pressing the foot-pedals with bare feet. Another allowed me to try on his ring, a huge, carbuncle-like polished pebble set in big golden claws. He told me he had come from Macao with a small gold brick taped under his scrotum. Later, in Macao, I was to see these gold bricks on sale : they are usually brought in by refugees from the mainland. He spoke respectfully of the " babas " and " nonas," old Chinese men and women whose families have been resident in Malaya for a long time. He said they are " good people, best Chinese."

Whenever a white person tells a Chinese taxi-driver where to go (in English) he nearly always says " Wah ? " Even if he understands first time he is so conditioned to the idea of not understanding what a white person says that he can't help saying, " Wah ? " When I learnt a little Cantonese I would give directions in that language but always the driver would say, " Wah ? " Though perhaps that was due to my bad inflections. Malay and Indian as well as Chinese taxi-drivers often didn't know where places were : one had to direct them oneself. Many of them did not know important public buildings like the Dewan Bahasa dan Pustaka, the Cultural Hall of the Language and Literature Agency or the Tengku Abdul Rahman Hall.

Shirley is a favourite name for Chinese girls. Bar hostesses and taxi-girls (professional dancing-partners) have names like Ava, Gloria, Shirley-Anne, Lily, Alice, Nancy and, of course, Suzie, the most popular of all.

Chinese youth dreamily fingering his smooth chin, moodily searching for a hair to pluck out. His latched lids flicker with interest when I sign the chit for our drinks : he leans over to see how much it is. Again that passionate curiosity about bills and money.

The pallid, round faces of little Chinese boys ; when their small mouths smile, they reveal perfect, tiny, pearly teeth, like the teeth one sees between a high-class doll's formally-parted rosebud lips.

I saw a Chinese wearing a tiny rectangle of black cloth pinned to the left sleeve of his shirt with a safety-pin. I stopped him, politely, and asked him why he was wearing that. He replied very courteously that it was a sign of mourning for his dead father. If he had been mourning his dead mother, the black rectangle would be pinned on the right sleeve. These tokens of respect and sorrow have to be worn for a whole year following the decease. Sometimes one sees blue or green oblongs being worn : these are for sons and daughters or for sisters and brothers.

The Chinese death-houses : racks upon racks of old, dying men and women brought there by weeping relatives to die. They lie there, emaciated, unmoving, silent, patiently waiting for the end in an atmosphere of decay and quiet suffering. They are brought small bowls of rice and soup by relatives, sometimes by little grandchildren. There is an unemotional nobility in such a stark and practical way of dying. There is the wish not to be a burden to the living, not to take up room in crowded tenements, not to bring ill fortune upon the household by dying in it. The death-houses in Singapore are sanctuaries of selflessness, where ugliness, pain and horror become, in their nakedness, eternal truths. The acceptance of death makes saints of the most ordinary mortals. Beside them, the living look clumsy, sinful, weak and helpless. The dying are the ones who are strong, for they have no fear of terror when it comes.

The wine made from the ginseng root is much valued by the Chinese. The root is forked, like a mandrake root, and the Chinese name, jên shên, alludes to this image of forked man. (Jên is Mandarin for " man.") The Chinese prepare it with great care, and it is expensive. Small bottles of the wine are sometimes given as gifts at Chinese New Year.

A Chinese cook-amah : an old lady of seventy, many times a grandmother. She visits the cinema every Sunday, and on Monday mornings regales her employer with an account of the film she has seen. For her, all films are divided into two classes : " velly cly " and " velly laugh." As for the characters portrayed in them, " all men velly bad," and " all woman velly solly."

The old moon, sinking through the black palms, looked like a suspended parachute of peach-coloured silk. I was reminded of the old Japanese teaching that literary composition is the best medicine for sorrow.

The girl on the switchboard at my hotel is a Hokkien Chinese. Her voice is abrupt and hoarse ; she speaks good English in clipped, rapid, deep tones, and is as matter-of-fact as any Chinese male. At first I was dismayed and terrified by her until I gradually realised that there was some sort of sympathy growing up between us. She usually shot out her phrases through clenched teeth, and the first time she smiled at me I was taken aback. It was something I had never expected, for in fact in order to stand up to her aggressive maleness I had been consistently rude to her. One day she told me that a certain person from the English Department at the University had telephoned, giving her a very strange message for me, to the effect that I had to go and see the Prime Minister next morning at eight o'clock. This I recognised as a feeble leg-pull. The message had, however, ended with two words which, the girl said, had made her blush. Surprised, I asked what they were. She became at that moment all girlish and coy and said : " I cannot tell you. It was that gentleman who has the Chinese boy-friend. You know, he is always drunk and shouting silly things. But I will write it down for you." She wrote the words on a piece of paper, slipped it into an envelope and handed it to me with a confused apology. The words were : " F—— off." It became plain to me then that I was not wanted at the University, and I decided I would leave before the year was out.

An elderly, dowagery, almost matronly Chinese " boy " at a hotel in Taiping had a swaying walk, slightly camp, toes turned in, head kept level. Some Chinese boys have an almost teetering walk, as if their feet had been bound from infancy. They take short steps and seem to stub their toes into the ground then rise springily upon them in a swaying, dancing movement that informs their whole body and is most attractive to watch.

How odd, all these magazines called *Male*, *Men Only* and so on, are full of pictures of the female only. They should surely be called *Women Only*. This reminds me of the periodical Southey was expelled from Westminster for editing, *The Flagellant*, which was against, not, as one might imagine, for corporal punishment.

The thin-bearded Chinese beggars are like old ivory carvings of sages and hermits. I saw one wearing an old solar topee, his ragged shirt open on a flat, bony yellow chest and wrinkled belly, his neck all veins and tendons, his hands trembling, emaciated claws. I admired his very lovely, soft, whitish beard, the drooping ends of the thin moustache round a curiously youthful, pretty, dry, sad mouth ; the extinct yet seeing eyes, the legs like sticks, the feet like brittle parchment fans slightly open, slightly broken. He trots a little in his walk : this trotting in such an ancient and decrepit person is heart-rending—as appalling as Lear going off-stage at a run.

To-day I saw an old blind beggar man led by a young Chinese girl in rosebudded samfu in a hardware shop. He bought a bright pink enamel pudding-basin, his new begging-bowl. His old one has had a hole worn through the bottom. He sits with his new bowl on the bridge; it is a pretty bowl, with the label of gold paper still sticking to the inside. I drop a one-dollar note silently into the bowl, as a first offering or handselling. But he has heard the soundless fall of the note : I was reminded of those Buddhist mystics who can hear the sound of fallen snow. He seized the note and felt 't all over, rapidly. I realised he might have been hoping for a five-dollar note. I didn't have one : all I had was a ten-dollar note which I laid carefully in the bowl. Again he heard the note fall. This time he seized the bowl, got to his feet and hurried away across the bridge, his skinny hand on the balustrade.

At a very rowdy Chinese restaurant full of shouting cooks and bawling waiter-boys I ordered some tea while I studied the menu. "Wah ? " said the boy. He didn't understand, and brought me a glass of iced lichee water—sweetened iced water with a few canned lichees which the Malays call " cat's eyes." I had some chicken stewed in a paper bag, followed by sour-sweet langsat fruit. While I was eating this a singer-beggar came with his one-string fiddle made from a broom shank and half a coco-nut shell and wandered round the restaurant and the pavement outside singing and playing a weird music. The song over, he went round the tables again, leaving on each a small packet wrapped in old Lucky-Strike carton-paper. Inside the packet, when I unfolded it, was a small nut. (No one, I later learnt, ever opened a packet or took one away : it is courteous to the beggar just to leave it for him to collect.) Then the man came round and everyone gave him a small coin, ten cents, " for the packet," which he took away. The packets were really to save the beggar's face and to make it easier for us to give him some-thing. Also it makes his begging legal. When he had collected his handful of small coins and the packets, he went off to the next kedai kopi to try it on again.

A visit to a Malay kampong in a fairly rural area, not quite jungle. I was taken to the headman's house where I sat on the veranda sipping tea thickly laced with condensed milk. There were many faded family photographs on the walls.

Across the compound (our English word is derived from the Malay " kampong ") is a small, plain wooden mosque. A piece of hollow tree-trunk hangs from its eaves; this is beaten by the headman to announce the beginning and end of fasting hours in the fasting month. There is some joking about the fasting period, shortly to begin, and about Muslims who secretly sneak a meal of Chinese noodles in back streets.

"Bad words" had been scrawled in coloured chalks on the sides of some of the huts: "Saleh plays with his brother" was one of the inscriptions, which had obviously been there a long time. When the phrases are translated for me, there is great hilarity among the kampong boys. Which of them, I wonder, is Saleh? It's just a great joke to everyone.

The headman's wife was stirring oblong pans of latex with a square piece of metal. Acetic acid had just been added to the latex, freshly-tapped early that morning, to make it curdle. Then it will be rolled through the iron rollers of two small mangles. One of these has grooved rollers which impart a goffered surface to the rubber. One boy says that the rubber grown in his kampong is the poorest in all Malaya. But the village is surrounded by golden rice-fields, producing about three hundred piculs a year, more than enough for the forty inhabitants who sell the remainder at a good price.

I met some local girls, rubber-tappers with lavender hoods, blue smocks and black trousers: they looked so pretty, I wanted to take a colour picture of them but they rushed past on their bicycles with heads averted, too shy to be snapped.

There was a little café with some handsome boys and young men lolling about in it; they wore nothing but chequered sarongs and lit the cool dusk of the interior with their broad, friendly smiles. They gave, as did the whole village, an impression of indolent happiness, playing their rustic games under the glittering, blackish-green spokes of the coconut palm-trees' feathery wheels of foliage.

It is amusing, in the newspapers, to see a certain well-known brand of food-drink advertised in Chinese terms. We are given the story of Willie Khoo, a badminton champion who is now a "has-been" because he is so tired and off-colour these days. . . . He goes to see a doctor who advises you-know-what. Next comes a delicious little drawing of the washed-out Willie tucked up in bed, his thick-fringed slant-eyes prettily closed as he enjoys refreshing sleep. One month later: the champion, managing to hold both a racquet and a girl, is being congratulated by his coach : " Well, you certainly gave Bong a trouncing that time . . . ! " Willie grins and (thinks).

A curious sign outside a shop in Batu Road, where the Indians are always having " Monster Sales " says : Business War !

A Malay, on waking, told me : " I dreamed of snow." Yet he has never seen snow, excepting on the moving pictures. He believes it is an omen of great good fortune. I, too, had dreamt of something white : my maid in Japan sticking a re-address label on an envelope with cold rice. The Malays believe white is a lucky colour, but for the Chinese it is the symbol of death. Red is the lucky Chinese colour.

Snow I have never known, nor seen except in pictures, to-night I dream of you in the dark, falling endlessly as the light of stars upon my pillow's lifted face, sealing my shut lids with white sleep, snow whiter and deeper than snow, whiter than opium, snow of my dream.

The moon like a bunched fist of bleached birds' bones, of cold-berried mistletoe.

Knees that smell of nutmegs, hands warm with spice, ears hot under the long hair.

Plump Bengalis in soiled white drapes walk excitedly on fussy, fat legs.

I woke at 5.30 a.m. and sneezed, once. The Chinese believe that to sneeze between 5 and 7 a.m. means that " you can either expect a visitor soliciting assistance or an unexpected windfall of money." I wish it could be both.

Two Chinese names on the front of shop-houses : Manpals (in Batu Road) and Man Kok (in Ampang Road).

Such a welter of people, of races : how will they ever " merge " ? In the words of Matthew Arnold, they are :

Between two worlds—one dead,
The other powerless to be reborn.

11. Flowers, Trees, Animals

The whole of the Far East is gradually being carried away by ants. Great termitaries are common sights in the fields and the secondary jungle. Telegraph poles are of cast iron or of specially-treated timber. Native houses, which once used to rest upon timber stilts, now often are built on concrete supports : planks and posts chemically treated to prevent destruction by ants and termites are now used in the construction of huts and houses.

But there are still ants everywhere, whole regiments of them marching unswervingly across roads, bridging streams by using fallen trunks, running in dense relays up and down the walls of houses, devouring whole sections of jungle and forest with their noiseless gnashings. The consciousness of this silent host everlastingly at their subversive activities used sometimes to give me a feeling of panic. Yet I liked them : I admired their determination, their undeviating purpose, their colossal strength and fearless agility, their quick intelligence. Some could bite and sting very painfully. There were all kinds : shy, modest, retiring ones, aggressive ones, eager gossipers and grim fighters. If ever I accidentally crushed one, I was struck by the atmosphere of concern and bewilderment, the grief, almost, that would immediately develop among his brothers ; often I watched the careful way they carried the crushed body away, returning again and again to the scene of the accident to confer, to gather up last remnants of the corpse and then to continue with their awful tasks as if nothing had happened. I felt they had a collective courage as well as strength of will. The world, I began to think, would not be too bad a place if it were taken over by the ants.

But I should hate a world taken over entirely by mosquitoes. Though their numbers have been considerably reduced in certain parts of the Far East, including Malaya, one lone mosquito in a room is enough to disturb my peace, if I happen to be composed.

From time to time in the Malayan newspapers there would appear angry letters from readers complaining that their particular part of town had been infested with vicious mosquitoes for weeks, and when was the Health Department going to do something about them?

About mid-February is the beginning of the new season for mosquitoes—young, inexperienced, long-shanked, coltish, black. When they are first hatched and have still not had time to learn the nasty ways of human beings, they sit dumbly on the wall at the head of my bed or perch on the matted floor beside my sleeping-roll, just inviting a swipe. They are sprightly and I am a bad shot: I nearly always miss, and hate it when I don't. But one of them alone with me in a bedroom without a mosquito-net is enough to agitate me and keep me awake all night. They always bite me on the knuckle joining my right index finger to the hand, or on the knuckles of the little fingers, which they seem to find especially succulent and tempting.

The young ones leave a big, white, irritable blister; they don't seem to draw blood. Whenever I manage to squash one —how un-Buddhist!—there is no trace of gore. But their high soprano scream in the hot dark is one of the most chilling sounds I know. In the jungle there are large, savage varieties called "tiger mosquitoes."

The giant Malayan cicadas sound like cats squalling: vast choirs of them can be heard chugging in the padi-fields, backed by the stertorous, mechanical croaking of frogs.

The climate, not really suitable for humans, is one in which these un-human and anti-human communities thrive. During Christmas week, when humidity was high in Kuala Lumpur and temperature was nearly above blood heat—humidity was 100 per cent and the temperature went up to nearly ninety-two degrees—I was interested to read in Dr. Fred Hoyle's book, *The Black Cloud*, that people who live in areas where humidity is high could perish if temperature rose much above the level of the body's normal blood heat, which is 98·4 degrees. For-tunately, in Malaya the extremes of humidity and heat seldom occur together : the highest humidity generally comes at night, when temperatures are lower.

The jungle, besides being extremely unpleasant at times, is also very dull. There are snakes, elephants, rare rhinoceros, tigers, but they tend to keep out of the way when they hear or smell a human being approaching. Jungle-walking is not really very adventurous. There are lots of existing trails, and even " jungle-bashing," that is, beating out new routes, though arduous, is hardly fraught with peril.

Jungle-bashing is a hobby practised by a few keen white men, and it is often included in training courses or initiative tests for troops. There is no danger, as long as everything is well planned. It is best to go in a small party with an experienced leader who knows how to plot and mark the track. The Malay boys are good trappers and keep one well supplied with mouse-deer or pelandok, porcupine or landak and various kinds of wild fowl.

The only wild life one sees is monkeys. Leeches are a problem when wading streams or pools. Land leeches also are unpleasant, like long dark loops that lope along the ground or drop from trees on to their victims. They usually attach them-selves to the leg and blow themselves into a bloated lump with blood. You can pull them off fairly easily : a lighted cigarette-end encourages them to let go. But they can leave a nasty wound. Big red ants called curinga, and giant wasps are also to be avoided.

On my first night in the jungle I went alone, taking a Lilo and some mosquito-netting which I slung over some branches above my bed. I was near a well-beaten track and had no intention of getting lost. Nothing happened. I slept quite soundly except when I was woken up by queer noises—the harsh screams and yells of flying foxes or fruit-eating bats.

One must be careful, however, not to pitch one's Lilo under the deadly upas tree, which drips a corrosive poison that turns one's flesh to a green jelly. (Upas is the Malay word for poison.)

When I got up just after dawn the Lilo was flat : I had put it down on a large thorn. Later I heard that five wild elephants had been in the area and had killed a farmer.

One animal which I did not get a chance to observe in its wild state was the giant monitor lizard which inhabits the islands off the coast of Kedah; they have been spotted on Songsong Island by men of the Royal Australian Air Force who say they have seen specimens over ten feet in length, though the average length is six feet. At least one of the species of lizards on Songsong Island is thought to be the same as that found on the Galapagos Islands off the west coast of South America. If this is confirmed, it will be a major discovery in saurian biology for Galapagos lizards have never before been sighted in Malaya.

Though I did not see any large lizards, I saw many of their beautiful skins displayed for sale in K.L. They are made into shoes, handbags and belts.

The aborigines, like the wild life, are chary of strangers: I never encountered a member of the remote tribes in his own environment, though longing to do so. They are small, friendly but timid hunters and fishers. I had dreamed of bare breasts and bodies painted like zebras, from whose embraces I would emerge covered with black and white stripes. Alas, it was not to be.

The delightful chichaks, of course, are everywhere, and I came to be very fond of one or two which inhabited the rooms of a Malay house I later occupied. There is a curious superstition current among Malays and babas that if a chichak gives a cluck while one is saying something, it signifies that one is speaking the truth or that the remark is prophetic. The creatures look like salamanders, but they love coolness. They adore the chill of a refrigerator, nibble at the curious rococo ice-cubes my model makes, sip drops of wine or gin spilt on its top. (So do the ants, which get drunk and rush round in dizzy circles: but drink never seems to affect the chichak's agility and presence of mind.) There are both fawn-green and black chichaks. I have both kinds, and am indeed favoured. The house they inhabit is a fortunate one. They often vanish before a death.

I miss my favourite insects, spiders. There must be spiders about, because I see the telegraph-wires simply cocooned in their webs. But I never saw one in my hotel rooms or later in my house. Instead, there were a number of quite large, pale-ginger, shining cockroaches which gave me the shudders, they looked so sleek and well-fed and sly. They marched intelligently about the house, exploring the floorboards and the furniture with watchful intentness. As soon as I moved they would freeze into immobility and if I threw a book or a shoe they would scuttle off at lightning speed. I bought some white pellets to put down in corners ; cockroaches find these tablets irresistible. They eat them then go away and swell up and die ; other cockroaches eat the dead ones and become poisoned in their turn. It was horrid to think of all that going on under my floorboards, but it had to be done.

I noticed that the ants wouldn't touch dead cockroaches when these had been poisoned : how clever of them ! But they would become mad with grief over a dead fellow-worker or even over another kind of ant. One tiny ant carried away a big black-and-red soldier ant, holding him high above his head like a weight-lifter with barbells. When these big ants sip drops of spilt wine they almost immediately begin walking about on their hind legs.

As soon as I arrived in my Malay house, which I shall describe later, two swallows started nesting in the metal cup which covers the place where the iron shaft of the fan enters the ceiling. Every morning I would find straw and feathers scattered on the table underneath. It was a happy omen, but useless, because I soon left the house, and Malaya, for good.

A huge, green, spotted grasshopper : its very low-slung, heavy, navicular body cradled on long-shanked, high-elbowed legs. It sways about on these spring suspensions as if dazed. Perhaps it is in the middle of some courtship ritual and has flown in from the hotel garden for a rest. When I wasn't looking, it suddenly flew up and landed very weightily on my hair. I jumped and the grasshopper jumped. Then it lurched through the air to an adjoining chair. It seemed exhausted. A large Bengali lady came into the lounge and was about to sit in the very arm-chair on whose seat the grasshopper had perched. I rushed forward and just managed to rescue the poor dazed insect in time. The lady gave me such a look. She had very nearly sat on my hand too.

The chichaks seem this evening to be glued on the glass of the fanlight and look like yellow paint-splashes, for I can see only the pale undersides of their bodies pressed fervently against the panes. Perhaps they are digesting a big meal. One was on the same pane as a large flying ant, with which it was courageously but unsuccessfully trying to do battle. It kept giving little jumps to face its brown-winged opponent's restless movements : the ant was small by comparison but its scaly wings looked fierce and unappetising and I really felt it was the little lizard that was at bay.

This morning, at breakfast, a large, milk-white, brown-and-red-spotted butterfly, its wings netted with jet-black veins or lines, was spreadeagled against the pane. The sky shining through it made it look like a segment of stained glass. Name : Lacewing butterfly.

I opened a book and a black butterfly flew out. It was one of those butterflies, dark and limp, that rise from the long wayside grasses like dead shreds of ash from a bonfire of paper fanned by summer draughts.

Pretty names for Malayan butterflies : Mapwing, Tawny, Harlequin, Netwing, Marbled, Mottled, Blue-branded, Banded Tiger.

An almost bat-like, dark-brown butterfly, at least six inches across its triangular, ragged wings. From the white tips of the upper pinions, two narrow white stripes traverse the whole of the top and lower vanes. I wondered at its absolute immobility near the top of the green wall, under the vast snows of the brilliantly-lit hotel ceiling. I leaned over the stair well and wafted a current of air towards it with a scented fan. The wings only just stirred, like dead leaves. Another gentle breeze from my paper fan and it detached itself from the wall and fell, softly fluttering, to the hall floor before gathering sufficient strength to rise again, weakly, sleepily. I felt it was near the end of its days and went and locked myself in my room, ashamed at having disturbed it.

Kept awake by a chichak beating its miniature alligator tail, that seems so tough and hard, against the wall in a febrile flagellation. It is the noise of a highly-polished boot being whipped by a well-worn leather bootlace.

The leaf-insect, like a withered leaf, blunders away, when I flick it off my brown arm, on roaring wings, its body big and heavy. To-night, swarms of flying ants, seeking their queens, cloud the sodium-vapour lamps, shadowing the roads. I find my navel full of discarded brown wings when I get home, and my hair is stiff with scales.

Nightfall here is not as sudden as one is told it is in the

tropics. A fairly long twilight lasts from 6.30 to 7 p.m. The same in the mornings. But at the end of twilight and with the extinction of the afterglow, it is quickly dark.

Enormous rubbish-bins, seven feet high, stand on the arcaded pavements. They are filled mainly with paper and broken strip-lighting tubes. A big black rat, almost as big as a mouse-deer, leapt out of one I was rummaging in near the Mosque.

Large white flatfish, about two dozen of them, laid out to dry in the hot afternoon sun on a deserted traffic-island in Old Market Square. A pi-dog with pointed, foxy ears and snout, sniffs at one, raises a leg just before he is hit by a stone cast by a small boy guarding the fish.

This morning a sky almost entirely covered by clouds like curdled milk. The clouds, packed together, were fairly regular in size and with a roughly square shape, like flocking or quilting. Occasional thin rents of blue, but on the whole the uniformity of the pattern was amazing.

Petaling Jaya is famed for its thunderstorms and sunsets and also for its heat. This is due to the lack of trees. The lately-planted ones look small and straggly in an artificial desert landscape of cement and riven stone, of basely functional architecture : offices and banks like vast, grilled, oblong beehives, box-like concrete houses, each with its concrete drive and car-porch, its heavily-grilled and padlocked doors. (These houses are always being burgled.) Dead-straight streets and roads ; everywhere scarred, churned, reddish earth, broken-down embankments between dual-carriageways, joyless seas of dull-green roofs.

A notice on a drab public lawn outside some government building says : " Kip off the grass." Lying beside it, the lurid egg-yolk-yellow cover of the *Overseas Daily Mirror*.

This is a happy land for some domestic animals. The soft-eyed, placid bullocks—one horn painted red, the other green for the festival of Thaipusam—ramble fearlessly about the roads, tugging at the ever-long, ever-lush grass.

It is a land of dogs and puppies : nearly every household has at least two. They are used as guard-dogs, and they are trained to bark at the slightest noise, at every passer-by, making the nights hideous and sleepless with their howlings. The dogs standing on the house-steps of Straits Chinese, looking this way and that along the road—how bourgeois, narrow-minded, unimaginative, intolerant and censorious they look! In these respects they resemble some of the owners. Or one sees them walking backwards and forwards in front of houses, looking like goody-goody school-children proceeding sagely to school. The dogs symbolise the smug owners of the houses, their self-satisfied, pampered children who are outraged by any departure from the norm. These guardians of respectability are somehow not real dogs : they have been degraded, but accept the degradation because they have known nothing else. They bark hysterically at everyone and everything and carry on savage vendettas with neighbours' dogs, but only with the dogs of neighbours poorer and therefore socially of lower class than their own masters. This class-consciousness in dogs is a horrifying trait. And if one stands up to them and defies their barking and bared teeth they prove cowards. Certainly they didn't seem to be much good at stopping burglars. I was burgled twice in two weeks when I was living in a house surrounded by the residences of rich towkays whose gardens were overrun by dogs. But more of this later.

One afternoon a big brown dog came and laid down by my front steps, in the shade. He died there, in complete silence, hounded to death by other dogs which ran away when they knew he was dying. Two boys dug a hole in my garden and buried him. There was an uneasy silence over the neighbourhood all that afternoon.

One evening, passing the large open doorway of the Station Hotel's kitchen annexe, I heard a pitiful mewing coming from the direction of a monsoon drain. I hunted round in the semi-darkness before discovering that where I was standing, right between my feet, was a new-born kitten. It surely couldn't have been abandoned by its mother. It must have been left there by someone who didn't want it. Just a few feet away in the hotel kitchen sleek cats were reclining, giving themselves an occasional lazy lick.

I picked up the kitten, which was surprisingly heavy. It was wet and dusty and sticky with after-birth. I carried it into the kitchen, to the great surprise of the Chinese cook-boys, and placed it beside one of the cats, which gave a start of surprise and immediately began to sniff curiously at it. Another cat came up to lick it.

I left the kitten to the cats and to the tender mercies of a few kitchen-boys and women. There was nothing else I could do, as at that time I was still living in a hotel and could not have kept the kitten in my room.

A few weeks later, on a car drive at night to Port Dickson, I saw some puppies lying on the road, struggling feebly. I made the driver stop. I got out and picked up the puppies which had obviously been thrown out of a passing car by someone who couldn't be bothered to find them homes. One of them was limping a little but otherwise they seemed all right. I wrapped them in a blanket and held them on my knees all the way back to Port Dickson where I bought saucers of milk for them at an open-air café and left them in charge of the proprietors. The event reminded me of my first night in Kyoto, when I saw a small white spitz knocked down and killed, in a yelping flurry of feathery tail, by a motorist who did not stop.

A long, boring, bruised-looking twilight, sinisterly still and faintly mad. A fortune-teller was squatting on the pavement, half-naked, with an emaciated kitten beside him, tied to a lamp-post by a length of string. The kitten was ceaselessly mewing with hunger, ceaselessly pacing or rather wobbling to the end of the length of string and back, walking over the beggar's dark thighs, pushing its face up against his chest, looking up at him and miowling in a desperate way, a sound of such horrible unhappiness and distress that I ran and bought a cup of hot water and condensed milk, poured it into an old tin and took it to the kitten, which drank avidly. The fortune-teller put out his hand. I only had a handful of small coins, which I gave him. He passed each coin through the oily flame of a small candle-stump. A few Indians gathered round, laughing mockingly, thrusting the kitten away from the milk with their feet, and laughing uproariously as it struggled back to the tin. I felt my heart was breaking. I went away, pursued by the sound of that unfeeling laughter, and of the kitten's renewed complaints.

Stumpy-tailed cats : Malays believe there was once a Prince who was in love with a Princess. She was very poor. All she had was a ring, and to keep it safe she knotted it in a cat's tail.

That is why Malay cats now have a lump at the end of their stumpy tails. The Chinese have long-tailed cats. No Chinese would ever tie a valuable ring on a cat's tail!

Long-tailed monkeys play on the green slope outside my hotel window. They sometimes enter the hotel rooms and steal fruit and cigarettes. Guests encourage them by throwing bananas and plums. Every morning, sounds of hard scrubbing come from the yard below my window, where the Chinese washerwomen chatter at their work, assisted by small girls and boys. They are watched over by a brooding old grandfather monkey, a baboon. He has fine grey mutton-chop whiskers and a backside displaying all the colours of the Union Jack. I throw him an apple : it is seized by a smaller, livelier monkey. I throw another and the old grandfather manages to snatch it away from one of his wives. He sits apart from the others now, on his furry hind legs, exhibiting his big pale paunch, and slowly, delicately eats the apple, chewing with closed lips, with great application and solemnity, all the time batting blissfully his sky-blue eyelids. He has reddish fur round his eyes and on the top of his head. He expertly cracks a pecan and with dainty fingers extracts the bits of kernel. A smaller monkey has difficulty in cracking the pecan I have thrown and with a squeal of rage he hurls it at a washerwoman. I throw him a banana as a consolation prize. He runs away with it, pursued by the rest.

Round the eaves of the hotel, nests of collocalia swiftlets. The Chinese boys dislodge and collect them by using long, sharpened bamboo poles. They make them into bird's-nest soup, a great delicacy which, I notice, never appears on the hotel menu.

The grass of lawns and pavement verges here, so rich, springy and soft, what can it be ? In the hotel garden it is tough, resilient, spiky, tinged with red. It is called " Serangoon grass " or *digitaria*. All sporting surfaces, for golf and racing and so on, are planted with this.

The strong, heady odour of verbena in the garden, after a thunderstorm. Its fragrance seems to be the very essence of my memories of Colette, of Claudine. Then comes the disgusting stink of rancid diesel fumes from the night express standing in the station.

The kapok tree's gaunt appearance, with its thin branches stuck out at right-angles to the dead-straight trunk, has earned it the nickname of P.W.D. tree. (Because people think it resembles a telegraph pole erected by the Public Works Department.)

Flame of the forest or *delonix regia* : a great abundance of magnificent crimson flowers. The nipa palm or *nipa fruticans* is the best variety of palm for attap roofing. Sugar can also be tapped from its inflorescent stalks.

Plants which are very fashionable to-day in European split-level contemporary-style dwellings grow almost as freely as weeds in Malaya : the castor-oil plant, for example, which has a rather attractive foliage. *Ricinus communis*.

Some ponds are covered with the large, waxy-pink flowers of the sacred lotus or *nelumbium nelumbo*, a heavenly Latin name. It is widely cultivated for its roots and seeds which can be eaten. Melon and sunflower seeds are also eaten ; the latter are delicious.

The durian, related to the West Indian soursop, is a fruit I developed a passion for. It is very much an acquired taste. It has a hard, prickly skin and is about the size of a very large coconut ; it tastes like peaches and cream but has a most peculiar, pungent scent. It should not be eaten with alcohol, or when one has a hangover, as the after-effects can be fatal.

The langsat, growing in bunches like small, pale-brown kidney potatoes is delicious when it is ripe and sweet. The interior has five milky-white segments, full of juice whose sweetness has a very special tang. The taste is like that of a pomelo.

The rambutan or *nephelium lappaceum* has cool, white, sweet flesh. It tastes rather like a lichee. It is very common in Malaya, and in December when it becomes ripe the spiky red-green outer shells or husks are scattered all over the streets. On all the main roads out of town there are small stalls selling bunches of rambutan and also mangosteen. (The name is derived from the Malay word " mangustan.") There is a Malay saying : " Durian is the king of fruit, and mangosteen is the queen."

I bought two " star-fruit " or *averrhoa calambola*. It is called *belimbing manis* by the Malays, though it is really a native of Java. It is waxy, greenish-yellow, with five sharp vertical ribs. It is a sort of large pod and is very sweet.

In the complicated drink called " gin sling " or " planter's punch " the full slices of lime and orange, studded with chopped pips, are as delicate, complex, translucent and crystalline as rose-windows. They glow in the shafts of sun splintering the long, light-rimmed glass in which the chinking cubes of ice go toc-toc like a couple of stained-glass diamonds that have worked loose in a rustling tiara.

A distant ceiling-fan, switched on at a low speed, revolves in a slow and stately way, like a three-legged dowager going upstairs. British soldiers singing at the bar a song that has the refrain : " Ro-oly-o, shit or bust. . . ." Later, a very improper version of " The Twelve Days of Christmas."

Outside in the garden the Artillery Plant accompanies them with its tiny detonations. This plant, *pilea microphylla*, is called by the charming name of katumpangan in Malay. When the plant is touched the stamens burst open with small explosions, giving off dense clouds of pollen like smoke from artillery. Another plant in the garden is the beautiful Javanese Ixora or *Ixora javanica*, a tall bush with thick upright clusters, flat-topped like cow-parsley, of vivid red flowers. There are wild forms of this plant in the jungle.

Waiting for a bus under a big, shady tulip-tree in Brickfields Road—what a name ! So typical, like Hose Road also, of this most prosaic of all tropical lands—one of the flowers fell from the topmost branches and hit me quite a thump on the head. I thought it must be a bird or grasshopper or a praying mantis. The huge, leathery red flower with hairy black stamens was a gross goblet of a thing. It was odourless and rather grotesque ; heavy, too. I sent it to someone in England by airmail and it cost a lot of money.

The netting round the tennis courts in Pudu Road is draped thickly with curtains of Railway Creeper or *Ipomoea cairica*.

Someone has sent me a basket of vermilion gladioli and large marguerites set in a round tin of damp moss and filled out with stiff branches of furry green fern. The Chinese girl at the hotel desk asks, in her deep, sharp voice : " Who sent you the basket of flowers ? " She thinks I am trying to hide something from her when I tell her the truth : that I don't know.

The rain-tree is so called because in the evening or during rain the leaflets fold together. On ancient rain-trees one finds all kinds of parasitical plants, particularly wild orchids and clumps of ferns. There are some lovely ones along the Ipoh Road : they afford good shade when I walk along there by day.

In the Lake Gardens there is a curious tree with immensely long, dark pods ; these wrinkled pods are about a yard long and two inches wide and the tree is very tall—at least sixty feet. It is a horse cassia or *cassia grandis*. Another tree with long seed-pods is a cassia called Shower of Gold. There is one in the Maxwell Road.

But of all the lovely trees in Malaya, the palm is the loveliest. They are always delightful to watch, whether the tall, straight, royal palms of official residences or the leaning, mop-headed lay-abouts of ulu and kampong. One of Malaya's most perfect sights is a clump of coastline palms spurring the crimson-sashed sunrise or the glittery silver of a moonwashed bay with their wind-wobbled, breeze-buckled wheels of shivery, shining, sharp, black, shagtop leaves. Or the traveller's palm : the breeze riffling through its almost geometrically-arranged leaves that are like a full hand of cards or a fan of greenback notes.

The Ramphil flower shop in Ampang Road is one of my favourite rendezvous. The charming, energetic proprietor sends gorgeous cartons of orchids to any part of the world for a very reasonable price. (I later discovered he was a most wonderful ronggeng dancer.) He has two girls in samfu preparing baskets of flowers—marguerites, yellow chrysanthemums, gladioli ; but the orchids are his great pride. He has queer, spidery varieties from Indonesia, Borneo, Sarawak, and Malaya itself. The names are attributive : Spider, Scorpion, Spotted Snake. Some dull yellow ones, spotted with brown, with very thin, crimped petals like ravelled wool, and some luminous white dove-orchids. The native ones are faintly reptilian, like small vipers, I don't know why.

This is a country of jungle. It is never far away. It keeps encroaching on fields and gardens, towns and villages, and only the ceaseless vigilance of armies of men, women and children armed with sickles and parangs and axes keeps it at bay.

I lie in a cane chair on the veranda of my Malay house, looking at my garden through the cracks in the bamboo blinds that are called " chicks." The wide-spreading rain-tree, the round-topped mango tree, the white-clotted frangipani and the toy-like papaya are all seen through the horizontal splits like trees ceaselessly fragmented and reassembled on the selective grid of a TV set. Screened, masked, riddled with dark and light, still the shapes and the colours come through the dim, cool, wooden curtain. But one day, I know, they will be carried away by ants and made one with the jungle again.

A character in Ivy Compton-Burnett's *Mother and Son*, says : " The jungle is never dead. It is a strange thought."

And a disquieting one, too.

12. A Cycle of Cathay

The astrologers say there will be a "fatal conjunction" when the Sun, the Moon, Mars, Mercury, Jupiter, Venus, Saturn and Ketu combine in the sign of Capricorn on 4th February, which is the Chinese New Year.

I took the bus to Kajang, a few miles outside Kuala Lumpur, to sample what is said to be the best satay in Malaya. There must be something wrong with me, I was beginning to think, because I didn't like this dish that Europeans raved about. The special kind of satay offered at Kajang—a pleasant little village with prettily-colourwashed shop-houses and a charming police station set among lawns and flowers—is made of chopped-up sinew and bone in minced and crushed meat skewered on bamboo and grilled over charcoal. It was indeed very good and appetising and extremely well-prepared. Outside the police station I admired the orchids and other flowers which were growing in brightly painted pots fixed on poles about a yard high. One sees flowers growing in this curious way everywhere in Malaya : I think it must be done in order to avoid the depredations of mouse-deer, rats and other vermin.

With my little lunch, served by friendly Malay boys—the country Malays are much happier, it seems to me, than those in the cities—I drank a bottle of Dog's Head Guinness which had been so chilled in the refrigerator that half of the bottle's contents had frozen solid. It very quickly thawed out in the lush warmth of noon. The familiar brown Guinness label was accompanied by a large scarlet one covered with Chinese characters.

At a Chinese bakery I purchased a curious white bun, large as a doughnut, round and greasy, and it was on a square of edible rice-paper. Though it had a curiously pallid outer casing, I thought it might be a Chinese form of the Japanese sweet bean-paste cakes. However when I bit into my dessert, I discovered that it was stuffed with very sticky, chopped, fried pork. It is really a pie, not a cake, and is called, I later learned, " chasiu bao." I'm sure it was very nourishing but I didn't like it and fed it to some bullocks on the roadside. They didn't care much for it either.

Discussing erogenous zones with a Buddhist priest, we agreed in the end that they were more of a blessing than a curse. He was wonderfully sane about it, and spoke of various afflictions with instant understanding and wisdom. " Love and the world are illusions," he said. " Love brings fear, and fear is the root of all that is wrong." I did so agree. Cast out love (if you can, in a world so cynically conditioned to accept it and even fight for it by the pressures of big business and advertising and beglamourising books and films) and you will cast out fear. Once the first step has been taken, the rest is easy. And I had no trouble in accepting the idea that the world is an illusion : life has always seemed unreal to me, or rather, not real enough, like one of those modern American plays that are so " natural " they appear false. We live in a lonely dream. The Buddhist priest, with earthly transcendentalism, clapped his hands and woke me from a trance with the sound of a fall in sleep.

At night in the Batu Road : the arcades and shop-houses, the shabby hotels with dim bars. Groups of Chinese in light underclothes or pyjamas sitting in wicker chairs, fanning themselves with bits of cardboard. In a furniture shop, two young Chinese boys wearing only vests and pyjama-trousers are snoozing on a double bed just inside the window : a small girl is curled up on a bamboo sofa. Two old, bearded men at the back of the shop are rattling mah-jong bones on a glass-topped coffee-table. They are smoking the long, thin, cheap, dark Malayan cheroots.

An Indian taxi-driver with dyed hair. It is tinted with henna, and his nails, too, are stained with it. If he weren't so sordid he'd be almost Firbankian. His tarnished smile : the silvered teeth rotted with betel.

Two little Chinese boys wearing only cotton pants ; they walk along, totally absorbed in each other, their thin arms round each other's bony shoulders. Their perfectly spherical heads have very short-clipped hair : the fine black stubble is like the down on a lichee. Touching, the shoulder-blades like butterfly-wings beating under the fine flesh on either side of bony spines as spiky as kite-pigtails. They are deep in conversation, and already they have the faces of old men.

In a flower-shop, the Chinese boy tried to palm off some disgusting gladioli on me. " Orchids are too common," he hinted. (And too cheap, while gladioli are expensive.) I said : " Gladioli would make my room look like a nursing-home." He understood, and giggled and wiggled with me, then got me out of the back shop some really gorgeous, dark, spotty spider-orchids from Borneo. Also some palest green ones, which I am going to take to the pastrycook's to have candied. A crystallised orchid, done while the dew is still fresh upon it—how totally titillating!

A Chinese girl looks at me with a face soundless as glass, empty as mirrors. The street girls here are more discreet than the few pan-pan girls who still lurk on the Ginza. Prostitution is frowned upon in Malaya. But most of the so-called " massage parlours " will cater to those who need " toning up." Some advertise " relaxing treatment " for " gentlemen suffering from nervous hypertension." These massage parlours are gruesome places. The girls who work in them are dingy and well past their first youth. A real Chinese massage, however, can be most exhilarating. It begins with the girl wriggling and shaking and pulling and cracking every finger joint. Then she proceeds in the same manner to manipulate your wrists, elbows, shoulders and neck—rolling, twisting, squeezing, pressing. The head is lifted and dropped until the spine at the base of the skull gives ominous cracks. She then attacks the toes, wiggling and pulling them as she did the fingers, and rubbing between the toes with a delicacy that oddly enough does not tickle but soothes. The Chinese gentlemen in particular are very fond of this kind of tender agony. Then the masseuse jerks at the ankles and presses the feet back until the big toes nearly touch the shins. She goes on to give the muscles of the calves, knees and thighs a thorough drubbing. Then she sits on your posterior and gives artificial respiration ; you turn over, and she does the same to your chest and any other vital part which you may feel is still not sufficiently relaxed. These Chinese girl masseuses, clad usually only in their panties, always reminded me of the beguiling Mrs. Yajñavalkya in Ronald Firbank's " Valmouth," who used to say : " I alvays try . . . to end off wid a charming sensation." But of course she was so much more vibrant a character than the bored, grisly harpies with hard hands and frog faces whom one encounters in the massage parlours of Malaya.

A night humming with stars, swooning with palms, odorous with the freshly-applied pomade of oriental youths yearning towards the amateur dramatic performance of "Playbill" at the Mauresque Town Hall. A night for succumbing to more than one temptation, a night when, before falling, it is pleasant to remember Bagehot's advice, culled from a popular pull-off-day-by-day calendar issued by a well-known local business firm : "It is good to be without vices, but it is not good to be without temptation." But why mention them in the same breath ? Vice is not nearly as tempting as temptation ; and what, indeed, is vice ? To the pure, all things are pure : to the vicious, all is vice. The Chinese, fortunately, like all Orientals, do not know what we mean when we talk about vice. I think of G. K. Chesterton's "Song of Right and Wrong":

> *Tea is like the East he grows in,*
> *A great yellow Mandarin*
> *With urbanity of manner*
> *And unconsciousness of sin. . . .*

A Chinese calendar is a picturesque affair. Everything is written in four languages : English, Chinese, Tamil and Jiwa, which is the Malay adaptation of Arab script. Pictures of racehorses indicate the days when race-meetings are to be held in Singapore, Kuala Lumpur, Ipoh and Penang. Red lanterns indicate the Chinese New Year, which this year falls on 4th and 5th February, and Chap Goh Meh, literally Fifteenth Night, the Lantern Festival. Gazing at this calendar which was presented to me by a Chinese pedlar in exchange for one dollar —grossly extortionate—I am reminded of Tennyson's absurd line in "Locksley Hall": "Better fifty years of Europe than a cycle of Cathay." I cannot subscribe to those sentiments now, and anyhow Tennyson didn't realise that a "cycle" in Chinese terms lasts only sixty years.

Name for a Firbank character : Baron Smegma. How darling Ronald would have adored the Orient ! (I love putting people off by appearing affected like this : even my future's affected. And curiously enough it always puts off the right people, never the wrong ones : the dunces, not the dotty.)

Tropic Temper

To the Mandarin Palace in Bukit Bintang Road, for a small collation of chopped chicken and nuts, a few shreds of spring onion and slices of bamboo shoot that had been pickled to taste like soap. A glass of pale-brown, weak, lukewarm tea in a gunmetal holder, constantly replenished by a Chinese waitress in cap and apron and bobby-socks : she is short and stocky, with unbelievably plump calves. With her spiky bang of hair and her urchin smile, she looks like a wildly pretty boy. On the way back to my hotel, I passed in Pudu Road a much better restaurant, the Kum Leng, where I enjoyed under the pretty red lanterns a large tureen of shark's fin soup. By the time I got as far as Cecil Street, in the centre of Chinatown, I was feeling hungry again, so I stopped at a street stall and sampled some re-establishing mahmee, with egg noodles, shrimps or prawns, bits of pork, liver and vegetable. Flaming chilli sauce and brown soy sauce. Bean shoots. An excellent, cheap meal.

Almost opposite the Malacca Rest House a Chinese shop-keeper had died and preparations were being made for his funeral. (It was typical of my Malacca friend, Hussein—a dreamy, ill-informed, unobservant, indolent, mendacious and utterly charming kampong youth—that he should have told me it was a wedding.) There was a very amateur band, the sort that the Chinese always have riding before them in taxis on the occasion of a wedding or a funeral. Drums, clarinet, trumpet, flute and cymbals were playing doleful music with absolutely no recognisable tune, but it was vaguely Western funeral-marchy, very deliberate and loud.

Dozens of guests and mourners were already sitting at tables in the arcades in front of the shop, eating dried peas and beans and sipping tea in a very subdued manner. They were all wearing white shirts and dark trousers. An elderly man—the dead proprietor's eldest son ?—was dressed in a loose black cotton suit whose floppy jacket was fastened in front by white tapes. It had no buttons or pins.

The ancient gold and black signboard tilted over the entrance to the shop and bearing the deceased proprietor's name was " crossed out " with two strips of white paper in the form of a St. Andrew's cross ; a few cars standing outside the shop also had these strips of crossed white paper pasted over their rear windows.

In one room open to the street was a very showy altar with tall paper dolls standing on either side; there were forests of big, smouldering incense-sticks and guttering candles, both red and white. It was all extremely pretty in its richly-mixed colour. On one wall was a pale-blue cloth embroidered with silver characters.

In another room, yellow-robed Buddhist priests were busy before another altar and wall-hanging. Sitting on the ground were many small boys with handkerchiefs tied round their heads so that a white triangle of cloth hung over their foreheads. There were also one or two small girls with them. I saw one of the little boys, delighted with the solemn music that ceaselessly, tunelessly brayed out into the stifling night, dancing a few steps, then remembering where he was and turning all solemn again.

A large notice said, in Chinese and English: "Funeral to-morrow at 10 a.m. All welcome." They have to bury people quickly here. The next morning the procession set off with scores of mourners, most of whom had been sitting up all night at the tables, drinking beer and playing mah-jong and dominoes. The dead man was enshrined in a big paper palace, gaudily decorated with coloured and gold and silver foil. There were sheaves of paper money for him to take on his last journey into the world of spirits. He also had a Cadillac constructed of gold paper, a paper refrigerator, sumptuous paper robes and other luxury consumer goods made of paper: he would not disgrace his family name by arriving destitute in his heavenly abode. Cakes, fruit, rice, wine and candles were also provided for his last journey. Soon, these status symbols would, with his body, be reduced to ash that would be sealed in an urn and placed on the hillside at Bukit China, in a horseshoe grave facing the western sea. His happiness thus insured, he would not return to haunt his family at the season of the dead with dismal complaints. The family business, too, would go on thriving, undisturbed by ill-fortune. It made me feel that if only things are done right, with proper ceremony at the right time, all will be well. Death, for the Chinese, is a ceremony whose forms must be exactly observed; they are not afraid of death: their attitude towards it is both formal and natural. That night, lying under the white mosquito-net, I appreciated this quotation from *Jude the Obscure*:

Tropic Temper

Teach me to live, that I may dread
The grave as little as my bed. . . .

There is a very kind Chinese student in the English Department who often gives me a lift back into town from the University on the back of his motor-bicycle. In Malaya, a boy on the back of a motor-bike does not hold the driver round the waist. I had to cling on to the back of the saddle, and anyhow I usually had an armful of books. It was exhilarating to tear along the Federal Highway—but look out for speed traps, the Traffic Police are murder!—with the spicy fragrance of my student's rich black hair blown across my nostrils by the warm wind. He always insisted on carrying on a conversation, even at sixty miles an hour, when even in K.L. the breeze caused by movement grew chill; then it was a relief to lean forward against his back for shelter and to catch his wind-whipped words. Once he said, to my astonishment : " I saw you last night outside the Federal Cinema with a Chinese girl, I think your sweetheart or your wife." I hadn't noticed him. He was the only person at the University who showed me any kindness.

At night in Batu Lane, amid the flaring lights of little open-air restaurants and shops, Chinese mountebanks hawk their " testicle and penis pills." The sizzling acetylene lamps emit that sour pungency that reminds me so much of my childhood. There is a big crowd, mostly Chinese, mostly the very old and the very young, gathered round the voluble quacks who are displaying charts covered with characters and numbers. There are photographs of beauty boys culled from the pages of physique magazines, all exhibiting overblown muscular development and what is called, in the modelling profession, " crotch-interest."

The leading saltimbanco puts on quite a show : he may be an elderly, plump, laughing Chinese keeping up a deafening cross-talk with an elderly, scrawny, laughing Chinese woman, both using hand-microphones and speaking non-stop at a very rapid rate. To-night there is a dialogue between a strapping, bare-chested youth and a wizened old man, bearded like a sage, who keeps making very discreet, not to say refined gestures at his flies and pelvic girdle. They keep up a well-rehearsed stream of patter, very fast and apparently very funny, judging by the smiles and laughter of the onlookers, who to-night range from sprightly grandmothers to sluggish street-girls looking half-heartedly for a bit of trade. There are numerous schoolboys and schoolgirls, as well as tiny, bare-bottomed infants squatting in the dust of the front row. They all follow the cross-talk and the by-play with rapt attention, gravity and glee. It is a charming, simple sight, this age-old street entertainment interspersed with cymbal-clashings and drum-thumpings. Soon television will come with its more sophisticated quackery. But I do not believe these popular semi-instructional sideshows will ever die out. In the East they serve a social need in a way that mass entertainment can never do.

I wanted a large red silk Chinese lantern, shaped like a pumpkin, and decorated with gold paper and a long red tassel, for the Chinese New Year celebrations. I went into a Chinese antique store in Batu Road where I had seen some hanging from the ceiling, long ignored among the cheap tourist frippery, the piles of junk made from bamboo, bone and ivory. When the assistant took down one of the lanterns, I saw that its top was covered with thick dust, and that some of the gold-paper ornamentation was broken ; it had obviously been hanging there for years. He asked fifteen dollars for it, an exorbitant price for such a shoddy, shop-soiled piece of goods. I was suddenly seized, for the very first time, with the bargaining rage that had so often appalled me in others. I spoke terribly scathingly and impolitely about the lantern, and cast doubts on the value and authenticity of everything else in the shop. I couldn't believe my own ears : the things I was saying were outrageous. I deliberately insulted the proprietor by offering one dollar for the lantern, though of course I knew I should never get it for that price. He smiled disarmingly at my ridiculous offer and shook his head regretfully, as if apologising politely for my own unreasonableness and lack of diplomacy. I felt like a bull in a China shop but went on haggling. Finally I beat him down to seven dollars, then in paying only gave him five dollars and walked out of the shop with the lantern. I had still paid too much. But my extraordinary behaviour had shocked me : I was shaking all over.

A visit from the " baba " poet Ee Tiang Hong, a nice, quiet and very intelligent person speaking perfect English (and writing it too). Although born in Malaya (Malacca) of Chinese parents he speaks no Chinese and only " bazaar " Malay, that is, the popular everyday form of the language as opposed to the " pure " or formal Malay which the government is trying to make everyone learn. Ee Tiang Hong seemed to me the best by far of all the Malayan poets writing in English : he has a vivid, colloquial style and uses imagery in an almost surrealist fashion. He is the only poet who writes convincingly about his native land, and his word-pictures of the old Chinese sections of Malacca like Heeren Street and Jonkers Street show a very individual view of the world around him.

It seems to me a great pity that the Malay tongue should be officiously emasculated, deprived by academics of its invigorating colloquial freshness and wit and poetic originality, all of which characterise the common Malay idiom. Speakers of the gusty, jolly, irreverent, disrespectful and picturesque bazaar Malay are afraid to create works of literature in that racy tongue for fear of being laughed at by " pure " Malay speakers. This is a great pity : deprive a language of the living roots of common speech and it will become a dead language. Fortunately, though those holding government posts now have to take examinations on their proficiency in Malay, these government directives about the purity of the Malay language are not taken seriously by the majority of the people. And indeed how could they be, when everywhere one sees Chinese, Tamil and English words, and hears them used in ordinary Malay speech ? The first word a foreign visitor sees on arriving is " kastam " (Customs). Then he finds that " officer " is " opsir," " stamp " is " setem," " electric light bill " is " bil letrik " and " college " is " kolej." (The out-and-out purists argue that " college " should be rendered " maktab," but even this word is of Arab derivation.)

Though Western-style painting and sculpture are encouraged, writing in English, whether poetry or prose, is actively discouraged. The University magazine is practically the only place in which a Malayan writing in English can reach a public, and such writing is always attacked in the Press. Any Malayan writing in English finds that his " loyalty " to the régime becomes suspect. It is a saddening and narrow-minded attitude. If the writers of Malaya, whether Malay, Chinese or Indian, are to present their new country to the world, they must obviously write in English. Though all languages are international,

English is the most international of all. I advised frustrated students and writers to adopt my own methods in order to reach a wider public : casting poems into the sea in bottles, tying them to kites and balloons, dropping them into the streets from upper windows, chalking them on walls and pavements, reciting them over the public-address systems at railway stations and airports and leaving them in public library books.

Malayan smells : last night, an actual bonfire, under some trees in Pahang Road, a smudge of fire whose smoke however did not smell like English bonfire smoke, harsh, sweet and soft. This was a sharp, unpleasant odour, like the gamy market's perpetual hum of ripe fruit, overripe durian, flyblown pork and smegmatic fish.

The Chinese carpenter's house stands in a Kuala Lumpur slum not far from a main highway lined with modern office blocks : in the distance the new Parliament Building is going up, at great expense, among the spacious carpet-bedding of the Lake Gardens. The carpenter's house is a haphazard series of walls and roofs. A main room, bare-floored, is cluttered with bits of humble furniture ; two food safes standing on circular " ant-puzzlers." Hanging from the dilapidated wall are bunches of red or white candles on bamboo sticks, for ancestor worship. The interior is darkly lit by few windows, unglazed, covered with tough wire netting. Outside, the broad leaves of banana trees sway over the whole of the window's sky, drowning the rooms in glaucous light.

Two or three better, smaller rooms lead off this main one. Some of these have sleeping-spaces which are rented out to poor travellers and workers. One, where the old man sleeps, next to the shrine for the ancestors, is where his wife died. His family tell him he ought not to go on sleeping there, but he does not like sleeping anywhere else, and he feels his wife sometimes returns there to be with him.

The old man has a great fat bouncing daughter, huge as a wrestler, her face broad with healthy smiles ; she tells him again he ought not to sleep in the bed where his wife died. Perhaps she wants the bed for herself, or to rent to travellers and pilgrims. There is something tragic and universal about the argument. But the old carpenter just quietly nods and draws on a cigarette while the great hoods of his lashless upper lids jut down over his wrinkled, faded eyes. He is seventy-five. It is a fine, heavy, manly, marked face, deeply lined. From his sparse, smooth eyebrows sprout one or two long, dark, shining hairs. His brown-spotted hands are still strong and capable. He pours me out some of his best brandy, though it is only ten o'clock in the morning. He is poor, he tells me, but he has good things, if only very little of them. He is like a small, simple, quiet island in the midst of an ocean's turmoil as he sits surrounded by the energetic bustle and shouting of his great fat daughter, by the games and complaints of his numerous small grandchildren, by the fantastic conglomeration of things in the house. One has the feeling that they have never thrown anything away.

On my way out, I glance into the big kitchen which is almost filled by the daughter's cheerful, mindless clatter, chatter, laughter. The all-inclusiveness of the East! It is almost impossible to take in such a welter of things, yet I must—the big, round, shallow metal bowls in which some fish and vegetables and noodles are being fried; the enormous, thick, round chopping-block with its vicious-looking chopping-knife, the plate of pork dumplings ready to be stewed, the bunches of plain brown wooden chopsticks, the sieves and strainers, grinders and squeezers, the huge bottle of soy sauce, the hanks of straw, dried fish, noodles, the basins of rice . . . all the cups and bowls and china soup-spoons, the metal ladles, the wooden spatulas . . . the chests and boxes and baskets . . . the chickens and ducks wandering in and out. . . . No, I can never take it all in, with only the space of half a second in which to look. The eye can only take in a certain amount in the West, but in the East, where nothing is excluded in an all-inclusive culture, one trains oneself, over the years, to take in everything, to accept it and be overwhelmed by it, emerging at intervals as if from drowning. In Chinese paintings, it is what is left out that comes crowding to the imagination's eye. But English prose is not Chinese art: there is so much of Asia that however much one puts in there will always be something left out. That is why Kipling says, in " The Man Who Was ": " Asia is not going to be civilized by the methods of the West. There is too much Asia and she is too old." Asia, thank goodness, will always be too much.

13. Kung Hi Fatt Choy!

Beaumarchais says : " That which is not worth saying is sung."
The ignorant might think that this statement would be particularly appropriate in the case of Chinese Opera, which to the
uninitiated is an almost endless succession of squawks, screechings
and yowling recitatives. Every morning about 8.30 Radio
Malaya gives extracts from Chinese opera for half an hour or so.
People who had just got up and switched on their wireless sets
would rend the morning air with this appalling din, with its
accelerated crescendos of high, hysterical gong-beats, the sweet
insipidity of the songs and the Chinese girl singers, the endless
narrative arias of shocked description.

Nurtured on Noh, Bunraku and Kabuki, I used to find these
performances ineffably tedious and vulgar. But I was afforded
a better insight into the nature of Chinese Opera when I saw
a performance of " Princess Kwei Ying " in English, acted and
sung by Malayan amateurs, mostly Chinese. This was a traditional story which had been brilliantly translated and adapted
by one of the many Jesuit fathers in Kuala Lumpur, all of them
superb linguists and Orientalists. The translator was Father
T. J. Sheridan, S.J., and he revealed to me the wit and humour
of this particular dramatic form. There were, as one might
expect, many jokes about money, and there were biting sallies
about diplomacy and rather uncharitable remarks about personal
appearances. I had always been taught that " it is rude to make
personal remarks," and therefore this latter type of joke struck
me with additional force. The Chinese, it appears, have no
such scruples about giving offence ; but the savagery of the
criticisms of human shortcomings was always accompanied by
polite smiles. I was amused to hear that for a marriageable girl
the worst disqualification is a square chin.

This was easily the best and most entertaining amateur

dramatic performance I was ever to witness in Malaya. The costumes were authentic, borrowed from a professional Chinese Opera troupe, and they were dazzling in their brilliance, their bespangled colour. A few days later I attended a performance of part of the Ramayana in English blank verse, done by Indian students. Compared with the Chinese Opera, it was lamentably dull and badly performed. For some reason the Indians in the audience were convulsed with laughter at the most inappropriate moments, and there was something unkind in their mirth, a sneering note that was most unpleasant. This sneering, superior attitude, I was to find, was a common characteristic among Westernised Indians in Malaya. But I had already noticed, in Europe, that Orientals there suffer very often a degeneration of character when they come into contact with Westerners. They seem to discard their native grace of manner and adopt all the worst attitudes of the West, becoming casual, flippant, shallow and putting on a horrible pretence of knowing smartness.

Chinese popular songs are reminiscent, in their sweet, naïve sentimentality, of Irish tunes. On the radio the other morning I heard a Chinese song which had many melodic phrases like those in " Jeannie with the Light Brown Hair " or " I met her in the Garden where the Praties Grow." (Though this was better than what followed : half an hour of American wide-screen credit-title symphonic sound-track interspersed by the drone of dive-bombers, the crashing of bombs and the whine of bullets.)

Decorations for Chinese New Year have been going up in front of many shops during the past week. Brightly-painted flats are fixed over doorways and studded with electric light bulbs in crude Chinese Opera style. Vermilion silk lanterns bearing the characters for " Happy New Year "—" Kung Hi Fatt Choy "—hang over the windows in the five-foot ways. Sellers of melon seeds have already set up a few pavement stalls.

On a Chinese restaurant menu, among the list of " European Dishes " is Joe Ackerley's *bête noire*, Chicken Maryland, mis-spelt as Chicken Marylamb.

During the past week, the one that precedes Chinese New Year, the whole hotel has been cleaned and painted, the lift overhauled and its gates gilded. This is a traditional Chinese custom : the New Year must be welcomed in a clean house, otherwise the family will have bad luck throughout the coming year ; after the cleaning, all mops and brushes and brooms are hidden away lest someone inadvertently pick them up and sweep away the New Year luck. Everything sparkles in the February sun. All sharp, cutting things like knives and scissors are also put away lest the threads of good fortune be severed.

At the bank, before I left for Singapore, the clerks gave me clean new notes : New Year is the time to give " ang pow " or presents of money in bright red paper or envelopes, and it would be disrespectful to hand over dirty notes. (I have never seen such filthy bank-notes : the one-dollar notes in Malaya are sometimes almost black with grime. The five-dollar notes, about the same size and colour as the one-dollar ones, are often confused with them, especially when they're ragged and dirty.)

I had an air-conditioned compartment in the train. It was so cold that when I went to bed I had to ring for the boy to put another blanket over me.

The first thing I noticed this time about Singapura, the Lion City, was the deliciously fresh, cool breeze that blew from the sea in the early morning and evening. I had almost forgotten what a breeze was like.

When I got off the train the station was crowded with holiday-makers but a taxi-driver came up to me immediately and said he would take me to my hotel for two dollars. This was far too much, and I asked him to use his meter, but he refused so I had to walk out into the main road to find a passing taxi. The fare by this taxi's meter was one dollar. The Singapore taxi-drivers, like the Bangkok ones, have another dodge if they want to rook you : they say the meter is not working. This is the sort of misery that can ruin a holiday : one doesn't want all this awful, dull haggling. Sailors from H.M.S. Something, tourists and visitors for Chinese New Year and delegates for Malaysia Week are fleeced right and left. And one can't so much as look in a shop window without the proprietor and his assistants, usually Indians, coming out and pestering one, with oily smiles, to buy expensive rubbish. There are even trishaws loaded with cheap toys and tourist junk ; the driver peddles along beside one, offering dirty pictures under cover of a barometer covered with painted shells. It is no better walking through Change Alley, the celebrated arcade whose cluttered shops spill out over the narrow lane and where Indian money-changers pester one to change money at rates which give them a handsome profit.

In Empress Place, the statue of Sir Stamford Raffles gazes out over Telok Ayer Basin where the liners are lying ; off shore, tankers and warships. At night, in honour of the Malaysia Week delegates and the magnificent display of native dances outside the floodlit City Hall, ships are dressed overall in fairy-lights. Batteries of army searchlights are trained on the vast stage where performers from every part of the future Malaysia—North Borneo, Sarawak, Singapore, Malaya—exhibit their local dance-rituals in brilliant sarongs and turbans and cheongsams. Among the dancers is a team of Malay aborigines dancing the Siti Dayang, accompanied by chanting led by the halak or medicine-man. It is a dance of thanksgiving for the harvest. There is a display of koontau, the Chinese art of self-defence, and a selection of old Portuguese dances from Malacca performed by Eurasians. There follows the Tarian Nyonya, a dance performed to the tune of " Gambang Semarang " by Straits-born Chinese girls from Malacca. Dressed in sarong and kebaya, they represent a community from abroad that has absorbed a Malayan way of life while retaining some of the rich cultural heritage of their ancestors.

These were just a few items in a long and brilliant show. Throughout the performance there was a perpetual fizzing and hissing and ear-splitting banging of fire-crackers and sparklers set off among the dense crowds of spectators covering the padang. Boys were throwing jumping-crackers under the feet of girls whose cheongsams had such long slits in them that their legs were revealed right to the top of the thigh.

In a small bar : three drunken British sailors roared in, fighting with a tiny taxi-driver who in his efforts to get more money had torn the white sweat-shirt of one of his clients right down the back, from the collar's narrow blue border to the broad, stiff-looking white band, the corseted waist of the sailor's floating, wide-bottomed whites. These were now rather soiled at the back ; the side pockets were torn and frayed, and there were some traces of vomit on the front flap.

I left for Bugis Street : bright lights, loud music, drunken sailors, tattooed old ladies and savagely-painted, hard-faced young ones. There were swarms of little shoe-shine boys; other children were selling papers and cigarettes. At food stalls they were frying mee; hanks of dark-red meat were hanging from others. Everywhere there was the stink of burning coconut oil from satay roasters basting their savoury titbits with rancid oil. I met a Malay soldier on forty-eight-hour leave, a mild, lonely little creature who clung to me for the rest of the week-end. He was afraid of the fireworks, and so was I.

The trouble with Singapore is: too many British—civilians and tourists and troops. Every foreigner is treated like a tourist with money to burn.

And what's the good of buying things cheap in this free port if you have to pay tax on them when you take them home? On my way back to K.L., the customs officials even tried to make me pay tax on the camera I had taken with me, and which I had bought some months before in England. Tourists entering Singapore from the mainland should always declare any dutiable articles they may have, and receive a signed chit for them, to avoid confusion if they are going back to Malaya.

Shariah—that was the soldier's name—sat with me for a long time at an open-air café table in Bugis Street, drinking Carlsberg and watching the passing scene. I have rarely known anyone so timid. He shrank away from exploding crackers, yelping dogs, roistering sailors and loose women. He was like a little mouse-deer, with big, frightened eyes.

Two huge British sailors, their white caps tilted well forward, went by lolling in a trishaw pedalled by a sinewy little old Chinese who was understandably going rather slowly. The seat was too small for two grown Western men; they were crushed together and forced to sit with their arms round each other's shoulders. Touching and funny. They were hurling crackers and streamers in all directions, a wonderful exhibition of extro-verted gusto.

Tall-spired St. Andrew's Cathedral stands bone-white in the dark. There are many courting couples and wandering youths strolling across the dark lawns under the rain-trees surrounding it.

A barrowload of glutinous-looking cakes for New Year, stamped with a big, bright-vermilion seal signifying Keong Hee

Huat Chye (Hokkien), or Kung Hi Fatt Choy (Cantonese), or Kung Hsi Fa Tsai (Mandarin), meaning, of course, A Happy and Prosperous New Year. Beside the cakes, a row of six pairs of freshly-blancoed tennis-shoes drying in the sun.

Early morning, seven-thirty. Swarms of dark-skinned Tamils are picking up what looks like a coloured snowstorm of paper left by last night's crowds on the padang in front of the City Hall. Later Shariah and I go into the cathedral, as bone-white inside as outside. Stained glass at the east end and in a few other windows. There are narrow lancets shuttered against the tropic heat. About twenty large metal three-bladed fans are suspended on elbowed rods from the tops of the high nave walls and revolve at full speed over the gathering congregation —mostly mems in flowery dresses and shady, light summer hats.

One of the nice sights in Singapore to-day : the lovely faces and figures of country people in town for a day's holiday. (Though it's strictly a Chinese holiday, the Malays, leisure-loving, have taken the day off too. But all Indian shops, businesses and restaurants are open.) Whole families of Malays are garbed in beautiful new sarongs and songkok or in Western clothes, very smart. Streets are thronged with boys and girls and little children with Chinese mother and father and grandparents, all wearing pretty new clothes. Some are riding in rickshaws or taxis. The children are enchanting in their solemnity, very conscious of their new little cotton suits and frocks— cheap but stylish on their stylish bodies, so neatly cool. The boys have been cropped and the girls newly permed so as to start the New Year with a " new head."

Shariah and I saw a man riding to market on a bicycle with a large flat wooden board in front of the handlebars. On this board were big green knobbed fruit, a sort of gourd, and three dark-grey ducks, their feathers ruffled by the sea-breeze and the wind of motion, their bright intelligent little heads constantly turning sharply from right to left to right. They are not in cages : they are not even tied. It doesn't occur to them to fly away. They are off to market, to be placed with scores of others in large round wickerwork baskets, awaiting purchasers who will eventually take them home for the New Year feast and kill them just before dinner by biting through their plumy necks. Or they may be bought by a poultry merchant to be roasted and lacquered and placed among the glazed piles of ducks in the shops of Chinatown.

Though I disliked Chinatown on my first visit to Singapore, I can now see its wonderful vitality and charm : it is a most exciting experience to walk there on this fine Sunday morning in my new pink silk shirt with my new gold plastic belt glimmering like a luxurious snakelet, familiar of my loins, through the diaphanous material. I have a peacock-green scarf and new, tight white pants. Gold kid sandals with no heels slip-slopping along : the Malays accept you more willingly if you slip-slop slowly along as they do. They, like all Orientals, tend to smile at anyone hurrying and bustling. As Kipling says in " The Naulahka ": " A Fool lies here who tried to hustle the East." Besides, it's much too hot to hustle, and I've forgotten my paper fan, never mind, I can get one anywhere, yes, that one painted with a tiny dragonfly, only fifty cents and perfumed with paregoric. Delightful to observe the grave and happy faces of the Chinese, their labile hips, the delicacy of the palpebral curve ; the bones of their fine hands in languid agitation, the soft shine of their perfect teeth as they play fan-tan in moucharabied dusk.

South Bridge Road : scores of small Chinese children setting off fireworks on the covered five-foot way. They stick the half-inch-long red or green slugs of the crackers in the pavement cracks and light them with the glowing tip of a smouldering brown incense-stick. (One five-year-old is using a cigarette.) Only the dramatic passage of a scarlet fire-engine, its firemen in black, its siren howling, stops for a moment the bang-bang-banging and the children's screams of delighted terror. Outside the Sincere Dispensary some little boys are improving the racket by placing " repeating " crackers under inverted tin boxes. The boxes jump about to the tune of the explosions while the boys dance and laugh. Some of the squibs seem damp ; they fizzle out in a meagre shower of sparks.

A bedlam of gongs, trumpets and crackers as we approach the Haw Par Villa—a fabulous and unintentionally comic wonderland of strange characters from Chinese mythology and all kinds of fish and birds and animals in coloured cement—an Oriental Disneyland of staggering vulgarity. It was a relief to enter the air-conditioned quiet of the Van Kleef Aquarium and cool off beside its immense tanks of tropical fish.

Tropic Temper

The Sri Mariamman Temple in South Bridge Road : it has a lovely polychrome tower over the front gate which is decorated with banana leaves and small bunches of miniature bananas. There are also polychrome figures of sacred cows as well as statues of topee-topped imperialist soldiers in British uniforms with sloped arms.

I took Shariah to the Tiong Hoa Restaurant, opposite the Cathay Cinema, for an extremely good Indonesian curry—nasi padang and nasi goreng. One chooses from a large array of dishes : a little of each, with rice and jambals (rice crackers) and lager makes a satisfying and delicious meal. There are about twenty dishes on the side tables : chopped chicken, shrimps, chopped eggs and brains, curried giblets, various kinds of local vegetable including the ubiquitous okras, sliced cucumber salad. The curry has a wonderful re-establishing heat that is just right. It is far from insipid, which is the fault of many Malayan curries ; but it does not burn : it just radiantly heats. Its glow sends jets of joy and sunshine down into a belly jaded by a diet of milk-shakes. A perfect meal, both stimulating and relaxing, for two dollars each (about four shillings).

All this, and Cliff Richard, who, with the Shadows, is Shariah's idol since his personal appearances in Malaya. Cliff on the record-player sings " Outsider (that's Me)." I adore the way he pronounces " lurv " in " Fall in Love with You." But not as good as Eartha Kitt singing " Got that l-lurvin-bug itch." Sounds as if she'd been suckled on cyanide. Good.

All day the spitting and spattering of fire-crackers loaded the air with sour fumes. As evening fell the palm-laden sunset crackled with them ; they were growing in volume and sounded like thunder beginning and never reaching the final orgasm of a heavy sternutation. Sometimes when lots of fireworks were going off at some local temple it sounded like a burst of distant applause.

The pavements, five-foot ways and gutters along the Esplanade are deep-drifted with dull-red cracker wrappings, like bloody confetti.

A little boy with sparklers waves them up and down, brushing the warm air with the scented stars of ceremonious fire.

The " Happy World " funfair on New Year's Eve : almost deserted and very dismal. All these big funfairs in Malaya have a shoddy, seedy look ; their drab and dingy stalls have none of the excitement and glitter of an English fairground.

The only cheerful thing that evening was the Chinese Opera troupe from Formosa rehearsing for their opening on New Year's Day. The old man at the door kindly invited me to go in and watch. There were about a dozen other interlopers round the footlights, holding up the bottom of the pleated red nylon flounce on the bespangled curtain to peep underneath and watch the " practice " as the old man called it.

I went round to the back and on to the stage itself. There were some powder-clouded mirrors and lacquer make-up boxes near the back entrance ; on the other side of the stage, in the wings, was the orchestra—fiddles, cymbals, drums, flutes and trumpets.

On stage there was a scene of the utmost confusion. The cast of about twenty were in ordinary clothes and wore no make-up, which in Chinese Opera is very complicated and takes hours to put on. But they were using a few props—spears, sticks, fans, wooden swords, scarves. There was a large number of children, presumably part of this great acting family : they were watching the rehearsal in a half-hearted way, as if they knew all the lines and moves already. But they sat quietly. Later they would have walk-on scenes and perhaps a few words to say : they were serving their long apprenticeship to the theatre ; it was not a question of being gifted—they had been born into the theatre and it was their life work. This prosaic attitude was impressive : to them acting was just a job, no better, no worse than any other. There was no room for emotionalism or displays of temperament : they were born professionals, and at the end of the rehearsal they would have to sweep the stage, unpack the costumes and cook the supper.

It may have been a play the company had not done for some time. (These troupes have scores of plays on their travelling repertoire.) Most of the cast members were reading from long, narrow scripts like toilet-rolls. There was a director with script and staff ; he kept banging this on the floor when anything was not right. I think he must have been combining direction with playing the leading role.

Various small boys are shoved around, more or less into correct positions, by a stage manager. They stand there for a few moments, blinking drowsily in the scalding-white neon working-lights. Then the stage-manager leads them off and at once rushes on himself, reading something from his script. An older boy wearing only cotton underpants and a Hawaiian shirt is asleep on a chest behind a flat representing, in crude colours, a palace interior. The director thumps his stick, the boy is called, woken hurriedly; he goes dazedly forward into his part, mumbling mechanically. The other actors take no notice of him, or of each other.

There is no scenery, only a very solid table and two very solid chairs. I noticed that the latter had tubes of bamboo, about one foot long, nailed to them—two on the front table legs, one on each chair. Bales, crates, baskets, all half-unpacked, litter the open back-stage.

In all the confusion, a little girl and an old granny are sitting on the floor stitching bits of cloth together. A youth in pyjama-trousers and nothing else is lettering the posters in green and red paint: it is lovely to watch his long, thick, loaded brush rising and falling as he does his neat and careful calligraphy. He brushes the paper first with some transparent liquid—is it glue-size?—before drawing the elegant characters, some of which look like castles, others like flowers, swords, ships. He is watched by a very old man who never moves but sits silently cross-legged, absorbed in the young man's artistry: perhaps he is his teacher of calligraphy.

In the neighbouring theatre, the company had barely arrived. There was no scenery, but I saw children mending some drop-cloths; the bottom rollers of these were made of thick bamboos. The stage was strewn with wicker baskets. An electrician walked across, filled a bowl with cold rice from a communal tub of the stuff and went and sat morosely in his corner among the switches and wires to devour it, along with some savoury titbits of pickled vegetable, using giant chopsticks. A girl actress was combing out a long, artificial switch of hair. Others were removing day make-up, using hand-mirrors. A little boy was carrying round the day clothes of a chief actor who was wearing nothing but his drawers. Someone spilled a basket of green oranges and they rolled over the stage into the footlights.

In both theatres there was a brightly-painted and illuminated shrine at the back of the stage containing the polished image, in dark wood, of a little Buddha. Offerings of oranges, grapes, peaches (with wafers of red paper laid on them) and a great bowl full of burning joss-sticks. Everywhere red good-luck papers were stuck up with hastily-calligraphed New Year greetings on them. In a number of rooms at the back were dozens of big plank beds where one or two babies were sleeping or playing quietly.

Back into town in a demented taxi ; the driver was hurrying to avoid the crackers which boys kept throwing under the wheels. One flew through the open window of the cab ; the driver leaned over and threw it out again. It exploded in mid-air but we were well past it by then. The night was a frenzy of crackers.

It is the " Year of the Tiger " which will begin at midnight to-night. This year Chinese astrologers say it will bring good to all mankind because for the first time in history its beginning will coincide with a total eclipse of the sun and the extremely rare zodiacal combination of seven (not eight as the Hindus claim) planets.

But millions of Hindus throughout the world are praying that world disaster may be averted during this alignment of the heavenly bodies. Something like panic has seized the population of India.

The Year of the Tiger is also traditionally the year in which it is unfortunate to wed and which brings little luck to maidens in search of a husband. In Japan, the wedding-halls are packed with couples hastening to tie the marriage knot before the Tiger Year begins.

A roaring crowd rushes round a corner, followed by an enormous, undulating dragon—no, it is surely a lion with a fiercely-painted head and long body borne along by at least a score of youths who are making it writhe grotesquely on the ends of long poles. The bearers are running through a perfect hail of exploding crackers, to the accompaniment of gongs and drums and trumpets. Two stalls, selling Mandarin oranges, water-melons and melon seeds, were knocked over in the frantic rush. Next a stall selling an astonishing variety of greeting-cards, mostly in brilliant red, teetered over and would have fallen if the proprietor had not thrown a lighted jumping-cracker into the crowd.

Tropic Temper

Outside a Chinese temple in Philip Street there were swarms of worshippers pushing their way towards the altars with fistfuls of burning joss-sticks and plates of oranges : they were hoping to make peace with the gods. Volley after volley of fireworks were going off outside. The night sky was reddened with the multitudinous explosions of rockets. Banner-writers and greeting-card writers are hard at work inscribing good wishes on scarlet paper. The flash-bulbs of thousands of photographers add their lightnings to the glare of exploding crackers. Well before midnight the traffic in the densely-thronged streets is at a standstill.

The full lunar year in the Chinese calendar is one of thirteen months and it has become a custom that salaries are paid on a thirteen-month basis ; as there are only twelve months in the Western calendar the salary for the thirteenth month is paid at Chinese New Year. It is really a New Year gift to employees. They are certainly spending their money fast to-night. All debts must be honoured before midnight and all financial accounts brought up to date. Ten-cent pieces are put in red envelopes and presented to children as " lucky money." The notorious secret societies are also demanding their " ang pow " protection-money from rich towkays. Gangsters and thugs in Ipoh, Penang and K.L. have been sending polite extortion letters to rich people. But very few people report these demands to the police. They prefer to pay up, believing that if they report the thugs to the authorities the secret societies will take their revenge by kidnapping children, destroying property, slashing car-tyres and by committing every imaginable kind of violence.

In K.L. and the Federation, crackers are banned. The police warned the public not to let off any fireworks or the dangerous sand-crackers known as " Sha Pau " or " Kam Chin Pau." But even before I left K.L. I heard a number of crackers being exploded behind my hotel, in the Christian graveyard, to frighten away foreign-devil ghosts and evil spirits.

The ceaseless crepitation of millions of fire-crackers lasted well beyond 2 a.m. It filled the whole sky over certain predominantly Chinese areas of Singapore with an unearthly chatter. On the Esplanade boys were setting off small " whirligig comet " crackers, letting them whizz out over the grimy little breakers of the Singapore waterfront. Some of them snaked quite a long way out into the luminous dark before falling into the sea. The stink of gunpowder and sulphur permeated my clothes and hair and my hands and face were covered with the floating grey smuts.

After midnight I walked along the deserted North Canal Bank. There it was dark and quiet. The lighted river was black with shifting and rocking boats of all kinds—sampans and junks and lighters and rowboats. As I leaned on the rail gazing at this eerie, sombre sight I could hear the groan and creak and knock of boats heaving slightly on the lazy swell. It sounded like drugged, uneasy sleepers stirring and moaning in the empty boats. There was none of the day-time animation, none of the gaiety and merriment and lively noise of the rest of the cracker-mad city. It was a sad place, haunted by the day-time ghosts of weary working men now sighing in sleep over remembered toil and sweat, hunger and poverty, disease and sorrow. The distant brittle brattle of fireworks. A few exploding on the opposite bank, at the foot of a massive, impersonal skyscraper.

I wandered back along the Esplanade, where the high tide was gurgling up through small gratings in the red-and-white-chequered promenade, throwing up small bucketfuls of water. The gardens were white with lovers in the shade of the tropic trees. The Year of the Tiger had begun.

14. *Semper est in Oriente Virtus Movens*

So there has been no dire calamity caused by the maleficent influence of the combined planets. The Indian astrologers were wrong, the Chinese ones right. This Monday morning of New Year's Day is gay and sunny and everyone is very happy. The first thing I saw when I emerged from my hotel was a bevy of six or seven small Chinese children looking like a perambulating basket of flowers riding with mamma in a trishaw; the driver was pedalling along slowly, but patiently and good-humouredly.

Heads of businesses and proprietors of shops as well as parents and relatives are handing over small red envelopes containing a clean dollar note or perhaps a new-minted ten-cent coin to young employees and children. One thinks of all the preparation that goes into this small ceremony, often performed almost in passing (at the most with a slight bow and smile by way of thanks) in the streets where nearly all the Chinese shops are shut. An exception to this is the row of glittering jewellers' shops in South Bridge Road, open presumably for New Year present buyers.

I entered a café for some iced tea : on the walls were two enormous, fantastic gold-paper dragons with crimson mouths and huge, red, popping eyes lit from within. They were beautifully, joyfully made.

I never saw an Indian boy or girl playing with Chinese firecrackers (nor a Malay, for that matter.) Naturally, perhaps, as the Chinese New Year has no real significance for them. But I did happen to see a Chinese boy innocently letting off a cracker in the vicinity of an Indian household. As the firework fizzed and exploded, a little Indian boy and girl skittered away to their mother, a plump virago who shot out of her doorway, nose-ornaments flashing, earlobes like pierced wattles positively flapping with outrage, pursuing the fleeing Chinese boy with gabbled threats and shrewish screams.

A small incident, but significant ; it indicates a deep problem confronting the inhabitants of Malaysia. How can the three main races ever unite when there is this total lack of community, of common language and religion, customs and temperament ? The Chinese would never give way : they are so flexible, have such powers of lying doggo and playing possum in awkward situations that they are actually the most inflexible of all races. Like water, they find their own level, and then it is impossible to shift them.

The Indians would never give in : a dreadful thing that would be for a nation so conscious of imagined inferiority. It might seem to be the Malays who would be in danger of being swamped, as indeed they are at present by the Chinese communities. The Malays are apparently the weakest. But the power of Islam is tremendous, and Allah is great. "Islam—such a noble, powerful and bigoted religion," as Aunt Dot says in *The Towers of Trebizond*. The Malays, with all the fierce strength of their religion behind them, could never be overborne. What results ? Impasse. I believe all the talk about a "United Malaysia" is pointless. Merger may indeed one day be effected, for purely political ends ; but these people and their religions can never merge. They will simply go on existing side by side, together but apart, as they have been doing now for the last century.

The Tengku's visit to Macmillan in November 1961 had the expected outcome, though merger was to come sooner than expected, in 1962. The disturbing feature of the conference in London was the British Government's insistence that her naval and military bases should be retained in Singapore for "the defence of Malaysia, for Commonwealth defence and for the preservation of peace in South-East Asia." The Tengku has agreed ; the Malays are apparently indifferent, but they still distrust the British and British intentions. They want to be left alone, to be a neutral country. The whole world could be neutral, and at peace, if it were not for the machinations of a handful of insane power-politicians. Something is very wrong with our systems of government when these men can destroy the world without reference to the wishes of humanity. " Better Red than dead ? " I'd really rather not be dead.

The Malays, of course, have been exploited not only by the white man but also by the Chinese and Indians. From my observation it seems to me that Malays feel intensely inferior and uncomfortable in the presence of Chinese, who are so industrious, money-loving and business-like, in direct contrast to the leisurely, good-natured, spendthrift and totally uncommercial Malays.

The Chinese are intelligent, capable and loyal to their own race : this latter quality makes them " exclusive " and " communalistic." They do not care to work with or to employ people of other races. It is rare to see Chinese and Malays forming friendships and walking together in the streets. The Indians rarely make friends with anyone. The three races tend to keep apart, and the division is primarily religious in origin, for the various religions and sects have nothing in common. The two most closely related are Buddhism and Christianity, but even so they are far apart in the manner of their religious observances.

The Chinese in Malaya are like worker and soldier ants. Nothing derogatory is intended by this comparison—ants are an example of mass genius. They are continually milking the Malay aphides whom they have successfully domesticated on their own ground.

The Malays regard the Indians not as ants but as lice on the body of their land, and the fact that they were imported *en masse* by the colonial British is not forgotten by the country's rightful inhabitants. The Malays, always cautious, mild and slow to rouse, show no resentment ; or rather they show on the whole less resentment than they show towards Westerners. Even this is faint and ill-defined.

The majority of Malays, so gay and uninhibited within their own strict but easy form of moral elegance, are, I believe, as depressed as I am by the present-day Indian's accusatory self-righteousness, his fussy primness and church-hall nosiness and censoriousness ; these traits are surely an unhappy backwash from life under the British in India ; they must also be partly due to the severe trauma of their long and agonising Indian freedom movement. They have their freedom now, but at great cost to their minds and souls and bodies. It is to be hoped that the younger generation of Indians, born in free India, will grow up without this ghastly imperialist hangover, and that Indians will not always feel compelled to rectify an inborn sense of inferiority, to compensate for slights (often imaginary) with aggressive, shrill self-justification and denunciation of the short-comings of others. This narrow and rigid moral outlook, how surprising and unhappy it is in a great Asian nation !

Disraeli wrote, in *Contarini Fleming*: " The practice of politics in the East may be defined by one word—dissimulation." Well, if you must have politics, what can you expect ? And we must not forget the old saying : *ex oriente lux, ex occidente lex,* which Bailey transforms so marvellously in his great poem " Festus ":

> 'Tis light translateth night; 'tis inspiration
> Expounds experience; 'tis the West explains
> The East; 'tis time unfolds eternity.

In some Malayan Chinese restaurants they give you hot, steaming towels, but offer them dangling from the end of tongs : if they're too hot for the waitresses, aren't they too hot for us ? It's probably due to some antiquated notion that a servant's hands, however clean, must not come even indirectly into contact with an honourable customer's. In Japan the hot towels are placed in little baskets and are often opened, flourished if too hot, and handed to the customer on the bar-boy's open palms : much more human, refined and civilised.

The Chinese in Malaya, Singapore and Hong Kong are *abruti*. The restaurant owners are sharks, always trying to shove a few extra dollars on the bill. The businessmen are the hardest in the East : making even a small profit out of a Straits Chinese is like squeezing blood from a stone. But individual Chinese are often delightful : they are faithful friends and good lovers.

I remember the old amahs at New Year, off to the Chinese Opera or the puppets wearing nice new black " figured " satin trousers and coats, hair neat, neck shaved. There were throngs of them with their small charges at the New World Amusement Park in Singapore on New Year's Day. They stood watching the " Chinese " variety show with its Western-style crooners and strict-tempo dance band and queued up to get on the Dodgems and the Ghost Train.

On my last evening in Singapore, I was walking through the Capitol Arcade and was stopped by a Eurasian woman—was she drunk or mad ?—who kept smiling wildly, giving short bursts of maniacal laughter, swinging her large hips in a would-be seductive way, flourishing a large, very hard handbag which caught me on the hip, leaving a big bruise. It seemed to be made entirely of metal. The passers-by gazed wonderingly at her and a few Indians stopped and laughed. She frightened me, the way she kept arching her eyebrows invitingly and throwing back her head, widely-grinning, to give full-throated cackles. Her eyes, rimmed with black, were never still. Then it suddenly struck me : she must be a mild case of " amok." I expected then to see her bring a parang or a keris out of her monumental handbag and lay about her. Someone must have bewitched her with a bad spell. She was not a very attractive sight, so I went away when my curiosity was satisfied. Heaven knows what happened to her.

The Malays say : " Berchuchi mata " which means literally to wash the eyes, that is, to go sightseeing. For the Malays, seeing new places is a kind of spiritual elevation, the opposite of the accidie and melancholia that afflict them if they stay too long in the same spot. Sightseeing is for them truly a refreshment of the soul and a recreation of the body.

They also have a lovely phrase, " Tida apa " which, said with a rueful shrug, means " It doesn't matter." It might almost be the national motto of the Malays. They frequently use the little word "la," which gentles a command, softens a statement ; a kind of persuasive particle which intensifies meaning and civilises speech. Or it can be a cajoling addition to a statement, encouraging a reply, like the Japanese " *neh* ? "

The Sanskrit word for a circle, mandala, which Jung made a common part of English speech, is used by the Malays to mean area or district. It must have been brought into their language through the Hindus.

A Malay proverb : " The water in a coconut is round ; in a monsoon drain [1] it is straight." Meaning : adaptable. But the title of my next—and last—book of poems will be : "Refusal to Conform." Shariah, to whom I said farewell this evening, told me this Malay saying : " Friendship of men : inseparable as ink and paper." I shall never see him again. He is being sent to the Congo with his unit. We were " close as the fingernail

[1] This is not a gutter but a deep straight trench made of cement generally alongside the pavement but sometimes across it.

and the quick "—an Arab proverb which has been adopted by the Malays.

There is a sad feeling of anticlimax in the air after all the excitement of the great festival. I am glad to be going back to K.L. But there will soon be another festivity. Every day now at the bottom of the Stop Press column in the local newspapers there is this announcement : " Fasting Hours—Kuala Lumpur 5.18 a.m. to 7 p.m." The Malay fasting month has begun.

Not many days after I arrived back in K.L. the shops along Batu Road began putting up big notices saying : " Hari Raya Puasa." Puasa is the Muslim fasting month of Ramadan. The Hari Raya is the festival of rejoicing and celebration held to mark the end of the fasting period.

15. Some Pleasures

Dancing is second nature to the Malays. One sees this at once in their easy, relaxed way of walking, that contrasts so remarkably with the Chinese walk—busy, aimful, directed. The Chinese always look as if they are going somewhere, the Malays as if they have nowhere to go excepting to the regrettable end of some pleasant, careless dream. How often I have admired and envied the grace of the Malays: the beautiful balance and modest elegance of the Malay girls, and the swaying, gliding saunter of the supple, witty-bottomed Malay boys. Even when they are standing still, their bodies seem to be doing a silent dance.

I first saw popular Malay dancing at the Albert Hall in London in 1955 during the performance of my masque, " The Triumph of Harmony." This required some dancers from the East, and the producer was lucky to be offered the services of a group of Malay students who were on a course at the Malay Teachers' Training College at Kirby, near Liverpool. They came up to London one very foggy week-end, when they must have been feeling the cold of England keenly, and rehearsed willingly. I was entranced by their beauty and gentleness: gentleness is such a rare quality in the modern world that I felt deeply moved by those Malay young men and women. And when they danced together, to the music of a melodeon and a fiddle, the impression of sheer grace and kindliness and charm they left on me was unforgettable.

Never did I think that one day I should live with Malays and see them dancing in their own land. But just six years later, that is what was happening. It was like the realisation of an impossible dream. Next to the Malay people, their dancing was what I loved most in Malaya.

All the big amusement parks or " Worlds " in Malaya have one or more open dance halls for popular-style Malay dancing, which is called ronggeng. The place where the dancing is done is called a joget. There is no admission fee : anyone can wander in and sit down at one of the tables round the dance floor. One orders a coffee, a beer or a bottle of Green Spot orange squash. But if one wants to dance, one has to go to a counter and buy tickets. A ticket costs forty cents and entitles the bearer to one dance with the girl of his choice. The professional dance-girls, or taxi-girls as they are sometimes called in Singapore and Hong Kong, sit in a long row in front of the band, and when the place is crowded you really have to run across the floor and claim a girl if you want a dance, because then the competition is fierce. But the best dancers—not always the prettiest girls—are always in demand.

One of the jogets in the B.B.—for Bukit Bintang—Park in K.L. is called the Chindra Mata Joget. It stands surrounded by cheap clothes shops and eating booths, between an ancient picture-house called " Sun Talkies " and a Dodgem track with a very loud amplifier and a warning notice to drivers saying : " Please do not Dash ! " But the music from the Dodgems does not seem to disturb the very rowdy joget band and its often amateur singers ; nor does it affect the tempo of the dancers. During the very brief intervals between dances, the Chinese Opera troupes or the music of a shadow-play or wayang kulit may be heard. There are two jogets in the B.B. Park, as well as a covered dance hall with an excellent dance band where Western-style dancing is the rule, with strip-teasers shaking glittering fringes during cabaret demonstrations of a very volatile Twist.

But the Malay joget knew all about the Twist long before the Twist became popular.[1] Popular Malay dancing is all twist— a twisting of hips and knees and shoulders and an unashamed, totally uninhibited working of the bottom. The best ronggeng dancers are those whose movements all stem from a free-swinging backside ; that is why most Europeans cannot do this style of dancing properly—they are too self-conscious. And usually their bodies are too big : they cannot accomplish the sensuous motions of the dance neatly or swiftly enough ; in a big white man these motions look merely sexy and gross. But the Malays can make the most sexy movements in the dance,

[1] Western-style dancing was banned in Malaya in November, 1962.

because of their lissom, compact physique, look delicate and pure. And white people are too earnest, trying to do it right, while Malays when they dance have a smiling self-forgetfulness. Even when large, fat Malays—there are some—do this style of dancing they do it gracefully and wittily. The secret lies in the Malay's labile loins.

The first thing one notices about this style of dancing is that the couples do not hold each other, and never touch. The man may advance upon the woman but she will always retreat : it is proper to keep apart. This is partly traditional modesty— the Malays never give displays of emotion in public, and of course never publicly embrace or even hold hands, though male couples, occasionally, can be seen holding hands as they take their evening stroll : that is permitted. Indeed, the Muslim religion prohibits any form of public contact, or even private contact, between men and women unless they are married.

So the couples dance together without touching. Sometimes they can barely be said to be dancing. They stand facing one another, smiling and chatting, and making a few rhythmical movements from time to time or just walking casually round the floor more or less in time to the music. The tunes are nearly always quick-steps, cha-cha-chas, rumbas, tangos, slow-fox ; there is usually at least one native tune played during the evening, on a fiddle, but the same casual steps are used by the dancers, though at the end of this native tune they will give cross-kicks with the feet in a curious, sprightly jump and these steps obviously have a folk-dance origin. It is a universal folk-dance step and could be either aboriginal Malay or Javanese or Portuguese or Dutch. In fact, when these steps are performed, they remind one of the movements of a Dutch clog-dance.

The man leans slightly forward when dancing, in order to give full play to his behind. (This is when he is dancing properly, not just walking around chatting, with a cigarette in his mouth.) The energetic working of his forearms and hands and the back and forward movements of his feet are sometimes reminiscent of a sailor's hornpipe, especially when the man is wearing tight trousers flared at the bottom in the Singapore style.

The girls, in tight sarong sheaths, follow the man's move-ments, but in a more muted way ; they are amazingly responsive to their partner's moods and can shadow and foresee all his movements and variations of steps perfectly. These professional girls get a rake-off on every ticket they receive so it is in their interests to dance with anyone who asks them, even if he is drunk. The girls frequently looked bored and tired; but if a partner comes along who is a really good dancer they can put on virtuoso displays that are enchanting to watch. They never refuse anyone, and always treat their partners politely: they never try to " show up " a bad dancer and, as I found myself, they are patient and encouraging with beginners.

Sometimes a man will buy a clutch of tickets and give them all to the same girl at the beginning of the evening, thus virtually booking her services. It is a respectable profession for a Malay girl, though in some cases it may be combined with prostitution. Most of the girls are willing to meet one outside the park after the dance, which lasts from about 9 p.m. to 1 a.m. They are utterly charming.

There are, surprisingly, no male professional dancers. Occasionally a girl will buy tickets and dance with one of the professionals.

It is relaxed, happy dancing. There is none of the tension and cheap sexiness of a Western ballroom. Even when the girls are weary and bored there is still beauty in the purely mechanical movements of their bodies. These pretty, fairy-lit open-air dance halls are the nicest places in K.L.

There are two jogets in the amusement park at Malacca, where another of the attractions is an open-air cinema that often shows Japanese films and the violently-coloured, melodramatic, lushly romantic Indian ones. One of the jogets is an indoor affair but apart from that it is truly Malay in character, with the girls all in sarong and kebaya.

The other joget is out of doors and the girls here wear Western dress: it is called the Chee Yean Keong and as the name indicates is under Chinese management. Here one meets all kinds of girls—Chinese, Indian, Sinhalese, Malay, Eurasian and occasionally Filipinos and Thais and Bruneians.

The twenty or so girls all wear identical short, bouffant pink dresses; they have beehive, bouffant and urchin-cut hair-do's. They begin the evening by sitting in a long line under the dance-band's platform. At the first notes from the band they stand, turn round and bow to the musicians. Then the girls advance in fours till the whole floor is covered ; during this opening display they dance slowly, with little shuffling cha-cha steps, gently-swaying hips, gestures of thin hands and thin, splayed fingers with thumb and forefinger joined. Their reserve and delicacy contrast strongly with the half-tipsy British and Australian soldiery sitting at the tables round the dance floor. Each soldier has a big bottle of Tiger or Anchor or Carlsberg beer in front of him.

Here there is a male M.C. who collects the girls' tickets from the customers ; he wears a pink shirt of the same material as the girls' dresses.

The girls are charming to their Western partners who look coarse and raw-boned and clumsy, clod-hopping in front of the pretty, good-natured girls who have all their work cut out to prevent the men touching them. There is a great crowd of Malayans standing outside, watching the antics of the foreign devils.

After a few moments of this, it is nice to go to the other dance hall and watch the Malay girls dancing with Malay boys whose slender, willowy hips and quick, neat footwork and quietly manly bearing are tributes to a deeply moral yet gay and instinctively graceful tradition. One begins to realise that the purpose of the Malay ronggeng is mainly to afford opportunities for men to show off their bodies and their dancing skills and other social charms ; but it is all innocent and unassuming in its light-hearted ease. Watching the Malays dancing, I knew they were one of the world's most highly civilised races.

Ronggeng is popular dancing. But there is an even more formal type of dancing, much admired in Malaya, which is extremely intricate and requires long practice. I saw some of these splendidly-performed, gorgeously-dressed national dances at a " pesta budaya " or grand festival of the arts to entertain the delegates to the Colombo Plan meeting. It was held in the vast Merdeka Stadium in K.L. which on that occasion was packed with thousands of people. It is a truly magnificent modern arena. There was a central covered portion in the stands to accommodate the delegates to the conference. I glimpsed some of these swilling brandy at the bar. I couldn't help marvelling at their undistinguished banality : these professional conference-attenders are like the " professional undergraduates " of to-day.

They have simply made a profession of conference-going, representing various bodies or governments, perhaps uttering a few official banalities from time to time, making all-too-predictable statements, living it up at smart hotels at someone's expense, never their own.

The dances were performed on a large stage which looked extremely tiny under the arc-lights trained on it from the sides of the colossal auditorium. There were dances by Malays and Indians—the latter did a superb "Seethaswayamwaram," a dance depicting an episode from the Ramayana performed by one of Malaya's leading Indian classical dancers, Gopal Shetty, and his students. Equally fascinating was the "Berhala Lima," or Dance of the Five Idols performed by dancers from Kelantan on the East Coast of Malaya. Then there were pretty Portuguese dances from Malacca: the "Farrapeira," or Dance of the Beggars, the "Viva Extrapasado" and "Les Lavandeires," the Portuguese Washerwoman's Dance. These were followed by "Tarian Pancha Irama," a "pot-pourri" of five Malay folk-dances by members of a celebrated folk-dance society in Kuala Lumpur, the Badan Kesenian Melayu.

I did not stay for the Merdeka Choir singing the Colombo Plan Theme Song (March tempo) nor for "a play depicting the ideals of the Colombo Plan."

The performance of folk-dances by Malay amateurs was the item which remained most vividly in my memory. They were performed to the music of drums and a sweet-sounding stringed instrument called a biola. The men wore black velvet songkok and brilliant samping, which means the whole ceremonial outfit worn by Malays on special occasions: the baju seluar, bright blue or yellow or rose-pink, which consists of a high-collared, full-sleeved shirt and loose, wide trousers of the same material; round their waists they wore vivid red or purple kain songket which is a silver or gold-threaded sarong reaching down to the knees and tied on the left hip in an especially intricate knot. The women wore long, dark, gold-threaded sarongs with calf-length pale-blue kebaya or overmantles. They all danced bare-footed.

The dances nearly all begin with the men and women facing each other in separate rows; as the dance proceeds they move towards each other and slowly interweave, going through the most complex evolutions with flitting eyes, shifting heads, fingers and hands making delicate, meaningful gestures : this form of stylised dancing is referred to in Malay as " fingers and eyes that talk." I have rarely seen any dance so subtly refined, so gently gay, so gracefully grave in its controlled perfection. It had an almost ritual atmosphere, and indeed in the old days these dances, which often went on all night, depicted the lives of deities and demons and their supernatural deeds. To-day the dances are kept short and are mainly courtship rituals or dances celebrating a good fishing catch or a fine harvest. Some of them are delicately romantic, like the " Tarian Mak Inang," where the men approach the women and claim their selendangs or long gauzy stoles which are used most effectively in the dance movements. I liked also the coy negative used by the girls in this dance when modestly denying the men's approach : the right hand was raised waist-high, palm facing the men, and moved slowly from side to side. One often sees this gesture of negation in ordinary life in Malaya ; sometimes the hand is waved in front of the face to indicate " No."

Unfortunately the Colombo Plan exhibition in the Chin Wu Auditorium was a very dull display, consisting mainly of out-dated photographs tacked on to pinhole board, lit by glaring electric lights and violent spots. The best exhibits came from Indonesia and Thailand, whose stalls had a few real things, interesting and unusual folk-craft articles, not just dead photo-graphs. I went outside to watch the boys swimming in the fine Olympic-size pool. For a few seconds there was an explosion of grey and salmon-pink sunset clouds in every conceivable formation over the green hill behind the Majestic Hotel and the Steshun.

I was constantly being disappointed by the lack of imagination shown in the arrangement of exhibitions in Malaya and Singapore. In a country with such wonderful resources of natural things for decoration and display, it was distressing to find beautiful folk-art objects uninventively presented.

In Singapore, for example, at the United Malaysia Exhibition in Victoria Hall, the pensive, conformist statue of Sir Stamford Raffles outside seemed to have cast a philistine chill over the exhibits and their arrangement. Again there were interesting and lovely things, like the brilliant photographs of bird's nest collectors in the Niah Caves of Sarawak, but these were all jammed together in a small, hot cubicle. The rest of the exhibition was very shoddy and badly laid-out, with harsh, unsubtle spot-lighting, acres of pinhole board covered with dead charts, dull official maps, yards of statistics and boring " Government Documentary " photographs. Upstairs, in a vast pillared and balconied hall, a postage-stamp-sized screen showed scratchy, noisy, " scientific " documentaries. I was pleased most of all by the visitors, who behaved with a hushed solemnity ; they were mostly country folk from all parts of Malaysia, nearly all wearing their brilliant local finery, some with tanjak or gold-threaded turban. It was lovely to see real people from Brunei looking at, and beautifully animating, the moribund Brunei section of the exhibition.

At the cinema in Malaya, all seats are bookable, and men and women have separate box-offices, I suppose to avoid unseemly contacts when buying tickets. I went to see " The Long and the Short and the Tall " at the Odeon, and found the mainly Malay and Chinese audience convulsed with uncontrollable giggles at the more " suspense-filled " moments of the film. Audiences here, particularly the young, cannot take any kind of heroics seriously. I felt sympathetic. After all, a giggle is the best answer to the horrors of modern life.

Friday, 18th May : Vesak Day, the name given here to the birthday of Buddha. The observance of this day is much more formal than in Japan, where it often seems to pass quite un-noticed. Here it is a public holiday. Temple Buddhas are drawn in ceremonial processions through the streets, accompanied by chanting monks who sprinkle spectators with some sort of holy water : a nice, saffron-robed monk simply drenched me with it as he slowly passed by on a decorated float in the Batu Road.

A royal marriage is being celebrated, and all kinds of public festivities have been laid on. The traditional use of bomohs and other magicians to bring fine weather and good luck for the marriage conflicts very much with the Minister of Health's recent statement, given as he was opening a rural clinic, that the country people should put their trust in modern science and medicine, not in ancient magic and superstitions.

But these die hard. Almost every day in the newspapers there are reports of magical ceremonies and superstitious rites, performed by bomohs, pawangs and kampong bidans or old-style native midwives. But educated Malays no longer believe that love-potions prepared by the local pawang or medicine-man can win a wife or a husband. In the case of sickness, religious leaders disapprove of seeking the help of bomohs and have ruled that this is an " un-Islamic " practice. Even on the East Coast where many old Malay customs are still retained, some of the practices and ceremonies performed by pawangs have been banned. Yet the practice of seeking the help of a bomoh or pawang for a good harvest or a good catch of fish still persists in remote corners of the country.

For the royal wedding in Kuala Lumpur, the services of a woman bomoh were sought to ensure fine weather, and apart from one short shower she was successful, in fact too successful, for after the wedding there was a long period of crippling drought.

In honour of the royal pair, the streets were decorated, buildings floodlit and the Lake Gardens illuminated with thousands of fairy-lights. For three nights there were wonderful performances of Malay songs and dances and displays of bersilat and koontau, the Malay and Chinese forms of self-defence. On the makyong stage troupes of players presented the oldest form of Malay drama. With the exception of two clowns and a sort of medicine-man, all the players were women. Rajas and their princesses, giants, ogres and djinns mingle freely and in these dramas nothing is incredible or impossible : for example, in one of them, a magic kite takes the hero to the Land of Giants.

In the manora, the ballet of old Ligor, all the parts were taken by men. Country boys who perform the parts of the heroine and her female companion grow their hair long. In a mixture of ballet, mime and slapstick comedy, the young men and boys acted out fantastic and romantic adventures. There were vivid costumes and many of the characters wore grotesque painted masks of tree-bark or wood. Both the makyong and the manora were accompanied by orchestras of drums, gongs and other instruments. But undoubtedly the most memorable of all the entertainments was the shadow-puppet play or Wayang Kulit performed by a team from Kuantan on the East Coast.

The screen was about eight feet square and was set up at the foot of a natural amphitheatre. I was surprised to see that the transparent figures of the shadow-puppets, only about one to two feet high, were always placed right at the bottom of this big screen. The large native orchestra as well as the sole manipulator or Tok Dalang, Father of Mysteries and his assistants were sitting behind the screen.

The bamboo ladder to this back-screen room was guarded by a Malay policeman; we had a little chat and without my asking he invited me to go back-stage. Holding me with his strong brown arms, he helped me to climb the very tricky ladder. Having safely reached the top—the whole stage and screen were on eight-foot-high stilts—I saw that the floor inside, where the musicians and the manipulator were squatting with crossed legs, was covered with woven straw and leaf mats, so I removed my sandals and gave them into my policeman friend's keeping. The team of musicians bowed and smiled and I bowed and smiled back. They were nearly all young men, wonderfully virile and handsome, and were smoking home-made, match-thin cigarettes. They were all wearing resplendent yellow baju seluar and loosely-coiled tanjak turbans.

They had a sort of gamelan orchestra composed mostly of gongs and drums, wood blocks and flutes, and the Malay-style violin, the biola. With these obviously native-made and well-preserved instruments—some of them seemed quite ancient, worn smooth by constant, loving handling—they kept up an extraordinary music, plangent and highly rhythmical, but to my obtuse and obfuscate ears without any kind of melody, though I soon began to recognise some regularly-repeated, brief phrases.

It lasted for five hours. The most extraordinary thing of all was the performance of the puppet-manipulator, who selected, arranged on the screen and agitated all the puppets as well as speaking all the lines in a virtuoso repertoire of voices, at times improvising dialogue and putting in improper words that made the audience on the other side of the screen, and the musicians, roar with laughter.

The good-looking young manipulator was obviously a great wit and a genius at poetic extemporisation; yet he was an ordinary workman, like the rest of the musicians. He tilted the flat, translucent shapes, patterned with bright colours and intricate cut-out decorations, against the bottom of the white calico panels of the screen so that their heads and the one movable part—the left or right arm and hand—were the most clearly-defined features. He would press the movable hand against the screen by means of a bamboo rod attached to its back; he prodded the screen quite vigorously, so that it bulged. Some of the smaller, grotesque figures of old men also had movable bottom jaws, worked on an elementary spring principle by a piece of elastic. Even such primitive devices and movements gave convincing life to the puppets. The sharp bamboo sticks to which they were attached were stuck into two long logs of soft green banana wood running right across the stage just behind the screen. There were scores of other figures dangling from bamboo poles slung under the roof. When one of these was required, a boy assistant would take it down and hand it to the manipulator, who usually seemed to have both hands full of sheaves of flat puppet-figures and bits of scenery that were also mounted on bamboo sticks. Sometimes these bits of cut-out scenery would represent a palace, a throne or a temple; they, too, were stuck at a slant in the log behind the screen, and their tilted shapes cast pretty, sloping, rather mysterious shadows, much bigger than the pieces themselves, across the calico panels. A strong white electric light was used, and the manipulator wore sun-glasses to protect his eyes from it whenever he turned round to pick up a new figure. He worked non-stop for five hours, chanting and singing and speaking, adapting his remarkable voice to every part, and constantly arranging scenery and sheaves of fantastic, mythological figures in veritable armies, that sometimes did hectic battle, on either side of the screen. No one else was allowed to manipulate the puppets, though one boy was mending any that suffered damage during the frequent epic battles and another was making and painting new ones from what looked like parchment or waxed paper. (It is actually buffalo hide.)

The Tok Dalang's enormous repertoire of stories is taken from the Hindu epics of the Ramayana and Mahabharata. He presents to the audience the tale of Prince Rama and his bride, Sita, who have been banished to the forest. There they encounter the demon Rakasasa, who abducts Sita. Then Hanuman, the

Monkey God, discovers where she is held prisoner and leads Rama to the rescue. The drama is spiced with earthy humour from the peasant clowns as they argue with the demigods.

Some of the prettiest shadows on the screen were cast by night butterflies and dragon-flies, moths and bats and beetles attracted by the strong light, which hung behind a dark shade about a foot from the bottom of the screen. The sound of the unseen audience stirring and laughing on the other side of the screen was a lovely and thrilling thing, so reassuringly, ordinarily human after too long a contemplation of the extra-human and sometimes terrifyingly real forms and movements of the shadow-puppets. I went out front once or twice to chat with my policeman friend and watch the show from the right side of the screen. Those small figures " carried " in the most exciting way. This was due to their very clear but not unsubtle colourings of reds and greens and blues and yellows ; the cut-out bits within the clear-cut outlines of the figures also helped them to make a telling effect on the spectators. With my policeman friend I walked right to the top of the amphitheatre slope, and from this great distance, at least a hundred yards, those tiny shadows were still distinct, their movements recognisable.

It is a great art, but unfortunately one that is slowly dying out. Perhaps the advent of television to Malaya will bring greater opportunities to this traditional native dramatic craft, and reveal its tremendous range and wide possibilities of development to an increasingly large number of people. It seemed to me that it would be perfectly suited to television presentation.

Dinner with a European living in an exquisite Malay house. It is of wood, raised high off the ground ; stone steps up to the front door and big, unglazed windows on a dusky veranda and a palmy garden. The place was a tonic to the spirit after some of the European deserts, both cultural and domestic, it had been my misfortune to encounter in Malaya. For one thing, there were actually some books in the house, all well chosen and displayed in specially-built shelves of local wood. There were two off-white rugs on the cool, dark wooden floor and a magnificent, ancient red-lacquered and gilded Chinese bed with pretty silk embroidered hangings : it had a Dunlopillo mattress in a vermilion cover. A Portuguese-style cupboard stood in one corner, and there were good chairs, some pictures by Malay artists and charming glass light-globes, melon-shaped, the kind one sees in mosques. All these items of furniture were picked up cheaply in the antique shops in Heeren Street and Jonkers Street in Malacca. Impoverished Chinese aristocrats and once-rich merchant families keep selling their treasures to make ends meet.

The house's occupant tells me he's leaving the house to move into a larger one. Shall I take it ? I had practically decided to cut my losses, throw up everything and fly back to Japan, leaving Malaya for good. Yet this house tempts me to stay, though the thought of buying furniture and pots and pans bores and frightens me. But already I am thinking what I could do with the place : instead of glass globes on the lights, I would have Chinese paper lanterns, those big round cheap ones on sale in temples. And standing on the polished floor, Japanese paper lamps.

The dinner, served by a Chinese boy in spotless white uniform, was delicious : Chinese noodle soup ; a whole roast merau, the good, sweet-tasting local fish, something like cod but more delicate ; grilled lamb, hot meringue pie, Stilton. Chilled Hungarian wine. For dessert we had some curious fruit looking like dark, grey-brown little potatoes with soft, sweet, fibrous pulp and large, almond-shaped, glossy black seeds. The taste was between a pear and a lichee, a quite distinctive sapor. I thought they were sapotillas, but the Chinese boy called them " chiku." Two Malay poets were also present, whose work I have been translating for an anthology of modern Malay verse. One of them had been to Swansea and he amused me by saying how astonished he was to find all the Welsh people talking English like Sikhs and Bengalis.

Shall I, shan't I take the house ?

In the Bukit Bintang Park, a Chinese Opera Company from Formosa is performing in the Hokkien dialect. They are said to be exceptionally good, so I went along to see them.

The large, semi-open hall was only half full. Many people were peeping through chinks in the side walls. I walked round to the back of the theatre, where the stage door was wide open on the backstage area. This was a vast space hung with sequinned silk costumes, wigs, pigtails and row upon row of beards—white beards, grey beards, black beards, orange beards, red beards, all in the same long, wispy, tapering shape. There were stacks of metal trunks for storing and transporting costumes. In one of the wings there was a large bed with a hard, rice-stuffed pillow, perhaps for the repose of the chief actors after a strenuous scene. Or perhaps it was a prop ; but it could hardly be this, because I remembered hearing that it was considered improper to show a bed without hangings on a Chinese stage.

There were trestle tables at which some of the cast and scene-shifters were eating and drinking. Out in front, I could just see the carmined faces of three girls performing a lengthy scene of explanation and expostulation, uttering hoarse, sharp, bitter cries of shock and outrage and satisfaction at various points in the narrative.

Three men in bright scarlet satin trousers and sweatshirts were daubing their faces and necks with wet-white, all the time strolling up and down and chatting with members of the company, which numbered about sixty. There seemed to be no call-boy and there were certainly no dressing-rooms ; the actors made-up and changed wherever they could find a quiet corner. Some actors and actresses, privileged beings, appeared from behind folding screens and stood in the wings waiting to go on.

The orchestra of about ten players was accommodated, as usual, in the wings. These players of cymbals, drums, flute and fiddle never stopped chatting and quietly cracking jokes among themselves ; from time to time, as if they had one abstracted ear on the stilted dialogue they must have heard thousands of times, they would give a bash and a clash on cymbal and drum at apparently casual, irregular intervals.

Nearby was the small shrine which such troupes carry everywhere with them : bunches of big fat joss-sticks and a number of candles were burning before the Buddha.

Next to the orchestra, in full view of the players who ignored her completely, an actress was changing and making-up. Her cheeks were a vivid carmine, shading away to dead white : the carmine covered her cheekbones and eyelids and stopped at broad black eyebrows. She had thickly-rouged lips and well-linered eyes. She had a long pony-tail of hair which she was combing and brushing carefully, straight back from the forehead, trying to make it lie as flat as possible. She flattened back the front of this sleek black hair with kirby-grips then painted a large black widow's-peak on her forehead : this is a sign of great beauty and distinction among the Chinese. She made a queue of her pony-tail and wound it into a compact bun : her head now looked very boyish, for she was playing the part of a young prince. I watched her put on a great, glittering head-dress ornamented with two yard-long, sweeping and swooping Oriental pheasant's feathers. Then I went round to the front of the house.

I stood among some old amahs peeping through a gap in the wooden wall. (The word amah, by the way, comes from the Portuguese word for nurse, *ama*.) The whole of the proscenium arch was quite dazzlingly lit with rows and rows of naked electric light bulbs picking out the vividly-painted designs on the panels framing the stage. It was painful to the eyes, though I was wearing dark glasses. In order to counteract this dazzle, the lighting on the stage itself has to be blindingly bright. The scenery was composed mostly of back-drops gaudily and primitively painted. The costumes, the best part of any Chinese Opera, were extremely costly and heavy, being made of silk covered entirely with sequin embroidery in many colours. These costumes glittered and sparkled like great barbaric jewels. Even the children's costumes were encrusted with spangled embroidery.

The heavily-spangled crimson curtain was not drawn between scenes. We were able to watch the stage-manager and a scene-shifter, in crumpled brown slacks and frowsty yellow shirt, a cigarette dangling from his lips, bring on the rare props, which included a very solid and prosaic modern wooden chair, pale-brown, with a medium-brown Rexine seat, and a pseudo-Jacobean sideboard on twisty, fumed-oak legs. I could not see the point of this article of furniture, which no one ever used.

The performance was hardly what we would call acting, but rather glorified story-telling, with very little movement apart from the characteristic twirlings of the long, flowing sleeves of the main characters and stylised placings of hands and fingers in admonishing attitudes. But there are great subtleties of inter-pretation, skilful eye movements and head-tiltings which a person as ignorant as myself could not appreciate to the full.

Nevertheless, compared with Noh and Kabuki, it was crude

in the extreme, lacking all subtlety and psychology. Seen from the front by one who couldn't understand the story or the language, it was almost painfully slow, static and boring. Indeed, the most interesting performances were the unrehearsed ones going on back-stage.

Apart from football and cricket matches on the padang, under the watchful eyes of the British mems, very few games were played. The heat was too much, and in the end I even gave up my callisthenics, for they weren't doing me any good. After several months in K.L. I was struck by the fact that I'd never seen a single student playing games on the many football and cricket pitches, the badminton and tennis courts in the super-modern University grounds. There was no swimming-pool and no bookshop. There is a large lake, but I have never seen students rowing or punting on it. The only people who go near the lake are a couple of workmen in a dilapidated boat hauling up stinking hanks of grey-green weed from the brownish depths.

The University also lacks a good restaurant and a bar. The canteen, though housed in the most modern of structures, is not capable of providing decent food and drink. It has spittoons like tin flower-pots under the tables. Birds pop in and out of the holes in the lacy cement-screen walls as they do in the broken open-worked and undercut stone-carvings of leaves, flowers and fruit round the north door porch of St. Mary Redcliffe Church in Bristol.

Malay saying : " If the teacher passes urine while standing the pupil will do it while running." The power of example in a good teacher-pupil relationship.

When he is in a dilemma, a Malay might say : " By swallowing a thing your mother dies and by ejecting it from your mouth your father dies."

Another saying gives a vivid description of a country bumpkin : " Like a deer entering a village."

Other attractive and entertaining proverbs of the Malays : " Give him the calf and he will ask for the thigh : like the Dutch asking for a piece of land."

A precarious situation : " Like an egg on the tip of a bullock's horn."

Tropic Temper

The past months' news from Goa and Algiers made me remember and re-read Evelyn Waugh's *St. Francis Xavier's Bones* and Albert Camus's *L'Esprit d'Algers*.

A visit to Templer Park, about sixteen miles from K.L. It is the jungle in its natural state, a splendid reserve of trees, game and wild orchids. The waterfalls are stupendous. Lots of Malay boys bathing in the pools at the foot of the falls : I sat on a rock, took off my shoes and let my hot feet hang in the chill water. Delicious. Then there came a simply tremendous rainstorm which soaked me to the skin. A bottle of beer at the little café near the entrance to the park. Many foreigners with butterfly-nets and fishing-rods. It is a popular spot for picnics. A few monkeys were the only animals I saw.

By the time I got a lift back into K.L. my clothes were fairly dry but I felt the need of something warming inside me so I went to have an excellent Ceylonese curry in a small shop-house restaurant (with Chinese nameboard) in Scott Road (off Brickfields Road).

The hot-spiced and well-cooked, tender mutton was served on a broad palm-leaf with plenty of rice and three kinds of vegetables, together with chillies, pickled tomato and other pungent delicacies. There was also chicken curry gravy and a dish of sliced cucumber.

First washing my hands at the basin behind a screen, I ate the curry with the fingers of my right hand. I took bits of curried vegetable and mutton and pickle and played with them, moulding them with portions of rice to make a small, rough ball of stuff which it was quite easy to thrust into the mouth without much mess. All the customers—mainly Ceylonese but also some Chinese and Malays—ate thus, though forks and spoons are provided. It is a curiously satisfying thing, to eat cooked food with one's fingers : it seems to be tastier, and more easily digested, when one eats this way.

Unfortunately the Anchor Beer was warm. But it was an extremely satisfying meal : I was given generous second and even third helpings. It was the best curry I ever ate in Malaya. It left me with gloriously burning lips, mouth and tongue— Hotlips Hassan I called myself, dabbing on a few drops of "Naughty Time" scent.

Some Pleasures

After the meal I washed my hands. This is a country where "I'm going to wash my hands" is no euphemism.

March 7th: this morning signed a two-year lease on the Malay house. I paid £140 in advance rent and for redecorating the interior. I'm tied to Malaya now.

Or am I?

16. General Knowledge

In Malaya there are no typhoons, nor earthquakes, no tidal waves : compared with Japan, it is a comparatively safe place to live in. But Malaya has floods as bad as those experienced by the Japanese, accompanied by terrific storms of thunder and lightning, especially during transition seasons. The monsoon rains and gales on the East Coast from October to January are often very severe, closing roads and making rivers impassable. Transport is brought to a stop because ferries cannot cross the swollen rivers. (There was a grave situation in Kelantan at the end of December 1961, when floods washed away roads and ferry-landings.) On the West Coast, winds known as " Sumatras," presumably because they originate in that area, can reach gale force.

The word monsoon is derived from the Arab word " musim," meaning a season, and is a corrupted form from Portuguese and English.

Here, as in Japan, mental counting is done by doubling the fingers in towards the palms and then unfolding them.

Often during an electric storm, the book I am reading seems to be suddenly alive with images of fire, death and destruction. To-night there are blinding, long-protracted overhead flashes accompanied immediately by such staggering detonations that it seems the air itself is being rent asunder. I am reading J. Christopher Herold's book about Mme de Staël, a most absorbing piece of scholarship called *Mistress to an Age.* (How very much Germaine reminds me of Simone de Beauvoir !) I always try to find some such riveting book during a thunderstorm, hoping it will help me to forget my terrors. But just after a particularly violent crash of thunder I read this : " At night, she could hear the rain falling on the roofs like a deluge. ' It penetrates into the houses, and the water pursues you with the energy of fire.' "

Then, talking about August Wilhelm Schlegel, Sismondi says :
" One allows him four paradoxes per day at the utmost, and
when he starts on the fifth, the oncoming thunderstorm can be
heard rumbling." My thunderstorm is right overhead, and the
rain is coming down in tearing sheets, flooding the courtyard
balcony outside my room !

A few days later, as I sit reading James Purdy's "Eventide"
in his miraculous collection of short stories, *Colour of Darkness*,
I hear a sound like frying. It is a shower of rain that suddenly
gets heavier : another monsoon thunderstorm coming on !
I fling myself on the bed with my book, because I have the
mistaken idea that if my feet are off the ground the lightning
cannot touch me. As the lightning whizzed and the lamp and the
air-conditioner kept dimming and gasping, my wincing eyes
read this : ". . . There was a darkness all over the city. The
fire department had been coming and going all afternoon. There
were so many fires in the neighbourhood—that is what she was
saying to Cora on the telephone, too many fires : the fire chief
had just whizzed past again. . . ." Just as I read that, there was
a sudden dimming of my bedside lamp and an electric shock ran
through me as I lay shuddering on the bed, followed at once by
a perfectly spine-splitting detonation. I cast the book away and
picked up my oiled-paper Malay umbrella which I used to press
the electric bell to summon my room-boy. While I was waiting
for him to come, there was another chilling flash and a brilliant
blue spark leapt from the telephone which at once started ringing.
The blue fire wandered rather lazily round the room and went,
as far as I could make out, down the plug-hole in the wash-basin.
(Fortunately, I had for once let my dirty water run away by
pulling out the plug.) When my room-boy arrived I was in
a state of hysterical giggles. Fortunately he is used to my goings-
on and when I rang for him knew what I wanted : he came in
bearing a bottle of iced sparkling hock with a huge bow of pink
satin ribbon tied round it—I had provided the ribbon myself
for use in such emergencies—and a kaleidoscope. (Because of
my nerves, he had opened the bottle before bringing it to my
room.) We sat sipping hock laced with brandy—a kind of
campaign shocktail—while he shook the kaleidoscope for me
and held it for me to look at whenever he got something really
pretty. I recommend this to all you who are, like me, mortally

afraid of thunderstorms—and who isn't, let's face it? Later
I learnt that a thunderbolt had fallen nearby.

Income Tax—how sordid, how unappetising, how completely
incomprehensible! I received my Malayan Income Tax form
from the taxman—my taxes were apparently in a " go " condition
—and the only nice thing about it was that it was addressed to
" Inche " (Mr.) J. K. The very stiff covering letter—why must
they always write them on that horrid dun-coloured paper, why
couldn't it be rose-madder?—begins " Tuan " (Sir) and closes
with " Yang benar " (Yours faithfully). Riding in a bus, I let
it be blown out of the window, and at once feel relief at having
lost it. Now I can forget all about it. But that evening a little
Indian boy announces himself; he is carrying the missing
form. I feign untold delight and give him a dollar, which he
doesn't want to take, but finally I slip it in his shirt and he
beams all over his face. I also offer him one of my Japanese
dolls, which he accepts with wonder and joy. I close the door
before I'm tempted to give him anything else. What to do with
the form, though? It reminds me of the time in Kyoto when,
weary of carrying a lot of dirty washing round with me on one
of my rambles round the ryokans, I threw it all in the river. It
was fished out by a missionary who thought someone had com-
mitted suicide. But I was traced through the laundry-marks
and some weeks later, back at home, the postman brought me a
parcel of dirty linen.

I put the form eventually inside the hotel piano when no
one was looking.

A Malay matchbox. The name : Chilly Brand, with a picture
of a bright red chilli on the label. " Damp Proof," I read, incredulously. Kelantan Match Factory. But matches and the
striking surfaces of matchboxes do not disintegrate here in the
humidity as they do in Japan. Most matchboxes are very tiny,
about one and a quarter inches by three-quarters inch, the
matches, always safeties, very thin. Usually made in Sweden :
Annebergs Tändsticksfabriks : Paraffinerade Säkerhets Tänd-
stickor. How that brings back Sweden to me, the match factory
I visited at—where was it? By a vast lake, in icy snow.

Envelopes in Malaya are sold with small slips of transparent,
grease-proof paper placed under the gummed flap, to prevent
them from sticking in the damp heat.

A letter from Japan, containing a small pressed leaf of Sendai Hagi, on which is written "I love you." In return, I send a Malay calendar: it is made of black velvet with a picture formed by sticking on bits of golden rice-straw. It is very neat. The picture shows a couple of kampong houses on stilts, with the moon behind palms, burnishing a rippled path across the water of a padi-field.

Like the tops of very hard-frozen ice-cream cones, the twin domes on the towers of the Istana Negara, the local Buckingham Palace.

Afflicted by melancholia, nostalgia, algolagnia—all the big words. It's no good: I must return to Japan.

Since the opening of a new, ultra-modern bank building in Market Street, swarms of Malayans have been staring fascinated at its two moving staircases leading to the first floor, and riding on them in dense throngs. These are the very first moving staircases ever to appear in K.L., and for that matter in the whole of Malaya. I wonder how the leisurely Malays would take it if moving pavements were installed in Mountbatten Road?

Boys are swabbing the outside of the Chartered Bank with whitewash, using huge fat brushes on long handles. Though they proceed at a civilised, slow pace, it is extraordinary to see what swift progress they make. They are using their whole bodies in their painting motions, and this is what gives the brushes such a wide, easy, rapid sweep. I spent a delightful two hours sitting on the Victorian fountain, wearing a big, shady straw hat, watching them at work.

A visit to the nearby town of Klang, where the Klang River is spanned by the Jambatan Kota or Castle Bridge, an impressive double-decker span, the only one of its kind in the country. Klang is the old royal town of the State of Selangor and there is some talk of it being made once more the capital of the Federation of Malaya. It is in an ideal situation, linked to K.L., twenty-three miles away, by fine highways. The Klang Gates Dam, a reservoir which supplies absolutely pure water to K.L., is a favourite spot for bathing picnics. Here on Sundays Malay body-builders, including the national stars, Clancy Ang and Osman Ali, can be seen in training, making the most of their inches. There is a radiantly cool, white royal mosque, a truly heavenly building with ethereal white domes and delicately-fretted stonework. It is a refreshment to the spirit, after a long, hot day in the capital, to enter this mosque at sundown and recline on one of the reed mats strewn over its quiet floors, then to go on to a moonlight bathe from the grassy slopes of the Dam. Another fine building in Klang is the newly-completed royal palace of the Sultan of Selangor, the Istana Alam Shah, with its up-to-date installations that include a private wide-screen cinema. It is set in beautiful grounds, commanding superb views of jungle hillsides and the green-topped limestone outcrop of Bukit Takun near Templer Park.

I paid an interesting visit to the Muslim Theological College at Klang, where Malay youths, and a few Malay girls, come to study the Koran, Arabic, Malay history and many other related subjects. Unfortunately English is not on the programme of studies, and so the students' knowledge of English is rather limited. I shall never forget the look of polite bafflement on those charming faces when they were confronted with a linguistics specialist who had been flown out from London to give some lectures on the science of language and phonetics. They didn't understand a single word of the lengthy lecture : it was sad, but also funny, to see them missing all the lecturer's little academic jokes. In its way, it was a perfectly good lecture, but for these Malays it was totally useless. In the library, the female students are segregated from the males by a high trellis.

Afterwards, to Port Swettenham, for a meal of baked crabs, the justly celebrated local specialty. A number of liners and cargo-boats call at Port Swettenham on the way from Penang to Singapore, and it is one of the ports from which Muslim pilgrims leave, in jam-packed ships, for the long, steamy voyage to Mecca.

Shortly after I arrived in Malaya, I read in the newspapers that Aladad Khan bin Taizullah Khan, a cowherd, had discovered a " magic spring " of healing water at Kampong Dalek Kechil, near the railway line which carries modern diesel trains from Klang and Port Swettenham to the capital. The cowherd said he discovered the spring after a " vision." Soon hundreds of people, including the lame, sick and blind were crowding to the healing spring, bringing empty medicine bottles to fill with the magic water.

This was followed by a warning from the Klang District

Officer that the water was heavily contaminated and advising the public to boil the water before drinking it. The cowherd countered this statement by declaring that if the water were boiled it would lose its magical properties. Finally, the spring, which was in fact a broken drain, was sealed up, but not before use of the water had been condemned by the religious authorities as "un-Islamic."

A few weeks later a Selangor princess was drowned in the Klang River between two crocodile-infested tributaries. Two pawangs or medicine-men were hired by the missing princess's family to find the body when all other searches had proved fruitless. The magicians went out in a motor-sampan and found the body.

About twenty-five miles from Klang are two attractive coastal resorts, Morib and Kuala Selangor. The latter overlooks the broad rice plains of Tanjong Karang and is famed for its old lighthouse and Portuguese fort where ancient Portuguese cannon on a stone-walled emplacement still cover the mouth of the Selangor River as they did in the old days, when they were used as a defence against Burmese pirates. There are fine beaches at these two places, but sea-swimming here is said to be rather dangerous because, as at Penang, the waters are sometimes infested by poisonous sea-snakes whose bite can be deadly.

Kuala Selangor was the subject of an interesting news item in that best of all Malayan newspapers, *The Malay Mail*. I quote verbatim : " A calamity was expected in Kuala Selangor yesterday. The deadline was 7 p.m.

" But after going into a trance at the ancient Royal Mausoleum here yesterday evening a police constable, Raja Hamzah, announced that he had managed to arrange for the disaster to be postponed until ' three Fridays from now '—that is, Nov. 17.

" Weeks ago Raja Hamzah, who says he is a great grandson of a Malay chieftain, Raja Hitam of Bernam, claimed he had a dream.

" He predicted a calamity in Kuala Selangor unless one of the cannons which had been taken from the port there to adorn the grounds of the Sultan of Selangor's new Istana in Klang was speedily returned.

" Three days ago, while in a trance, Raja Hamzah learnt that the date for the disaster would be Nov. 3—to-day.

" Yesterday morning the Kuala Selangor Territorial Chief, Dato Pengahwah Permantang, and religious officials went to the Istana in Klang to see court officials to have the cannon returned.

" A P.W.D. lorry stood by to bring it back to Kuala Selangor.

" Yesterday afternoon Dato Pengahwah telephoned to say the Royal approval had not been given and that the State Government would be asked to investigate.

" Raja Hamzah promptly went into another trance at the Mausoleum at the foot of Kuala Selangor Hill—and announced the postponement of the catastrophe."

At night in Kuala Lumpur, car headlamps blaze through the translucent white and pastel-shaded cheap nylon shirts, short-sleeved, of strolling youths, outlining most touchingly their frail chests and shoulders, their slender, belted hips in a sort of shimmering aura. I, too, wear such shirts ; they are non-absorbent, so do not show the sweat. Some people say they make you feel hotter than cotton or silk or linen shirts, but I never found it so, perhaps because I was hot and sweaty all the time. Like the boys, I wore my nylon shirt like a jacket outside my trousers. Like them, I kept my money in the transparent breast pocket, so that people could see how much—or how little—I had. I liked to have the raspberry-pink or the lime-green of a ten-dollar or five-dollar note glimmering through the fabric as a delicate indication of the means at my disposal : bored bar-hostesses, glancing up from some cheap comic book, would suddenly have a light in their eyes when they observed these hinted rewards.

I found a most extraordinary magazine at the Universal Book Store : it was American and was called : " Famous Monsters of Filmland." It was only thirty-five cents. The hilarious cover announced : " More Mad Robots This Issue ! " And : " He's back ! "—(coverpic of a gruesome, semi-decomposed maniac)— " He's back—to judge our make-up contest—Zackerley. . . . See Page 30 ! " Inside, a " Fang Mail " column with pictures sent in by readers of themselves in elaborate and would-be-scarifying but ludicrous " monster " make-up. There was also an amusing advertisement for " Venus Fly Trap." (" This plant actually eats insects and bits of meat ! ") Let them " rush " it to me ? No fear.

The evening of a riotous festival : I can no longer bear the loneliness of spirit that afflicts me on such occasions, which are so frequent in Malaya. I lock myself in and play with a mah-jong set, inventing my own rules and cheating constantly. At midnight, the sound of mosquitoes in my sleepless room is like distant revelry, a faint, far-off singing that has nothing to do with me.

Aloneness, stillness, a long book, inducing gradually, like ether or cocaine, a feeling of rapt suspension, a sense of exquisite remoteness. Then, all of a sudden, to dash out into the shattering street, wearing my rare apartness like a precious cloak of the winds to view close-up the distant spectacles of life, the immediacies of death.

I was born lonely. It is my only birthmark, hidden in my most secret place, but one that sometimes shows.

I have learnt to get along with my affliction, as the psychiatrists and ministers of religion advise. Increasingly I yearn to be alone and solitary, especially when surrounded by the East's vibrant crowds ; to have no friends, no servants, no colleagues, no enemies, no relatives, no acquaintances, but only the most casual of passing contacts : in the thronged festival street I brush my hand gently in passing against the robe of a stranger, against a girl's hand—so gently, they are not aware of my passage, my ghost-wandering.

Loneliness is a habit-forming drug, and I have become its incurable addict. I take deep draughts of it, increasing the dose, in heart, soul, mind, spirit and body, day after day, night after night, until eventually I shall at no moment be able to do without it. And with its accumulating brilliance goes silence, ever denser and stiller. Soon I shall attain a barely-animated absolute, if indeed I have not reached it already.

The entrancing names of the authors of my " *Indonesian-English* " *Dictionary* (Cornell University Press) are : Echols and Shadily.

" Doing " Eliot once again : how ghastly, the awful knowingness of his poetry, the horrid, dated allusions and imagery, that feeling of the *Strand Magazine*. And those poems in that perfectly irreproachable French, so un-French, that seems to have been vetted by St.-John Perse. To have to go through it all again, next year, with another set of First Years, how appalling a prospect !

Tropic Temper

A lot of dead wood in the Mod. Lit. course. I want to hack out Orwell and Greene, neither of whom seem to me worthy of academic attention, and substitute Nabokov, Firbank and Ivy Compton-Burnett, with Elizabeth Taylor, P. G. Wodehouse and Colin MacInnes as "required reading." I really don't see the need for Snow and Wain and Amis : they are railway bookstall novelists, and my students ought to have them simply for light bedside reading. But I fear that they will read nothing beyond what is on the syllabus. It looks as if I must also make out for them a list of "The 100 Best Bedside Books," and warn them that they'll be expected to have read some of them.

Lolita, by the greatest living master of English prose, may not, I have been instructed, be included in a course on Modern English Literature !

Next, I am informed by my professor that the English Department "has to be run like a factory production-line." Again and again I hear phrases like "We must be a graduate-producing factory." I can hardly believe my ears. My students might just as well be taking a course from a Correspondence College.

And we must have more modern poets in the syllabus besides the eternal Pound and Eliot, Hopkins and Yeats. Please, not Dylan Thomas or that bogus Wallace Stevens ! I want to do F. T. Prince . . . his two volumes. . . . Not allowed ! Oh, to hell with the lot of them !

This morning I could not face the half-portion of chilled papaya with my early morning tea. Something about its green-stained yellow rind, and in particular the great spawn of gluey, grey-brown, caviare-like seeds and the pale, stringy fibres at its cleft heart made me want to throw up. I had a pressed orange, only, and the tea, made insipid, as always, by that dusty-tasting "reconstituted" powdered milk which is the only milk considered safe in the tropics. I feel weak and shivery and can hardly lift the heavy, thick china cup which is white with a green band round the rim and the seal of the hotel in green on the side : on the bottom, "Vitreous Ironstone, Dunn Bennett & Co. Ltd., Burslem, Made in England," conjures up additional miseries in my fevered fancy. Downstairs, there is fish for breakfast after the porridge and the tot of chilled tomato-juice. Toast made from bread like cotton-wool. The *Straits Times* again reports police raids during the early hours of the morning on private homes. I feel the depressed excitement induced by Ambler's thriller about Malaya and Indonesia, *Passage of Arms*, incidentally one of the best novels about this area, though spoilt by one or two *invraisemblances*.

Invigilating the Finals. Before the students enter, I spray the room and the papers with scent. Then they come in, poor things, so doomed and hangdog they don't notice the new Thai tie I have put on to cheer them up.

After a night of love, the early tropic morning, eight o'clock. The Geology Department. In the ultra-contemporary lecture room, the powder-blue plastic venetian blinds are lowered against the stacks of sun. Two lumbering ceiling-fans moodily revolve, just fast enough to beat a breeze out of the palmy air and leave the papers undisturbed.

Outside, a yellow gash in the jungle: there, in mashed bamboos, the new wing's sun-screens of white concrete lace begin to rise: the brown work-boys, innocent of all examination, the girls in black trousers and coolie hats shovel piles of grit and gravel into the cement-mixer's gruelling guts. Under an aero-relief map of the entire world I break the red seals on Eng. Lit. 1550–1700, excluding Shakespeare and Milton.

My students, too, look as if they had been up all night. There is something about them I had never seen before—an air of decision. The girls' neat, dark heads, the pleasant faces, the slim bodies in batik sarong, samfu, kebaya, cheongsam or sari; the handsome boys, white-shirted, cool, on whom I shall gently feast my eyes all morning. I feel I am a stranger to them; it is as if we had never met before, so strange an hour it is. It is like a film, in slow motion, of people meeting again after death. Unscrewing their expensive pens, they take the first wary look at the paper, out of the corners of almond eyes.

The little manias assert themselves: one sets up a travelling-clock; another aligns pens and pencils. My favourite lays out a scented handkerchief. Some ask distracted questions, as if simply to give themselves confidence by hearing the sound of their own voice, and mine in answer: where can I make my rough notes? May I write with a ball-pen? (No!) May I smoke? (If you wish.) Then please will you give me a light? (With pleasure.) Is there any water? (I'll send for some.) Have you an aspirin ? (Yes, I thought you might need one, dear.) Would you please put a wad of paper under the leg of my table ? (There, now, is that steady ?)

So they begin. I wish I could tell them that it doesn't really matter all that much. Only their living, not their lives, depend on it. Not even that. I wish I could tell them that it is all meaningless. But that would be cruel, they're so young, so pretty, so hopeful. . . . But why should youth have hope, ideals ? Why should the ghastly truth be hidden from them, just because they're young ? The sooner they know, the better. I would be cruel only to be kind, in a way.

I remember my own Finals, hell that was worse than war-time, hell in a hideous red-brick hall, hell invigilated by a mad professor who tore up my answers. Another world than this, another time.

The long morning disturbs and touches. A boy from the canteen brings undrinkable coffee, thick with condensed milk. I sink into the strata of time, love, sleep and memory, but always return to here and now, to these young creatures whom I admire and like, would want to help——

I gaze at them in sadness and in pity : the boys' scanty vests, their rich dusk of shoulders movingly outlined under shirts the golden skin glows passionately through ; the girls' thin, sandalled feet on the cool mosaic floor. The dark locks of hair that, like an exhausted answer, fall at the end of every question across brows so innocent of knowledge—how tender, serious and young !

How can I not remember that they write their answers in another, foreign tongue ?

Some of my first-year girl students have a rather amusing affectation : here in the tropics they pretend they are freezing with cold, and wear thick European clothes—sweaters and jerseys, woollen or tweed jackets, corduroy slacks. And sunglasses, which they hope makes them look experienced and depraved. I know it's a bit silly, but so are all affectations, and I like this one, which is so young, so harmless. Like the peroxided moustache of that Indian youth : camp as a row of silken pavilions. Though I do not think affectations in the young and foolish—and in the middle-aged and foolish—should be encouraged, I do think they should be tolerated and, if possible, appreciated. It often means there is an imagination at work—O rare and blessed relief, in this, the most prosaic of all Eastern lands! And it may even be a sign of—dare one breathe the words ?—originality, intelligence.

Marking exam papers : Poets and Critics, 1780–1950. Faced with hundreds upon hundreds of questions to mark in a very short time—as usual, I've left everything to the last minute— the despairing examiner in the end can only give a brief glance through each question, to see if it is literate. The handwriting influences me : I like it to be lucid and restful but not too monotonous, but on the other hand a loopy script like demented knitting often rouses my interest, for there may be some individuality behind that tangle of pasty down-strokes which my manual of graphology tells me indicate heavy sexuality. Hooray for a little idiosyncrasy!

If the student answers at least one question on contemporary writers instead of churning out what all the books about books say about the everlasting Blake, Wordsworth, Shelley, Keats, I upgrade him. I always hope for at least one original thought in every paper. And it fascinates me to see how my own lectures and tutorials emerge : sometimes I'm quite unable to unscramble the message I myself have tried to put across clearly and concisely in tutorial and lecture theatre. Then I give the student the benefit of the doubt : perhaps it was my own fault, and I tend to upgrade him.

One very intelligent Chinese girl, a victim of her own inverse lambdacism, writing about Shelley's " Ode to the West Wind," had constructed with great ingenuity two long paragraphs explaining a line in the second section which she took to be " The rocks of the approaching storm." Her imperturbable explanation of something that at the back of her mind she must have sensed was odd gave me so much pleasure that I gave her an alpha minus.

If any student answers one of the less obvious questions, I give him high marks, and if it's a man student I give him more marks than I would a woman, unless the woman happens to be quite outstanding.

I like and upgrade certain papers that indicate great mental turmoil. I upgrade students who express eccentric, anti-social and mistaken ideas, provided they do so convincingly. Anything,

anything, rather than all this dismal mediocrity in which the student never puts a foot wrong and never says anything that is not unexceptionable. For a dutiful, mediocre conformity seems to be, in the TV jargon so many students employ in their answers, " the final end-product " of present-day university education. Students certainly did not come to the University of Malaya to satisfy a raging thirst for knowledge : they came to get a piece of paper which will perhaps help them to obtain a decent living wage as an educational or governmental drudge : a wage that is ludicrously low by Western standards but which is at least above the low subsistence level of the majority of Malayans. I always have this in mind when I am marking their papers, and that is why I always give them the highest possible marks, often far more than their papers really deserve. But the other members of the English staff are much less generous, perhaps rightly so : standards have to be established and maintained, especially in a newly-emergent institution like the University of Malaya. But it is no good trying to run the place like a factory or a submarine: the highest standard, surely, is the human one, and a university should first of all be a place where humanity can flourish freely, not be regimented and chopped up into nameless and character-less units.

Above all, I encouraged my students to be as unacademic as possible in their approach to literature : to actually read the works prescribed on the syllabus, instead of reading too many books about them, or books about books about them. I would quote to them the admirable last page or so of Chapter Five in *Northanger Abbey*, to illustrate this point. And always I insisted that it was the original creators of works of art, not their critics and commentators, who were the really important people. This may surprise some of my readers, but I can assure them that it was necessary. Foreign students of English are so examination-conscious that they tend to become hysterical when confronted with a long list of set-books : their reaction is to ignore the texts and mug up the critical commentaries on the selected works. They persuade themselves that by so doing they are killing three birds with one stone : learning English, studying their set books and getting smart critical slants on future examination subjects. In tutorials their essays are often blatant cribs of critical essays by C. S. Lewis or William Empson or Dr. Leavis or of the hosts of other commentators who flourish to-day. It is good that they should read these writers, but they must also somehow be taught that criticism is a literary side-line and that an examination of the original texts comes first. I also believe that for foreign students of English it is better to start off teaching them literary appreciation, a much-abused term, before instructing them in analytical criticism.

One of the most extraordinary statements in the examination papers, and one which illustrates the desperate efforts most students make to conform and say the right thing was this, by a Third Year Honours student, a woman, writing about " Kubla Khan ": " A woman wailing for her demon lover is something only slightly out of the ordinary."

I was reminded of that excellent quatrain quoted by Geoffrey Grigson in one of his anthologies :

> " O Cuckoo! shall I call thee Bird,
> Or but a wandering Voice ? "
> (State the alternative preferred
> With reasons for your choice.)

The examination horror ended with the English Third Year Honours Viva, a waste of a beautiful Saturday morning. The students were either agitated, flustered, hopeless, despairing or desperately aggressive : it was interesting to observe which way the ordeal, a quite unnecessary one, affected them. Sweating armpits, Indians looking green, Chinese flushed round the eyes, Eurasians haggard, Malays terrified, one or two of the girls almost on the point of hysterical collapse. I wished again I might tell them : " Don't bother. It doesn't matter all that much. Nothing matters all that much. Nothing matters."

I was rather shocked by the brutal, inquisitorial attitude of some members of staff whose aim seemed to be to reduce the girls to tears and the boys to impotent, humiliated rage. Some of the staff obviously adored showing off their superior knowledge, not so much to the student, but to the other members of staff.

I asked as few questions as possible, trying to put the answers into the students' mouths and smiling in what I hoped was a helpful way. Unfortunately the gap between my two upper front teeth always gives my smile a sinister look, and I think they were put off rather than encouraged by the smiler with the knife. And the rest of the board had reduced them to such a panic state of fluster that by the time my own turn came they were either incoherent and bewildered or terribly, sometimes desperately, and once or twice I thought courageously, on the defensive.

Do these vivas do any good ? Are they necessary ? All our decisions about marks had been made beforehand, and we had already agreed that no one would lose marks on the viva. I suppose a viva may help in a borderline case ; but it depends entirely upon the temperament of the candidate and the attitude of the examiners. One must always be as encouraging as possible to the students. For those who already had low marks, the viva merely served to confirm their lowness. My own feeling was that vivas were a waste of time and an unnecessary ordeal for both student and examiners.

Well, we live and learn, they say. We learn, at any rate.

My own work at this time was not making much progress. I had taken on a vast translation which had to be finished within two months, but what with the climate and my own disturbed state of mind I had to throw it all up after the first two hundred and fifty pages.

Nor was my own education proceeding very satisfactorily. I had been able to teach myself quite easily a little elementary Malay, but as a language it bored me and I didn't really think there was any point in learning it properly. What I did most ardently want to learn was Mandarin or Cantonese.

I put an advertisement in a newspaper asking for a teacher who could preferably speak both Mandarin and Cantonese. It elicited a whole sheaf of eager replies : I selected about five of what seemed to me the most promising applicants. They had such pretty names, like Wong and Wang and Ching and Chong. The letters of application were well written in just slightly off-beat English. The applicants' voices, however, panting with painful hope and excitement over the telephone, distressed me : I couldn't bear to disappoint any of them ; I wanted to employ them all.

The first person I interview is a graduate of Taiwan University : so quick, intelligent, nice, so eager to be chosen, and,

I suspect, the best of the bunch. He says : " Give me a fee corresponding to the lowest offer you have had (which is forty-five dollars—about £5—a month, for three lessons of one and a half hours each every week). It's not good enough for him and I tell him so. (The highest fee requested, for three one-hour lessons a week, was 120 dollars a month.)

One of the letters ran : " I have my honour to inform you that I shall be glad if you will agree and appoint me to be your family Chinese language teacher, and I shall try my best to discuss and study with you during the night time. I may explain to you in English as it is necessary for you to get the knowledge easily. Thank you very much for your trouble."

I finally chose a teacher who offered three lessons of one hour per week at a fee of eighty dollars a month. He is bright and lively and intelligent, but I fear has not much idea of how a foreign language should be taught. His name is Ming.

We started off with a list of about twenty words which I had some difficulty in transcribing into English phonetics because of Ming's pronunciation : I thought he was saying " neck " when he meant " leg " and " loom " when he meant " room." After a while I sensed his mental exhaustion so we sat back and smoked and chatted for a while, then went over the vocabulary again.

For the second lesson he brought with him a small, paper-backed reader, brightly illustrated, which is used by Chinese children in their first year at the infants' school. He also brought two exercise-books, one for my Chinese vocabulary, the other for practise in making characters. This exercise-book has its pages divided into small squares. The teacher writes the characters the pupil has to copy in the top row of squares, and the pupil copies them, writing downwards, so that he writes out each character about twenty-five times before going on to the next. There are about 150 squares to a page, and each compartment is about three-quarter inch by half-inch.

Ming wrote out the characters for " I, we, you, he, up, down, sun, moon, work, human being, sky, and earth." He did this very rapidly, with a ball-point pen, and without attempting to show me in what order the strokes were made. But I knew there was a definite order in the arrangement of the strokes in every character : fortunately the children's reader showed some of these and then I got Ming to write more slowly so that I could see how he formed his characters. A ball-pen seemed the wrong instrument to use, so I made my first attempts at Chinese calligraphy with a Swan Calligraphic, which is perfect for this purpose.

I always enjoyed learning new characters and spent hours copying them out. In a couple of weeks I could write nearly a hundred but I had to go back and constantly revise the characters I had learnt otherwise I tended to forget them in the process of learning new ones.

Then we discussed the first picture in the child's picture book and I wrote down all the words we could think of : the picture was a Malayan landscape with palms, a kampong house ; and there were Chinese, Malay and Indian children playing on the country road. It was interesting to observe the proportions represented by the various nationalities. There were two well-dressed Chinese children in the foreground, one Malay wearing sarong and songkok in the middle distance and one Indian wearing shorts, very much in the background. There were no white children, of course.

After the lesson, Ming and I had a chat about sport—he plays basketball—and Chinese food. I was horrified to learn that he eats dog once a week. His round, good-natured face and his obvious eagerness to do his best as a teacher are very touching.

But after a month or so I began to realise I could perhaps make quicker progress if I taught myself. I bought H. R. Williamson's excellent *Teach Yourself Chinese* in an attempt to supplement the inadequacies of Ming's lessons. Now how am I going to dismiss him ? Fortunately in my letter to him I stipulated that he should be on a month's probation.

He accepted his dismissal with good grace, and we remained firm friends. He used to drop in about twice a week for a chat and a smoke, and often he would bring one of his Chinese friends with him.

When a taxi-driver in Malaya has a client he never switches off the sign that indicates the taxi is available. I am always flagging taxis with the " Free " sign showing, only to see them sail past with grinning driver.

The Chinese characters for " sun " and " moon " are derived

from primitive pictorial representations of these celestial bodies. Many other characters have been formed in the same way.

The juke-box in the Paramount Bar is always playing "our" song, "Once there were Green Fields," sung by a male close-harmony group that sound as if their voices have just recently broken. One can imagine their scrawny young necks with immense Adam's apples straining to get the high notes. But the words are rather nice. I hate the song on the other side, something about a time to be sowing and standing beside your wife at the moment of birth. If only there was one bar where one could hear some decent jazz! All one hears is " Sunday Night at the Palladium " stuff. Oh, for some Thelonius Monk!

A lovely name: *Amorphophallus campanulatus*, the curious " Elephant's Foot " yam, called " loki " in Malay. It is unusual in the Arum family with its huge divided leaves. It is sometimes eaten. Tastes rather good, something like a floury turnip, when boiled.

On my very first meeting with Ming, he asked me quite abruptly what my job was, how much I earned, how many children I had and how old I was. When I told him I was a grandfather, he laughed, as if that were a good joke, and said, politely: " But you too young, like boy." Chinese, in speaking English, often seem to us to be abrupt, tactless and inquisitive, simply because English has none of the subtleties of Chinese, in which one can ask the most intimate and leading questions with a most refined politeness that avoids any kind of offence being given or taken.

This is done by constant polite self-deprecation; it is polite to refer to oneself as " hsiung-ti," meaning younger brother, therefore an inferior, or as " ts'ao," or grass, to be trodden underfoot.

I was pleased to learn that " ying," meaning brave or illustrious, is used by the Chinese to describe England.

A question like " kuei chia tzu " or " what might be your esteemed age ? " would have its delicacy matched by a delicate or rather cryptic reply : a refined answer to such a question would refer obliquely to the animal which presided over the person's birth. " Chia tzu " in this form of question refers to the Chinese sexagenary cycle of sixty years.

In Japan, I often noticed that military, naval and air force personnel spoke English to me in a very loud, abrupt and rather rebarbative way. There is no need to be intimidated or to take offence if one is addressed in this way, because the speaker is simply trying to speak as clearly and correctly as possible, just as many English people tend to shout at foreigners, hoping to make them understand. But there is another reason for this manner of speaking on the part of Orientals : they nearly all learn English in big classes of a hundred or even more : practically the entire lesson is spent declaiming English sentences in unison, following the pattern of pronunciation set by the teacher. The teacher has to shout to make himself heard by everyone, and naturally the pupils shout back : English instruction is therefore a somewhat martial affair. Even more so, of course, in classes for the military. If one is shouted at by a Japanese or a Chinese, it does not mean he is turning nasty : he is simply speaking English as he was taught. He would be terribly puzzled if one showed any resentment.

All the same, I wish that this tendency to shout when speaking English could be eradicated. Learning Chinese : language of learned dialects, I tune my English instrument, that seems now too precise and hard, to your scale of a million tones, adjust the noun, unclassifiable, of myself to your all-inclusive classifiers. (In Chinese grammar the classifier groups under a common suffix certain types of objects, animals and people.)

Ko, meaning a piece of anything ; Ting, used with hats, caps, etc. Kuan, that refers to slender long things like pipes, pencils, etc. Chih, classifier with candles, pens, etc. Chan, used with lamps, wine cups, etc. Pa, used with teapots, tea cups, etc. Tso, used with hills, temples, towers, etc. T'ou, used with animals (though p'i must be used of horses).

K'o is the classifier used with small round things like pills, pearls, seeds, beads, etc. Ts'eng is used with layers, strata, slabs, anything piled up in tiers, etc. To, ear, pendant, is the classifier of pendant things. Chang is used with tables. T'ang, classifier of trains (which shall be referred to as " fire-carts ").

Teach Yourself Chinese goes on to say, rather suavely, I thought : " There are many others (classifiers), which will be found in any good dictionary. The student should exercise care in using the right classifier with nouns, as this is the mark of a good speaker."

The cinematograph becomes electric shadow, the gramophone a preserve-voice machine; the radio is no-wire-electric, and lightning the flash-electric.

Matches are foreign fire. Yung-hsin, to exert oneself mentally, means to use heart. And seek-not-get means cannot find.

To pass a stool is big-convenience, and to urinate is little-convenience. By all means becomes thousand-ten-thousand. Chang, ten feet, also means husband. Tobacco, snuff and opium are all yen.

A proverb that suits me: " If you boil an egg in a teapot you can't pour it out." (Meaning, I have many ideas tucked away in my mind but I can't express them.)

Lao-chia, a polite expression of thanks, literally means: " I have hindered your chariot."

17. Books and Journeys

Marco Polo refers to Malaya, by which he may have also meant Siam, under the name of Lokak. He describes it as "a large and wealthy province of the mainland. . . . The people are idolators, ruled by a powerful monarch and speaking a language of their own. They pay no tribute to anyone, because their country is so situated that no one can go there to work mischief. . . . It is such a savage place that few people ever go there. The king himself does not want anyone to go there or to spy out his treasure or the state of his realm. Accordingly we shall pass on and speak of other things. . . ." [1]

That is what most travellers seem to do : compared with other regions of the East, Malaya suffers from an unmerited obscurity. Though it is, as I have said before, the most prosaic of all oriental countries, it does have a kind of sinister, lugubrious fascination and, even, charm.

But it is not a country of immediate attractiveness. Its climate is tiresome and its people are difficult to get to know in a short visit, which is all that most Westerners have time for. Visitors staying for only a few days in this country tend to jump to ill-advised conclusions and make the most specious generalisations. Such people might do well to read Dorothy Wordsworth's *Hamburg Journal*, in which she comments, with her usual acuteness : "We were struck with the extreme folly of people who draw conclusions respecting national character from the narrow limits of common observation. We have been much with German hosts and hostesses and notwithstanding the supposed identifying tendency of national manners . . . these persons appeared in every respect as if made in contrast to each other."

That is very true. But it is easier for a Westerner to see the differences between individual Germans than it is for him to distinguish between members of an Oriental nation, who on short

---

[1] Marco Polo's Travels. Translated by R. E. Latham. Penguin Classics.

acquaintance all seem to look very much alike. It takes a long time in the East before one begins to recognise different types and becomes aware of what constitutes the unlikenesses between individuals of certain Oriental races and tribes.

Part of the fault lies in our mode of travel: flying by jet airliner from Tokyo to London in fifteen hours or even from Phnom Penh to Bangkok in forty-five minutes does not give us time to weigh and consider national characteristics with any depth, though apparently in Dorothy Wordsworth's day travellers with much greater leisure to observe their surroundings could also be too ready to jump to a quick explanation when confronted by something foreign to their own natures. Perhaps in the nineteenth century the time it took to sit down and dash off a " picturesque " water-colour of the Drachenfels or of some horrid chasm in the Alps was no greater than that required by to-day's rabid photographer, with all his impedimenta of wide-angle lenses, exposure meters, haze filters, lens hoods, tripods and self-timers, to take a colour photograph of Mount Fuji with a " picturesque " cloud just in the right position on those diffluent slopes.

One nineteenth-century person who had a good, long look at the East, including Malaya, was a most indomitable woman, a Miss Isabella L. Bird (Mrs. Bishop), author of *The Hawaiian Archipelago, A Lady's Life in the Rocky Mountains, Unbeaten Tracks in Japan*, etc., etc. So runs the title page of her finest and best-known book, the one about Malaya called *The Golden Chersonese and the Way Thither*, commonly referred to simply as *The Golden Chersonese*.

The Golden Chersonese is the Aurea Chersonesus of Ptolemy, and the " Golden Chersonese " of Milton, though it is unlikely that its Mount Ophir is the Ophir of Solomon. And as Miss Bird comments, " the supposed allusion to the Malacca Straits by Pliny is too vague to be interesting."

Miss Bird, though not an eminent was certainly a remarkable Victorian. She visited Singapore and Malaya in 1879, and anyone who has lived in the East, particularly in the tropics, will realise what insuperable difficulties stood in her way. It was hardly considered proper, in the Victorian era, for a woman to travel anywhere without an escort ; but for a woman actually to travel abroad, and to the Far East at that, on her own, was something unheard of. (Mrs. Trollope might go to America, but that was quite a different matter.) There was something of Gertrude Bell, Isabelle Eberhardt and that other Isabel, the wife of Richard Burton, about Miss Bird. She was tenacious, obstinate, opinionated, fearless, not to say foolhardy ; though when in England she enjoyed delicate health, once she got to the tropics she seemed to become a tigress and would put up with every kind of discomfort and unpleasantness. Her prose was rather school-marmish and commonplace, but her rattle was out of the ordinary indeed. Relating her experiences on a voyage from Singapore, she tells us that she garbed herself in sensible Scottish tweeds, the skirts of which swept the deck, a large solar topee and a jacket whose back and shoulders were solidly padded to minimise the penetrating rays of the Malayan sun.

After a dinner of curry, she retired to her cabin, but on finding it overrun by giant cockroaches basking in a temperature of nearly ninety degrees she had a mattress and pillows brought up on the bridge.

There she made the acquaintance of a Welsh engineer who had married a native girl and had sixteen children by her, all under the age of seventeen. They exchanged the stories of their lives and before she retired to rest the engineer left her with the comforting words : " If you want anything in the night just call ' Engineer ' down the skylight." Miss Bird's comment on that is : " It does one good to meet with such a countryman."

She paid a visit to Malacca which provided her with some of the best passages in her book. The Government Bungalow was rather limited in its accommodations so she was put up at the old Stadhuys, the residence of the former Dutch governor of Malacca. Miss Bird wrote : " It has enough faded stateliness to be fearsome or at least eerie to a solitary guest like myself." She was half eaten alive by bloodthirsty tiger mosquitoes.

She sums up Malacca as it is even to-day in two quite good phrases : " a place where it is always afternoon-hot, still and dreamy," and ". . . . where trade pursues its operations invisibly." She goes on to give quite a stunning account of Chinese New Year in Malacca, during which the beverages served were Mandarin Tea, then valued at anything up to forty-five shillings a pound, and sparkling hock from the finest Rhenish vineyards. Her long descriptions of the costumes worn by the children of wealthy Chinese for the festivities are vivid, detailed and exact.

A later writer, much more intimately associated with Malaya than Miss Bird could ever be, was Sir George Maxwell, K.B.E., C.M.G., one of Britain's old colonial administrators, whose fascinating work, *In Malay Forests*, was first published in 1907. It is composed mostly of articles which originally appeared in magazines with nostalgic period names : *Blackwood's*, *The Pall Mall*, *Macmillan's* and *Temple Bar*. But it is still one of the best books about Malaya, especially the Malayan jungle, the kampong folk and the wild life of the interior. The only things I don't like in the book are the horrifying descriptions of animal hunts. One, about the hunting down of a rare rhinoceros—significantly enough, to-day this animal is almost extinct in Malaya—is extremely well written, but appalling and upsetting in its bland, mindless cruelty. How such an intelligent and cultured man could have pursued the poor beast day after day through the jungle, occasionally ineffectually shooting it in the backside, is beyond my comprehension.

The classic modern book about Malaya is not by an Englishman, but by a Frenchman, Henri Fauconnier, who came to the Peninsula in 1905 and opened up 300 acres of land for rubber-planting. He called the simple native-style house in which he lived The House of Palms ; the estate he developed was named Rantau Panjang and it was his life in this place, on a remote Selangor hilltop high over the jungle banks of the Selangor River that he described in his lyrical prose book, *The Soul of Malaya*. To-day the house he lived in belongs to the Socfin Company, and has been greatly enlarged and improved and fitted with a vast, flaring-gabled Minangkabau roof.

The Argyll and Sutherland Highlanders fought in its gardens against the Japanese, who overran them and burnt down the house as it originally was.

Now, in the restored and modernised house, there is fine furniture in local chengai wood. The walls are beautifully panelled and hung with paintings by Schister and Le Mayeur. Couches are upholstered with vivid batik cloth.

I read an edition of Fauconnier's book—which was one of the earliest Penguins—published by Elkin Matthews and Marrot in 1931 and brilliantly translated by Eric Sutton. The best passages are near the beginning : evocations of jungle and rubber-forest and native life, including a haunting portrait of a lovely Malay girl, Fauconnier's mistress. And there are some very amusing portraits of English planters and hilarious accounts of their eccentric behaviour in the old Selangor Club in K.L. Unfortunately the book about half-way through develops into a book not about the soul of Malaya but about the soul of Henri Fauconnier, which is much less interesting. Fauconnier and his heavy French companion have hearty-troubled, man-to-man discussions about " life " and " the meaning of things "—important subjects, but treated here with typical French bourgeois after-dinner banality and self-satisfaction. Though the two Frenchmen are not quite as bad as that : rather they philosophise away at each other with a solemnity and a " seriousness " that is touchingly youthful ; they are ever-so-casually self-conscious, would-be intellectuals with the shatteringly " deep " thoughts of provincial *lycéens*, brilliant but solid : they can play as much as they like at metaphysics, but they can always be trusted not to be erratic. All this spoils the book. But there are incidental snippets of information : Malays call " kur, kur " when attracting the attention of their chickens, and the Malay word for foreskin is " kulup." No confusion with Kirkup, please !

On one of my bus-trips to Malacca, I started reading Richard Hughes's *High Wind in Jamaica*. I couldn't get beyond the first chapter or two, but I was struck, in that brilliant opening that the rest of the book does not live up to, by the references to tropical scenery which exactly echoed my own feelings about some parts of the scenery of Negri Sembilan—impressive in places—which the bus was then passing through. Hughes says : " Tropical scenery is anyhow tedious, prolific and gross : the greens more or less uniform : greater tubular stems supporting thick leaves : no tree has an outline because it is crushed up against something else." Another remark which is true of a good deal of Malaya is this : " It is vegetation which gives the character to a tropic landscape, not the shape of the ground." What character does a rubber plantation give to the tropic landscape of Malaya ? None. It might better be described by one of the four " humours " of the ancients : phlegmatic. The Malayan landscape, recently so well described by Alan Sillitoe in his novel *Key of the Door*, always filled me with gloom—

it is so unmoving, so uniform, so lugubrious, so dull. If there were not handsome people and beautiful animals to animate the stifling immobility, the prospect would be dead indeed.

I look out of the window of the Malacca Express bus and see languorous sarong-clad girls slowly descending, with indolent grace, the stone steps coloured like Neapolitan ices which lead down from the carved verandas of their tall-stilted houses. All around, acre upon acre of regimented rubber plantation. Then comes a small kampong, with wigwams of reddish wooden planks stacked outside the coffin-maker's. Up across the sky swoop huge, stepped red-stone embankments cut through jungle hills to accommodate the new highway. Near-naked labourers are chipping away at the various ledges with lazy picks. Some are wielding mattocks, which they raise with both hands on the shaft high over their turbaned heads, where the hoe seems to hang for a long, long moment before they bring it almost regretfully, sadly down. Young men wearing only faded blue shorts are cycling along with naked axe or parang held across one golden-brown, gleaming shoulder, the blades flashing with the same pristine whiteness as their lucid smiles. As we approach Malacca and the sea, there is a ship luffing into the little harbour, her vast, lateen sails spread, pale-brown and membraned like skeleton leaves.

Round the kampongs there are always a few small black or black and white and brown goats, their hooves delicate, their posteriors playful, and they run and bound, nibbling at everything—there is so much variety of green stuff for them to sample!

The dogs round the kampongs are pale-brown, with foxy noses and round, pricked-up ears. They seem happy, and I have never seen one ill-treated by the country people. They are not very tame, and are terrible fighters.

The cats look quite wild, and even the domesticated ones are thin and mangy-looking, constantly grizzling at each other with lustful hate. I was surprised to notice that many Malay cats, particularly if they are white, have one blue eye and one green eye.

While the bus was dashing and bumping along at full speed into Malacca, a young daddy got up and took his little baby to the toilet right at the back of the bus. On this occasion I had been unfortunate enough to get the only remaining seat, which was next to the toilet door. The door wouldn't keep shut. The daddy held out the little boy over the pan and made rhythmical hissing sounds, presumably to encourage the son and heir to relieve himself. But the little boy wouldn't do anything, though the handsome young daddy went on hissing like a trainer grooming a horse. Is this hissing an Oriental custom, I wonder?

Yes, if it were not for the people and the animals, Malaya would be a dead place, dead with the deadness of sad, living decay, luxuriantly-living decomposition.

Camoëns, sentenced to prison for his part in a duel, left Lisbon for Goa in 1552. He sailed from there to Malacca in 1556 on his way to the new Portuguese spice islands of the Moluccas.

In 1557 he went on with the Portuguese fleet to occupy Macao, and it was there, in a grotto, that he composed the " Lusiade." (I was later to pay homage to his shade in this grotto.)

He returned to Malacca by way of Cambodia, where he was shipwrecked off the mouth of the Mekong River in 1559. He is said to have swum ashore on a plank, clutching the manuscript of the " Lusiade " to his breast. Once ashore he wrote his " pearl of all poetry," entitled " By the Waters of Babylon."

He spent several months in Malacca, in jail, because he had been accused of embezzlement, before going back to Goa, where he was again imprisoned before returning to Lisbon.

Luis Vaz de Camoëns is one of the greatest figures Malacca has ever seen. But he was locked up there, a common poetic experience. I visited the site where his prison had once stood, or at least where I judged " A Famosa," the Fortaleza de Malaca, had once stood, and, turning to the sea, cast upon the billows, in his honour, a wreath of *Bauhinia Kockiana* which I had woven with my own hands.

From Conrad's diary at Matachi in the Congo : " Prominent characteristic of the social life here : people speaking ill of each other." How true that is of all ingrown colonial societies ! Especially of Malaya.

Conrad again : fascinated as I am by the luxuriance and decay of the East, he writes : ". . . the intensity of that tropical life which wants the sunshine but works in the gloom "—what a marvellous description of the Malayan jungle !—". . . (that tropical life) which seems to be all grace of colour and form, all brilliance, all smiles, but is only the blossoming of the dead ; whose mystery holds the promise of joy and beauty, yet contains nothing but poison and decay." (From *An Outcast of the Islands.*" One of his short novels, *The Shadow Line*, gives a harrowing account of foreign seafarers in Singapore.)

The blossoming of the dead seemed to wreathe that sunset I witnessed one evening in Malacca. It was one of the few sunsets I had seen in Malaya : usually it is raining or cloudy at nightfall, or else I am locked in my room, with curtains drawn. The sunset only really began when the enormous, orange sun had dropped behind an anchored dredger which was outlined, sharp and black as cut metal, against the sea's molten horizon. The long necklace of sodium-vapour lamps, pale, virulent green, had just come on along Banda Hilir Road and the embankmented ocean-walk known as Wisdom Drive : the lights were like lucent, phosphorescent pearls. Schoolboys, dark ghosts, were playing their last games on the padang and among the acetylene-lighted eating-stalls opposite the Rest House the stallkeepers' little children were running from table to table with steaming bowls for customers' early evening dinners. Some old women were tending flamboyant bonfires under the blackening banyans and rain-trees.

The faintly-rustling silence of some vast object slowly rotting away hung over the shore and the off-shore islands. Immense dark-grey shadows were for the space of about five minutes flung right across the western sky like spokes from the hub of the sun's foundering axle ; the shadows and their golden interstices were as regular as the markings on the old Japanese flag (recently made once again the national flag of Japan). The spoke-like effect was caused by broken cloud low on the horizon. Overhead there was one solitary cloud of white gauze, shaped like New Guinea. For a second it was all suspended, breathless, over the heavens, like a human life just before the soul takes flight. Then it was gone, a blossoming of death, bringing a brief, grey chill. The boys still playing on the padang were no longer visible. Only their faint, wild voices sped through the gathering darkness like the twitterings of innumerable swiftlets, the chat of ghosts.

I strolled over to one of the eating-stalls and had some

mahmee. The street-vendors of savoury rice were serving passing customers on bicycles or in trishaws. They wrap each portion in a piece of neatly-trimmed banana-leaf, then in news-paper which is tied with a length of tough straw, bast or phloem, looped for the finger.

A child's balloon goes " phut ! " The sound of the balloon bursting reminds me that " phut " is derived from the Hindu " phatna," to burst.

This strange, suspended evening in Malacca brings back to my mind the vivid descriptions of the ancient city as it was at the end of the Japanese occupation during the Second World War, in a memorable book, *Homecoming*, by the great modern Japanese novelist Jiro Osaragi. There is to-night the same feeling of impending dissolution left by the disintegrated sun. I walk past the twin white English village towers of the Church of St. Francis and along Jonker Street, a long, shop-house warren of swarming life and sizzling light. Under the covered arcades of the five-foot ways the pavements are continually going up a step and down a step ; drains, deep and open to accommodate the monsoon rains, run alongside the stepped pavements and sometimes right across them, when they are insecurely bridged by paving-stones. Mediterranean jalousies painted a sour apple green hang from the colour-washed walls of Portuguese Street. The mosquitoes are active ; so are the pimps on the cinema steps outside the amusement park, offering what at first I took to be dirty pictures but which were black-market cinema tickets for yet another wide-screen Biblical epic : seats are at a premium this Saturday night.

The car-park in front of the cinema is full of taxis and trishaws. In Malacca, trishaws are extremely pretty vehicles ; many of them are brand-new, with sparkling chromium mudguards and glittering black-enamelled spokes. On the back panel, beside the licence-plate—trishaws are not being discouraged in Malacca as they are in K.L.—there is often a brightly-coloured " Sunday painting," quite enchanting in its naïveté : a bay with palms, a Chinese temple, waterfall and red-lacquered bridge among rocks, a view through a moon-gate of a nine-storied pagoda, and so on. The pictures look as if they are all by the same local hand. Some of the new trishaws have lavish Rexine upholstery, batteries of electric signals and lights : the owners look terribly aged to be taking on such new equipment, some of which, however, is hired out at daily rates. Malacca trishaws are so made that the driver sits pedalling next to the client who reclines in a sort of awninged side-car on the driver's left.

A trishaw ride around town is a favourite treat for small children accompanied by granny in dark, flowered pyjamas. Amahs on their afternoon off wander about with an oiled-paper or silken pagoda-topped umbrella over tightly-arranged grey hair, wearing brocaded jacket and half-mast, very wide black silk trousers, glossily ironed, with their razor-sharp creases down the outsides.

Eurasian girls in bouffant sherbet-tone frocks dandying along Temple Street, on spike-heel backless shoes, that go " clack-clack " on the pavements—a curiously cheeky, provocative sound. Wolf-whistles from lounging Australian soldiers: the girls pretend to take no notice, but nudge each other with their luscious eyes ; gilt crosses dangle in their modest cleavages. They both have a full, " Hapsburg " lip and magnolia-white complexions. Their dainty, hip-swinging walk proclaims their confident knowledge that they are " it " : a cut above all these common Malay and Chinese and Indian girls. Their names, I would guess, are Daisy or Rosita or Laura or Marie. Under the crimped hair, a look of jaded gentility.

In Heeren Street, some Chinese are preparing a funeral procession : a rather large hearse stands outside a grocer's shop whose shelves have been cleared of tinned goods to make room for funeral decorations, incense sticks, candles. There is a coffin in the hearse. It is obviously a pause in the preparations, because one of the undertakers is lying in the hearse, sound asleep alongside his coffin.

The Sing Lian Express bus ticket has a whole list of " Conditions " printed on it in three languages. One of the conditions says : " Whilst every endeavour will be made to adhere to the time-table, the Company reserves the right to alter it without notice and cancel the running of any coach in the event of tempests, floods or any other cause which the Company considers sufficient." Each passenger is allowed thirty katties of personal luggage free. " The Company will not be responsible for delay caused by breakdown, accidents, ferry delays or any other causes."

Tropic Temper

The Malacca Express breaks down in Seremban. We all get out in the market; the ground is slimy with recent torrential rain which fell as we were approaching the town: the wooden shutters on the open bus windows had to be raised to protect the passengers from the drenching deluge. Now, boys and men crossing the muddy, puddled ground of the bus stop, pick their way between the fruit stalls, gathering up their trousers by the side-seams. Indians and Malays have lifted the hems of their jellabies and sarongs and the Indians have furled theirs round their waists, exposing their thighs; but the Malays do not do that: they are too modest. Old Chinese women wearing black lacquered flapping trousers, worn already at half-mast, instinctively pull them up too.

In the public lavatory in Seremban bus station, Malays entering and seeing me standing at a stall swerve away and use the free toilets. An elderly Sikh, grey-bearded, his bunnish hair done up like a granny's under a loosely-wound white turban, hauls up his skirts, none too fresh, and squats with his face in a corner to piss. Sikhs, and other Indians, resemble the Arabs in this respect.

After a four-hour delay during which I walked round the town admiring some of the pretty colonial-style buildings, the churches, temples and the Lake Gardens, we were all herded into another, smaller bus which set off at a spanking pace for Kuala Lumpur. The road from Seremban to K.L. is notorious for traffic accidents; we passed the aftermath of one in which an Indian, driving along nonchalantly with his elbow out of his car window, had had his arm ripped clean off by a passing lorry. The arm had been carefully laid on a piece of brown paper at the roadside.

Two little girls in an open hut near Alor Gajah are busily plaiting attap and chattering away merrily. Attap, from the nipa palm, is called "nipa" in the far north of Malaya and in Thailand.

Sourmilk Ghyll and Churnmilk Force, in Cumberland—what wonderfully descriptive epithets for the rivers and falls of Malaya in the tin-dredging areas, where the waters, all shades of brown, red, yellow, orange, cream, white, are constantly milky with mud.

On the road to Kajang, I passed that enormous, man-made

crater, about 500 feet deep, with a lake of milky jade-green at the bottom. It is the largest tin-working in the world. The sides of the vast bowl, nearly a mile in diameter, are stepped—the result of earlier levels of workings. The tin dredges have been perpetuated in many of the excellent modern Malay painters' works, as well as on Malaya's twenty-five cent stamp. At this strange, haunted working, the very tall, gaunt sluices of intricate and ramshackle bamboo are erected in black silhouette against the sky's glowing orange and lavender extinctions. An eerie place. The scarred earth is now overgrown with lush grass and wild orchids.

Tin has always been one of the main products of Malaya. The first writer of travel books to mention Malacca was Cheng Ho, High Eunuch to the Chinese Emperor Ch'eng Tsu, who visited Malacca in 1409 and wrote : " Tin is found in two places of the mountains and the king appoints officers to take charge of them. Labourers are sent to wash and smelt it and it is cast into small blocks in the shape of a Chinese bushel. Each block weighs one kati and eight tahils or one kati and four tahils. This is used as currency in all trading purposes."

Tin and rubber have brought wealth to the rulers, both native and foreign, of the states of Malaya, but not to the Malays themselves. To-day the market for tin is steadily falling and many of the great workings stand abandoned, their towering sluices smothered in lianas, already half-lost in the all-devouring jungle's stealthy approach. Natural rubber, too, is losing its markets to the various synthetic brands though a number of small tyre-retreading businesses in K.L. and Malacca and Ipoh still use natural rubber in their presses.

Tin was in former days thought to be protected by a savage guardian spirit. Anyone who wanted to open up a new tin-mine would hire the services of a pawang or medicine-man who would then perform ceremonies of propitiation. (Pawangs are supposed to have a good " nose " for tin deposits.)

The pawang in his rites uses a private vocabulary, as do camphor-hunters, and this is called " Bahasa Pantang " or anathematical language.

Before the performance of the ceremony, the pawang erects an altar where he invokes the " hantu " or spirit of the locality for assistance in the new enterprise. Then he hangs what the

Malays call an " ancha," a rectangular tray of woven split bamboo, under the eaves of the smelting-house.

Certain rules must be observed : a breach of these rules results in a fine. Raw cotton must never be brought into the vicinity of a mine-working. Only the pawang may wear a black coat. Earthenware, glass, lemons, coconuts or limes are prohibited, as are also water gourds. Coats are taboo in the smelting-house, as are knives, axes and other weapons ; the posts must not be scarred or chopped in any way. Charcoal must not be allowed to fall into the races.

Malays still have many superstitions about tin : besides believing that it is protected by certain spirits they also believe that the tin itself is alive and that it possesses some of the qualities of living matter ; that it can of its own volition move from place to place, and that it definitely likes or dislikes certain people.

I must say that I always felt unhappy and ill at ease near a tin-dredge or a mine-working. I am probably one of those people tin dislikes or runs away from.

Similar ceremonies of propitiation are used when country Malays are about to enter the jungle on a hunting expedition : this is well documented in Sir George Maxwell's book, *In Malay Forests*. There is also a spirit in the rubber, which must be treated with respect and kindness. Many Malays still believe that certain very large trees are haunted by earth-demons or tree-spirits called " puaka." A tree so possessed is said to be " berpuaka." No Malay will ever tap a haunted rubber-tree. " Puaka " is derived from a Polynesian word meaning a pig. In North Borneo the word means pig-bodied or pig-faced spirit. In certain parts of Malaysia the puaka is said to be a spirit which takes on the shape of a pig.

Malay bomohs claim that puakas move about the country in large bands. They hunt human beings, and have this peculiarity (which is common to many Polynesian spirits) that they cannot cross water without dying. If they cross water, they die by licking all the flesh from their bones with sharp tongues. Some kampong people still wear charms and amulets round their waists to protect them against possession by these evil ones.

After a walk in the jungle I came back to K.L. convinced that I had swallowed a tree-frog. I don't know what made me feel I had done so, but when I mentioned it to a kampong boy

he asked me if I had urinated against any big tree in the jungle.
I remembered doing so, and my friend told me that the tree
must have been " berpuaka " and that the spirit of the tree was
angry that I had defiled its home. He took me to a village
bomoh who told me I was possessed by the pig-spirit : the pig,
of course, is the symbol of all that is unclean to a devout Muslim.
The bomoh made me an amulet which he rubbed first on my
stomach and back, then told me to wear it constantly round my
loins. I was never to take it off, even when bathing or in bed.

The curious feeling of stifling nausea continued in my
diaphragm but I went on wearing the amulet, which was simply
a pebble wrapped in a piece of silk and attached to a silken
cord, for three weeks. One night I woke up feeling violently
sick, and spewed out some gluey blackish-green mess. The
silken cord had snapped while I was vomiting. I was all right
after that. I buried the stone in one of the large red-and-yellow
plant pots in the hotel garden.

I was interested to notice that in a day or two all the flowers
in that pot had died.

Two entrancingly witty and acute passages from Rose
Macaulay's *The Towers of Trebizond* have delighted me : " Where
is this free world they all talk about so much ? " Aunt Dot
would interrupt the News to ask. " *I* never went there. It
must be quite extraordinary, everyone doing just as they please,
no laws, no police, no taxation, no compulsory schooling,
nothing but a lot of people all resisting aggressors and longing
for a just peace. . . ."

". . . Father Chantry-Pigg thought it would be wrong to go
to Russia, because of condoning the government which was
persecuting the Christians. But Aunt Dot said if one started
not condoning governments, one would have to give up travel
altogether, and even remaining in Britain would be pretty
difficult."

After a journey of even just a few days it was always nice to
get back to my dear old Majestic Hotel in Kuala Lumpur, if
only to sit in the lounge and read on the large brown menus :
" Patrons are requested to reserve their tables for dinner before
ordering their pahits." The Malay word pahit means " bitter,"
and is used to designate a short drink before tiffin or a " sun-
downer " or stengah. This last word, so popular with Britishers

in Malaya, means a half-measure of any liquid, but usually whisky, with soda.

Under the bleak light of neon on the ox-blood walls of the Merlin Hotel bar, I am always appalled at the unsmiling dourness of the Chinese bar-boys. They never spring forward to take one's order or to light one's cigarette as Japanese bar-boys and bar-girls do, wearing a radiant and friendly smile. Such unasked-for attentions are so civilising. But here . . . in Malaya, the customer is always wrong.

To Ipoh for the races, with a little " untouchable " Boyanese friend who, like so many Boyanese, works in the stables with the touring Australian jockeys. He gave me a good tip for a couple of races, and for once in my life I won some money, nearly five hundred dollars : I gave my tipster a hundred.

I travelled to Ipoh by train, though not in an air-conditioned coach. With the windows wide open, it was quite pleasant while the train was in movement, but each time it stopped I sweltered, despite the overhead fans. However, it was worth it : the people in second class are so much more interesting than those in first class, and one isn't pursued by the booming voices of Mrs. Xeters.

Ipoh looked ravishingly pretty as I arrived in a burst of sunshine which suddenly played right down upon my golden hair from a sky full of rococo, inventively-broken cloud. The beautiful Moorish-style white station, less ornate and pretentious than K.L.'s, looks like a mosque with its silvered domes.

Pith-helmets too, and the oiled-paper parasols of trishaws are often silvered, presumably to refract the sunlight and diminish heat.

I was feeling rather frail, so I treated myself to a taxi to the Bali Hotel. The astute Tamil driver had obviously been running the taxi's motor before I got in, because after only a couple of yards the forty cents on the meter ticked over to eighty cents. (And he had the nerve to ask me : " Do you want the meter on ? " when I got in.) I gave him a dollar bill at the end of the trip ; he thought he was going to be allowed to keep the twenty cents change as a tip, but I stood there waiting, very pointedly —I am awful sometimes—with my hand held out, and he slowly and fumblingly produced the change.

Books and Journeys

Not a bad room at the Bali : no air-conditioning, only a big, old-fashioned ceiling-fan flogging the " Dutch wife " on the bed. Bathroom and toilet combined : no " long bath," only a small stone sink and a tin, and a shower which also sprays the lavatory seat.

A fresh pear dipped in brandy was all I had for my self-prepared lunch, followed by one violet cachou. (" Arabian Nightflowers " they are called, and taste like violet mouthwash.) Then I put on my pink-tinted sun-glasses—I can put unpleasant people beautifully in their place by raising them slightly and peering underneath, so much more effective than peeping over the top. Then, armed with a brolly and a small keris—Ipoh is full of Secret Society thugs, and one never knows—I sallied forth, as the gossip-writers say, to inspect the gigantic Reclining Buddha in the grounds of a Siamese temple in Kuala Klangsar Road, about three miles away.

I took a trishaw through the quiet, leisurely streets green with lawns and trees and brilliant with *Lagerstroemiae flosreginae*'s mauve-pink and *Cassia biflora*'s buttercup yellow blooms. I waved to lots of very goody-goody-looking Chinese high school girls and boys as I cruised slowly past, but they did not wave back.

The object of my pilgrimage was the Meh Prasit Temple. As soon as I had unfolded myself from the trishaw seat and told the driver to wait I was aware of the great, smirking moon-face of the Reclining Buddha in a dusky shed in the distance but I pretended I hadn't seen him yet and occupied my attention with a curious group of adoring figures round a merely life-size sitting Buddha : all these figures were made of white plaster. Eyes, eyebrows and mouths are painted on these dead-white pans in expressions of sweet surprise and delight ; the mouths are shocking-pink, the eyebrows and eyes jet black. All round the courtyard were long loops of festive chains made of ropes hung with thousands of gaily-coloured rags of clothing.

More figures, scores of them, were ranged round three sides of the main courtyard which contains the abode of the Giant Reclining Buddha. It is made entirely of concrete ; its gravely-smirking lips are shocking-pink and its robes are covered with gold leaf especially imported from Thailand. There is a caste-mark, a word or a letter, in red in the middle of the forehead.

The hair is formally curled all over, the sign of a Supreme Buddha.

The statue cost over £2,000, is seventy-five feet long, twenty-one feet high and fifteen feet wide. It rests on a concrete platform four feet high.

A drowsy, saffron-robed monk was also reclining, in the kindly shade of his Buddha, in a royal-blue deck-chair. His shaven pate looked almost green. He gathered his robes about him and led me to a large opening in the statue which I entered by climbing a bamboo ladder: the interior of the Buddha was hollow, and blindingly whitewashed, lit by neon strip-lighting. It was rather like being in the Underground. One can crawl right along into the big toe. The head end of the Buddha's interior contains an urn in a glass box swarming with small electric lights; the urn holds pieces of bone said to have been part of the body of the Lord Buddha. Special compartments behind the platform are used for keeping the ashes of the dead in. The statue, built entirely by Siamese workers, was completed in 1957; it is bigger and more beautiful than the rather dilapidated and remote Reclining Buddha which I was to see a few months later at Ayudhya in Thailand. It is said to be the biggest statue in Malaya.

Inside the body of the Buddha I had that same sense of happy security which I have in caves: Jonah inside the whale must have felt very much as I did then.

The young priest, when I come back down the ladder, switches off the lights inside the figure and lies back in his royal-blue deck-chair, fanning himself with a banana leaf and smiling at me with a face that seems all bone and ivory. He can go to sleep again now.

Turning round at the gate for a last look at the Reclining Buddha, it still gave me a shock of surprise to see that huge, gently-smiling face with its great curled stupa of black hair, the head resting calmly on a broad hand supported on a noble forearm and elbow. The smile, as one looks at it from a standing position, is almost vertical. I felt that after all I had not been reverent enough: I went back to the figure with my trishaw-driver and we lit joss-sticks, placed them before the altar, stepped back three paces, bowed our heads over folded hands and—did we pray? I don't know what my driver did—perhaps he just repeated a formula, which is something—but I could not think of anything. My mind was totally blank; that is maybe how it should have been.

We had a smoke and a bit of a chat and then he trundled me away to the Perak Cave, about two miles farther along the road, where there is a temple, highly ornate, inside a limestone cave. This is not as big as the Batu Caves outside Kuala Lumpur, but nevertheless very impressive. On the walls of the Perak Cave, instead of the disorganised scrawls in Tamil, Arabic, Malay, Chinese and English which one finds on the lower walls and ceilings of the Batu Caves there are beautifully placed, well-composed and brilliantly-painted pictures of landscapes or figures from Hindu and Chinese mythology. Two of these mythological paintings were done in 1957 by two British National Servicemen, Frederick J. Billings and Piers Plowright, who were stationed for a while at Ipoh. These are worthy companions of the other figure-paintings whose polychrome raiment undulates and flows so confidently across ceilings and walls. I felt very proud that Mr. Billings and Mr. Plowright had shown such devotion to art and religion : looking at their lovely paintings, for the first time in Malaya I was proud to be British.

A nice Indian in charge of a stall selling fruit juice and joss-sticks showed me round. He does not ask for a tip, but hopes you will buy a drink from his stall. I did, but he doesn't mind if you don't.

I watched a new sitting statue of Lord Buddha being constructed in the main cave : a huge steel framework like a dressmaker's figure for some giant lady was being built round with bricks that were being covered with cement pigmented by a special veneering process in varying shades of saffron. A gentleman who introduced himself to me in the friendliest fashion as the Rev. Chan Seng Woh was directing the operations of some Malayan bricklayers scrambling about on complex bamboo scaffolding round the outside of the figure. This when completed will be over forty feet high and will cost 10,000 Malay dollars, well over £1,000. The statue rests, I was told, on a heavy concrete foundation about eight feet high " hewn in the image of rock and touched off with a decorative motif of lotus petals." On its face it is hoped there will be the sort of smile " that makes infinity seem very near." Mr. Chan's whole being seemed to glow with proper pride in his work, and some of that glow entered into me : I felt very happy in his company. He pointed out to me the signatures of the two English painters beside their paintings, for which he had the very highest regard : " They are perfect," he said simply.

I returned to my hotel in a dream, exhilarated by my talk with Mr. Chan and by the handiwork of my countrymen. I was quite unafraid of the gathering afternoon thunderstorm that was piling its dingy *baluchons* of cloud over the limestone outcrops of the sacred caves. The trishaw drive was only three dollars, including long waits, but I gave the driver five dollars because he had been so perfect to me. On the way back, at a café we had a large bottle of Tiger beer between us and we drank to each other's health. He was a dear old man who was terribly concerned to see me sweating so much. " You have fever," he kept saying, but as I kept shaking my head, sending showers of sweat flying in rainbows all round me, he suggested that we go to a massage-parlour : " Nice girl, nice finish she sit on it." But I was feeling very weary by now and declined his kind offer politely.

I took a shower. As I tilted the mirror over the wash-basin in my room, a pale yellow chichak shimmered from behind it and up the wall in a movement reminiscent of a flight of bubbles in an aquarium.

In the evening, after the storm, I strolled round the busy Chinese quarter and was overjoyed to find, in a bookstore, under a dog-eared pile of lurid sex-thrillers, like some exotic butterfly, a very old and dirty copy of the Crest Book paperback edition of Nabokov's *Invitation to a Beheading*. I snatched it up, my heart pounding with excitement and joy, and in a shaking voice asked the Bengali shopkeeper how much, expecting to be charged the earth. (I'd have given it.) " I let you have it one dollar," he said, speaking with incredible rapidity, his concept of fluency. " Pay cash or account ? " " Cash." He flashed me a vivid smile : " Somet'ing else more ? " " No, thank you." He seemed unwilling to let the book go and I was beginning to get agitated. " It in bad condition," he smiled, and then, before handing it to me, read the " blurb " at lightning speed : " Another memorable masterpiece by the best-selling author of *Lolita*."

I prepared to go. " You like hot stuff? " he winked at me. " I have *Way of All Flesh*, very naughty, very cheap I let you have it two dollar." I said no thank you. " You want good dishionary, plenty rude word, groin, bellybutton, vagina, stockingtop, armpit, poppycock. . . ."

Pursued by an accelerating crescendo of vocabulary, I fled away. The last word I caught was " tomtit."

I haven't met any Secret Society thugs : where are all these bad lads the imams are always inveighing against? Where, in this Year of the Tiger, are the hide-outs of the gang leaders, the " Tiger Generals? " Where are the Siew Ying Hoong (Little Heroes), the Pat Sin (Eight Immortals) and the Hoong Hup (United Triad) members? Apparently they all merged into the Siew Pat Hoong Secret Society, sharing their secret code-words and signs in a big take-over bid. A pity that such charming names should have been lost. But the fate befalling all mergers overtook the Siew Pat Hoong : it has been banished from Ipoh by the tireless efforts of the local police and the People's Progressive Party. It was one of the most powerful secret societies in Perak.

The luscious, all-pervading smell, in the streets round the Perak Turf Club, of durian. There are scores of them, giving off their sweet, ripe stink, spread out over the sides of the roads, and their vendors are doing a roaring trade. One of them offers me a slice on the end of a knife, smiling at me as if he expected me to turn my nose up at it. Little does he know I have developed a shameful passion for the fruit, and I swallow the slice with gusto. How sweet and fresh it is ! Fortunately I have had nothing to drink, so I can gorge myself, like a fruit-bat, to my heart's content. I buy a good plump one and take it to the shadowy padang where the lovers meet, outside the railway station, and guzzle the lot.

The brilliant colours of the Sunday street-market in Ipoh : pots, pans, cloth, mops, fruit, toys. One man came walking along with a perfect pagoda of bickering tin-foil " windmills,' every colour under the sun. One for me, please, to hold out of the train window as I'm riding home ! Gorgeous bauble !

I have Sunday lunch at the Ipoh Station Hotel : as usual, it's chicken curry with all the trimmings, followed by that Gula Malacca. A few planters and their wives, all pregnant, have come into town for Sunday lunch, which they eat to the perpetual squalling of babies and small brats. The Chinese boys are very patient with them all.

Before the train drew out of Ipoh, I noticed a well-preserved carriage, made apparently of teak, standing on one of the platforms—one of the first railway carriages to be used on the Penang–Singapore line, and preserved here as a charming museum piece.

Well, Ipoh was nice. Sticking my " windmill " in the open window, not too far out, I don't want to lose it, I open Han Suyin's *And the Rain My Drink* which is to keep me company to K.L. (I'm keeping the Nabokov for a more exquisite solitude.)

Han Suyin's book has some very fine descriptions of the Malayan jungle, rubber plantations and town and hospital life. Unfortunately her characters are not very interesting and are always saying very predictable things and expressing the required sentiments. They keep meeting each other far too often, as people never do in life. (Novelists might do well to memorise this passage from *Jude the Obscure*, which runs : " Somebody might have come along that way who would have asked him his trouble, and might have cheered him by saying that his notions were further advanced than those of his grammarian. *But nobody did come, because nobody does. . . .*" My italics. How extraordinary that little phrase is, how true ! And how incredible, coming from Hardy !)

In real life, one hardly ever keeps on meeting people. So often, alone in a bar or a strange town, I have thought : now I ought to be meeting someone, if life were like a novel. But life is just not like that. Hardly anyone ever speaks to anybody, which is what makes plays and novels seem so false. If ever I meet people, it is always at unwanted and insignificant times and places.

Han Suyin's characters are very prosy in their speech, and she shoves them around like so many dummies. Each one " represents " something, whereas in real life nobody represents anything. A prosy book about a prosy land, but worth reading if you know Malaya.

Among modern novelists, I much prefer the hilarious approach of Anthony Burgess : he gives a satirical, true but somehow sympathetic picture of Malaya in his remarkable comic trilogy : *Time for a Tiger*, *The Enemy in the Blanket* and—best of all—*Beds in the East*. I believe these books will become classics of elegiac farce in a sub-colonial setting. Certainly they are the best books ever to have been written about Malaya and the Malayans by a modern author.

The train passes a mist-shrouded Bukit Takun, its green top floating immaterially on air, its limestone crags wrinkled like the face of a sage on a Chinese hanging-scroll. Soon we shall be drawing into Kuala Lumpur, " always my torture," as dear Ronald said of Aldous Huxley.

Wistfully I sing quietly to myself, as the train enters those Saracenic arches, a little Chinese Opera air :

> *Loaded with lotus-scent the breeze sweeps by,*
> *Clear-dripping drops from tall bamboos I hear.*
> *I gaze upon my idle lute and sigh:*
> *Alas, no sympathetic soul is near. . . .*

18. Feasting and Fasting

Although Malays observe all their religious festivals in accordance with the laws of the Islamic faith, the manner of celebrating
them is often influenced by Hindu traditions acquired in the past
centuries. On festive days the Malays hang their houses with
coloured fairy-lights, or put candles on their verandas; they
illuminate their compounds and even set off crackers and burn
incense.

For the leisure-loving Malays, any religious holiday, whether
Christian, Hindu, Malay or Chinese, is always an excuse for a
day off. They participate in these " foreign " festivals in their
own way: during the Indian Festival of Lights or Deepavali,
celebrated early in November, I noticed that many Malay houses
in Kampong Bharu, the picturesque Malay quarter of Kuala
Lumpur, were decorated with lights and burning incense.

There are really only two main festivals in the Islamic year:
the Pilgrimage, or rather the feast celebrating the successful
conclusion of the annual pilgrimage to Mecca and which is
called in Malay Hari Raya Haji; and Ramadan, or more precisely
the feast marking the end of the fasting period known as
Aidilfitri or in Malay Hari Raya Puasa.

A number of smaller festivals are still observed, chief among
them being the " Night of Grandeur " or, in Arabic, Lay'lat'ul
Qadar; the Malays call it Malam Tujoh Likor. It is one of the
most auspicious nights in the whole Muslim calendar and it is
marked by prayers and readings of the Koran; devout Muslims
sometimes spend the whole night in prayers. The Birthday of
the Prophet is also a time of popular rejoicing.

On the night before the twenty-seventh day of the seventh
month Malays commemorate the Mi' raj Night or Night of the
Ascension. They believe that on this night the Prophet travelled
from Mecca to the Great Mosque in Jerusalem and thence to
Heaven.

Feasting and Fasting

Malam Nisfu Sha'ban, the night in the middle of the eighth month, is when the souls of the dead are believed to return to their former homes.

One of the public holidays in Malaya is the first day of Muharam or the Muslim New Year. Like the Chinese, the Malays believe that as the New Year begins, so will it continue, so they always at this period like to have money in their pockets and a feast spread on their tables; all debts are paid and all quarrels patched up; new clothing is worn and the barbers are busy giving every Malay who can afford it a " new head " to start the year with.

Ashura Day is one on which certain solemn religious rites are performed. It is a day of mourning in memory of the tragic death of Hussein, the grandson of the Prophet, at Kerbala. In some parts of Malaya a special kind of cake is made, called Ashura Cake, portions of which are distributed to friends and relatives.

Friday is the Moslem holy day and each week at noon on this day the Mosque and its gardens are thronged with Malay worshippers. A few Europeans have adopted Islam as their religion, but I only met one, in a night-club, and never saw any at the various mosques I visited at Klang, Ipoh, Alor Star and K.L.

On my way to the Jame' Mosque in Mountbatten Road after my Friday morning lecture I saw many Malays in sarong and songkok, and some in baju seluar cycling slowly towards their devotions. Handsome Malay boys in checked sarong and spotless white shirts are waiting at bus stops for transport into town: it is amusing to see that they stand in a long line, not in order to form a queue but so that each one will have a small share of the narrow shadow cast by the telegraph-pole near which the bus stops. Some Malay girls, wasp-shaped in tight-waisted sarong kebaya, are sheltering from the noonday heat under their gaily-striped and pagoda-roofed parasols, but they are not going to the mosque for they are not allowed inside except on very special occasions.

The boys' lazily-displaced weight is rejected with the *déhanchement* of inborn elegance on one smooth hip; they make a delightful picture standing there with the girls—sarongs moulding lissom loins, tense waists and those firm buttocks which the Persian poet sings of as " moons that never wane."

A detachment of Malay soldiers in walking-out dress—white baju seluar and rose-pink, shamrock-green or gentian-violet silver-threaded kain songket—is marching past the Moorish-style General Post Office towards the mosque.

About a dozen police are on duty outside the wrought-iron gates of the mosque. I like the trim-bottomed, khaki-shorted Malay policemen with their navy-blue woollen stockings and white gaiters over big black boots. They shove their pens and pencils neatly down the outside of the left leg, the tops showing what looks like a regulation half-inch above the turn-down stocking top, just as do the big-bottomed, white-shorted, baggy-legged, busy-looking (always carry a piece of paper) bumptious British executives and academics. Mad dogs and Englishmen. . . .

By twelve-thirty a lot of men had arrived either on foot or on bicycle or—very rare—in a large car with two round, plump, silken cushions in the rear window. (I used to think these were for kneeling on, but they are merely for decoration, power symbols like our own stuffed animals or back-seat blondes.) Some had already bathed their feet and hands and were arrayed in fresh clothes. Others were just arriving from work and were going to use the lunch-hour for their devotions. These carried a clean sarong in a paper bag. Some wore the Malay national head-dress, a songkok of black, dark blue, dark red or brown velvet : it looks like a version of the fez.

Those who had to change into a clean sarong did so in the garden of the mosque, where there is a large fountain, a circular basin and other places for washing feet, hands and mouth.

The sarong is a three- or four-foot-wide cylinder of cloth, usually checked or striped cotton for a man. The man puts it round his shoulders so that it hangs like a tent ; sometimes, for extra safety, he holds the edge in his teeth. Then, having already removed socks and shoes, he undoes his trousers under cover of the sarong, lets them drop round his feet and kicks them off. Some also take off their underpants : I saw one or two pairs of underpants lying on the grass, drying in the sun after having been washed.

Then the man takes the top edge of the sarong in both hands, stretches it sideways and folds the sides one over the other round his waist, usually right to left, keeping the edges he has gripped fairly high on his chest before turning them down in a sort of neat roll-knot in front. The fullness falls from this roll and is what contributes—as well as the figure inside—to the grace of the sarong when it is worn properly.

By now the interior of the mosque and the outer courtyard are packed with men sitting on the ground with their feet crossed beneath them. They keep their hats on in a mosque, but of course they take their shoes off. One or two are smoking. The muezzin's hoarse, passionate voice is relayed from one of the minarets. I occasionally recognize a word: another, " Allah," is heard repeatedly.

Many of the men stared at me with a kind of blank curiosity as I sat apart in the garden, watching the ceremony as discreetly as possible. Some little boys, after changing, came and sat beside me, smiling and looking up into my face, but remained silent, then went away. A number of birds hopped round my feet and I threw them some cachous and bits of bun: they seemed to be mainly starlings and a kind of small blackbird called the magpie-robin or dhayal-bird. The latter has white-streaked wings and tail feathers and a lovely song.

Only one person spoke to me as I watched the Muslims elevating their backsides on their prayer-mats. He was a good-looking but rather scornful young man. " Are you a Muslim ? " he asked abruptly. " No." A pause. " What do you think of our mosque ? " " It is very fine." He nodded with satisfaction, a faint smile on his face, but added : " You do not speak correct Malay." I replied : " I only know a few words and phrases." " Are you a tourist ? " " No, I work in K.L." " Where ? " I did not reply. " I never see you round here before," he said in English. He is rather poorly dressed and I suspect he is a street-boy. " So you like our mosque," he says, and gazes up at the yellow domes as if seeing them in a new light. " Well, have a good look," he says, after standing beside me in silence for a while. " Thank you," I reply, then say it in Malay : " Terima kaseh." He smiles, showing his perfect teeth for the first time, and moves away, waving.

Two friends, meeting, hold hands as they talk. This religious ceremony attended only by men has a wonderful atmosphere—a solidarity, a calm, a friendly gaiety.

One or two wives are waiting outside the gates. I'm glad to

see them kept out of this male preserve. I shall go each Friday at noon and sit in the garden of the mosque, under the casuarina.

There is something horrid about a religion like Islam—" such a noble, powerful and bigoted religion "—when police have to enforce the daily fast and have power to arrest Muslims breaking it during the fasting month of Hari Raya Puasa. The police on the East Coast are particularly strict in this respect. I went out to lunch with Karim and Hassan one Sunday and observed how furtive they were about eating and drinking. Most Malays, at least the young and " modern " ones, seem to look upon fasting as something of a joke, but their laughter, when they hear tales of other Malays breaking their fast during fasting hours, always seemed to me uneasy laughter.

The Selangor Religious Affairs Department issued a warning that any Muslim found breaking fast during puasa would be arrested and fined. It warned that it was also an offence for Muslim shopkeepers to serve food and drink to other Muslims during the fasting period. A spokesman for the Department said: " The police, religious officers and ketua kampongs will co-operate to apprehend fast breakers. I call upon all Muslims who are unable to fast for acceptable reasons not to eat or drink publicly during the day."

The fast began with the sighting of the new moon in the month of February. The Singapore and Federation Governments made arrangements to watch for the new moon in both territories. If the new moon was sighted on 5th February, puasa would begin on 6th February. If it was not sighted then, puasa would automatically begin on 7th February. Electric and hand sirens and, in the kampongs, gongs were used to warn the public of the beginning of each day's fast, and also to advise them when it was over ; according to the Stop Press columns of the newspapers the fasting hours in Kuala Lumpur were from 5.18 a.m. to 7 p.m. on 7th February, when puasa automatically began, the new moon not having been sighted on the 5th.

Some business firms change their office hours during the fasting month to make the fast easier for their Muslim workers, but most businesses carry on as usual.

Muslims at Kampong Sungei, one newspaper reported, were asked to stop using loud-speakers during the fasting month as it was affecting those people who were reading the Koran.

Later in the month a newspaper reported that five shop-keepers—four Indian Muslims and a Malay, all living in Malacca—were fined at a religious court a total of thirty-five Malay dollars for selling food to Muslims during the fasting period. They were charged separately under the Malacca Muslim Religious Ordinance. A number of other cases of fast-breaking were reported during the month.

About this time it was announced that the religious laws of Kelantan, on the East Coast, were to be tightened to comply with a statement by the Sultan that the State Government was determined to carry on the administration in accordance with the teachings of Islam. A Government spokesman in the capital of Kelantan, Kota Bharu, stated: " At present, there are many loopholes in the Council of Religion and Malay Customs and Kathis Courts Enactment, for example." A committee of religious experts was to be set up to study the law concerning khaluat (close proximity between members of opposite sexes), the spokesman added. The present law did not give a clear definition of the term khaluat, he said. As a result a husband and wife could be charged with " close proximity " if found in a secluded place. Fines imposed for committing khaluat would be reviewed, and laws on divorce would also be tightened up.

One headline ran: " Couple found in room fined, told to get married," and the story, from Kuala Lumpur, went on as follows: " The Kathi's Court here to-day fined a young Muslim couple a total of sixty dollars because they were found together in a room in Kampong Bharu. . . . The court also told the couple that the best thing for them to do was to get married. The case was tried under the Administration of Muslim Law Enactment 1952 which makes it an offence for Muslims found in ' khaluat ' (close proximity). Under the existing ordinance those found guilty of ' khaluat ' may be fined up to fifty dollars or two weeks' jail. The Selangor Government has drawn up legislation to impose heavier penalties. . . . The Kathi fined Husni thirty-five dollars and Fatimah twenty-five dollars. He also warned them: ' Don't do it again.' "

These khaluat cases are often started by jealous suitors or by parents or brothers of a girl who spy on her movements in order to trap her with her lover in a secluded place. On such occasions the lover is often beaten up by the girl's uncles and brothers. Legally they need not be caught *in flagrante delicto:* it is enough if they are found alone together in the same room or in a secluded part of the jungle. I feel that young people ought to be allowed to be in " close proximity " if they wish : they do not always commit sexual acts under such circumstances. Apparently the Muslim law does not apply to persons of the same sex being found in close proximity.

But this fiercely puritan aspect of Islam was one that surprised me : compared with Buddhism, it is indeed a harsh and bigoted religion.

An Alliance Member of the Federal Parliament objected to boys and girls dancing " cheek to cheek " at school parties in Malaya, and raised the matter in Parliament. He said : " At a parents' day function, I saw boys and girls dancing, touching each other's cheeks. When they did so, women present blushed. Please look into this matter." He added : " The dance ' Che Mina Sayang ' especially should be discouraged."

On the other hand, there was a surprising headline in *The Straits Times* of 24th January which ran : " Bosoms : Minister defends aborigine freedom." Two Socialist Front members had urged that the Government should ensure that aborigine women " dress properly " and not " make an exhibition of themselves."

One Socialist Front Member expressed concern that bare-bosomed aborigine women had been used as tourist attractions. Another referred to a Malayan Film Unit production on rural development which spotlighted aborigine women in their " original shape." He added : " Surely this is not the way for the Government to do propaganda. The Government should not only see that these people are housed properly but also that they are dressed adequately."

Dato Ismail told the Member that the aborigines who had performed at the Happy World amusement park in Singapore had come from Johore Bahru. He said that the Government had strongly protested against their appearance at the Happy World, but little could be done because by that time the advertisement had already appeared in the Press. He added : " We try to protect the aborigines, but in doing so we do not want to adopt the totalitarian methods used in Communist countries. The aborigines have freedom. All we can do is advise and persuade them. We cannot force them."

Feasting and Fasting

The aborigines mentioned above are the Kon Seletar, friendly descendants of the ancient Orang Laut who peopled the mangrove swamps of the Straits of Johore many centuries before the arrival of the white man in the Peñinsula. The English navigator Peter Mundy passed through the Straits of Johore in June 1637 and recorded this in his log : " We saw sundry companies of small boates covered over with mattes, which is the ordinary habitation of those that among these Ilands dwell. Where they have their wives, children and household goods. Here they broughtt us more Fish, fresh and dried, which I conceave is their cheifest mayntenaunce, killing them with fishgaes (harpoons) in which they are very dextrous. And a pretty sport it is to see them pursue the Fish with their little boates, who scudd before them as porpoises doe before the stemme of a shippe in a gale of wynde untill they are strucke. They use allsoe netts, hookes and lynes."

When Stamford Raffles and William Farquhar landed at the mouth of the Singapore River in 1819 the Orang Laut were still there, at a place called Kampong Temenggong. But over the years they were driven from their homes as commercial enterprise took over their jungles and mangrove swamps. They became dispossessed and were driven inland, where they suffered from malnutrition and particularly from a scaly skin eruption

However, they did not die out, and great efforts were made by enlightened people to restore them to their normal surroundings and way of life. And the Orang Laut themselves began to adapt themselves a little to modern civilisation—a little too well, if we think of their women's bare bosoms being exhibited in public. It is sad to think that they were cashing in on their charms in a sordid commercialism taught them by the West, as the Balinese women did until quite recently. So the protests about these bare bosoms that were made in Parliament were not merely the result of Islamic primness ; it is good to know that there are some people who are concerned about the moral welfare of primitive tribes in Malaya.

To-night, a Friday, half-way through the fasting month, the interiors of the tall minarets of the Jame' Mosque are illuminated by white bars of crude neon which are misted by an endless effervescence of insects flying towards the light and being repelled by it in a sort of continuous silent explosion.

Tropic Temper

Inside the mosque, rows of men in sarong and songkok are rhythmically kneeling and lifting their chequered bottoms in the air as they bow their foreheads to the ground during an ecstatic, almost hysterical reading of the Koran by some person unseen. One or two dim figures are also attending in the open, roofed courtyard and the dark garden sweet with the sound of fountains and vivid with scents of jasmine and frangipani exhaling their perfumed souls upon the breathless night with a passionate fervour.

To-morrow there will be Koran-reading contests at the Chinwoo Stadium. The competitors have come from many Asiatic countries.

February 26th: " Selamat Hari Raya Puasa " the shops all cry now from their sales placards. The decorations outside the shops and in the streets are as always pretty feeble. I have received a number of greeting-cards for Hari Raya, all bearing the joyful greeting " Selamat Hari Raya Puasa ! " and the Islamic date, " Satu Shawal 1381." The stationers' shops are stacked with pretty cards. The nicest one I received was from the Oxford University Press in K.L. It had been designed by a Malay artist; the acknowledgment ran: " Dilukis oleh Syed Ahmad Jamal." The word " Selamat " is common in Malay greetings: for example, " good afternoon " is " selamat tengah hari." It is in fact the oriental salutation meaning " peace " and comes from the Arab word " salam." The Malay word is pronounced " slamat."

The finals of the Koran-reading competition are being held to-night, 28th February, at the Merdeka Stadium. The Islamic date is 22nd Ramadan, 1381.

The colossal open-air arena is packed with people, the majority of them young men and boys. Only a sprinkling of the female sex. There are many country people, and a large number of them are in national dress.

In the centre of the green arena is a very pretty, idealised model of a Malay house, all in blue and white and pink, with green roof and rose curtains and five big metal cocks at the five gable-ends of the formalised Minangkabau roofs. All round it are lacy verandas, balustrades, steps, banks of potted plants and tropical flowers. The interior of the house is lit by pastel-coloured lights, and the exterior is dramatically illuminated by two powerful white searchlights situated behind the Royal Box, where the king and his entourage are sitting.

One contestant would enter the house, would kneel, bow his forehead to the ground in prayer then read a passage from the Koran. In this International Competition there were men from Pakistan, Thailand, Sarawak, Brunei and Singapore. No entries this year from the Philippines. Some women competitors, all Malay.

Over the darkened stadium one feels the deep and reverent and yet critical attention being paid to these expert readers. Their voices, rising in plangent complaint, passionate, sexy, quavering, adorned with tremulous shakes, *appoggiature* and panting stops, interrupted by long, dramatic pauses, are weirdly beautiful, resonant and powerful. If a reader ends a phrase on a particularly lovely note, the crowd demonstrates its enthusiasm by humming a prolongation of the note. Recitals are often greeted by *strepitoso* bursts of acclamation when they reveal some particularly fine phrasing or subtle vocal virtuosity.

There is even—surprisingly—derisive laughter from the largely Malay audience when one performer reads with a nasal, sing-song, Tamil-like intonation. It is astonishing, the purely silly sound of the laughter. But the Malays often laugh, sometimes rather unpleasantly and loudly, at anything unusual, at human deformities or at injured or misshapen animals. Many of them were nudging each other and laughing at my European companion and myself, and using the rather insulting Malay term that means " Britisher." We walked all round the stadium and saw no other foreign devils, so perhaps our scarcity value prompted an unusual number of unkind remarks.

The end of the fasting month is 6th March. Again there must be a sighting of the new moon. Hari Raya will fall either on 7th March or the following day depending on the sighting or non-sighting of the new moon on the night of 6th March. The king, the Yang di-Pertuan Agong, will say his Hari Raya Puasa prayers on the padang at the Istana Negara, his palace. The gates of the padang will be open from seven to eight on the morning of Hari Raya. All Muslims are invited to the Hari Raya prayers which will be led by Sheikh Mahmood Khalil Elhusany, a religious leader from the United Arab Republic.

The new moon was not sighted on the 6th, so the official

Hari Raya celebrations will be held automatically on the 8th.
All shops are open and busy on the 7th: the great, sprawling
markets and the street vendors' stalls jamming the five-foot ways
on either side of the Batu Road are surrounded by swarms of
people. There are several stalls selling new songkoks and the
Indian stores have enormous displays of sarong kebaya and
baju seluar and kain songket. But I rarely saw anyone actually
buying something.

On the eve of the first day of Hari Raya, which most people
apparently assumed would be the 7th, a great maroon was fired
just after 7 p.m. to mark the end of fasting. All the main
buildings were flood-lit and flags and banners were flying everywhere. The Jame' Mosque was brilliantly illuminated and hung
with thousands of fairy-lights and flags, an entrancing sight at
night, when its lights flickered on the surface of the turbid,
rushing river that washes its flanks. I stood a long time on the
embankments round the mosque, gazing at the spectacle of those
floodlit lemon-yellow domes that looked so ravishingly arabesque
among the lissom, black-tufted palms.

At the station, there were large crowds of people, mostly
Malays, with motley collections of luggage, waiting for trains
to take them to their country kampongs or homes in other towns.
All were wearing their best new clothes, for it would be a disgrace
to return to one's kampong looking poor.

All evening the streets are thronged with country boys and
youths buying shirts and ties at the Hari Raya " sales." It is
a time when everyone wishes to look smart and elegant, carefree
and rich.

On the morning of 8th March, the Malays were all in their
samping finery, dashing leisurely all over town to visit friends
and relatives at whose houses they would eat cakes and sorbets
and take part in great feasts of fish and lamb and chicken in
honour of A Happy Hari Raya. They do look dignified in
their national costume : I wish they could wear it all the time.

Nine-thirty a.m. A staggering hangover. I sit alone in the
deserted station bar drinking Carlsberg and lime, pulling myself
together. It seems I have bought a second-hand M.G. Magnette.
What on earth am I going to do with it ? I could never learn
to drive, I'm too frightened. It will mean getting a driver.

I predict, not the end, but the beginning of the world.

Feasting and Fasting

I became a good listener in order to be relieved of the necessity to talk. My entire conversation consists of encouraging silences and occasional nauseated monosyllables.

Refusal to appear what other people think one ought to be—" serious," " dedicated," " knowing " or any other O.K. word.

My lost feeling, alone always at local festivals in foreign lands. But are the others less alone ? Perhaps they are even more so than I am, because, for better or worse, I enjoy my own company better than that of any other person. But I always feel lonely at festivals. Perhaps the Malays don't know the word for " loneliness " or " aloneness " : the thing can't exist for them if the word doesn't. The word " loneliness " has a peculiar intensity because I know its equivalent in many other languages and all these words are ever with me, if not at the front of my consciousness, then always in my Viking bones and blood.

The days of Hari Raya Haji were spoilt by dull weather, apocatastatic clouds, torrential fall-out rains.

The car I've bought is in a garage somewhere and I ought to go and have a look at it but I can't get up the interest : the idea of actually owning a car bores me to tears. I can vaguely remember talking to the owner about it, 1958 model, " only 1,500 miles," he told me. I thought that was rather a lot. I had to rack my mind for suitable phrases and I hit on : " Does it hold the road well ? " " She does," the owner answered pointedly. " All right," I said, " I'll have it." As I am going away on a two-month tour of South-East Asia and Japan it will have to be " laid up " in a garage for the time I'm away. I was really half-hoping I would not return to Malaya, but stay in Japan for ever. Now I'm saddled with both a Malay house and a car I can't drive. They say one can learn to drive quite easily in Malaya, only 150 dollars, including fifty dollars bribe to the inspector. " You can't fail to pass if you just pass him fifty dollars," they tell me. No wonder there's so much bad driving and so many traffic accidents in Malaya.

But neither fifty dollars nor fifty thousand would ever get me behind the driving-wheel of a car. I am getting into more and more of a muddle with things. Thank goodness I'm going away in a day or two.

The headquarters of the Malayan Buddhist Society in K.L. is in a picturesque but dingy little temple opposite the " Unemployment Exchange." It has two main rooms with large shrines or altars containing gold or gilded images and a number of black ones. In front of them all is a black seated figure, impressive as a black Pope. Sheaves of joss-sticks blue the air with incense.

There are kind, smiling invitations to enter from a Chinese woman doing some washing in the yard and from a middle-aged priest, in western clothes who, before I step over the threshold, struggles into a grubby yellow robe, kneels at the right of the main shrine, where there is a large brass bowl he uses as a gong, and begins to intone a prayer, all the while punctuating his phrases, apparently haphazardly, with the chime of a small brass bell on a stick held in his right hand. He strikes the bell with a rod which is also held in his right hand. On the table in front of the shrine, behind the bowls and gongs and incense and other impedimenta, stand an empty beer bottle and an old orange squash tin.

Joss-sticks in scarlet and gold and silver wrappers, agreeably pictorial and boldly charactered, are for sale at a stall. In the yard, a box full of freshly-made king-size joss-sticks like huge bulrushes and almost exactly the same shade of velvety brown : although they are made from bullock and cow dung, they smell of jasmine and spice.

I walked back towards my hotel along the quayside opposite the Jame' Mosque, which had red and yellow striped awnings over its Moorish windows. The river was very full and swift after the recent heavy rains, and, as usual, very muddy ; there was the familiar smell of drains beside the bridge. Then I went through Old Market Square, beetled over by towering modern banks—a gust of freezing air-conditioned air struck my sweated skin as I passed the Bank of Tokyo with its rifle-carrying Punjabi doorman—and along High Street, averting my eyes from the girls' interested stares.

I passed on my right the temple whose entrance gate is used by three outdoor Chinese hairdressers and then moved on to the temple on the left-hand side of High Street. Vermilion candles, thick incense-sticks, gifts of oranges and apples on Kelantan pewter stands, a few withered posies of tropic cottage-garden flowers.

The temple has a courtyard with high, massive doors opening on the pullulating street. The main shrine and three altars—

the first with a dirty, moth-eaten brown cushion in front of it—
are directly opposite the entrance, under blue-tiled, horn-finial
roofs surrounding the open courtyard which is stacked on one
side with pot-plants on rough *étagères*. On either side, rooms
open on to the courtyard ; one of them contains the ping-pong
table which is a fairly common sight in temples, another a long
dining-table with a perfectly black, solid, dull-mirrored sideboard
of western cut behind it. Next to this is a sort of office ; the floor
is strewn with broken shuttlecocks and old badminton racquets
converted into shrimping-nets ; there are racks of Chinese newspapers on reading-poles and files, dusty calendars, a dishevelled
copy of the *Christian Science Monitor* scattered with dried fish.

Beside the main altar, three men, vendors of the scarlet-
wrapped sticks of incense and the vermilion candles, in black
trousers and white singlets are smoking, reading Chinese newspapers, idly scratching themselves. An excited Chinese woman
rushes past me with a fistful of blazing paper, imitation bank-
notes. A gong somewhere sends out giddy ripples of hallucinating sound.

Big clutches of red and white paper lanterns, very dusty,
netted with cobwebs, are suspended like clumps of balloons
from the beamed roof where the undersides of broken tiles are
showing. There is a festoon of paper hats, very sun-faded,
with dishevelled green and white pie-frills sticking out of the
crowns. Some faded ceremonial draperies are thick with
incense ash ; lanterns with drifts of ash on their bamboo ribs.
Between them a gilded Buddha with lips rouged like a film
starlet's ; another with a wispy black beard. As in nearly every
Chinese temple, there is an atmosphere of frowsty squalor, casual
reverence and unsuccessful commercialism.

The Buddha Jayanti Temple in Circular Road is, however, a
fine, modern and attractive place, its outer walls festooned like
the Meh Prasit Siamese temple in Ipoh with strings of gaily-
coloured bits of rag.

Outside, two wedding processions in taxis with brilliant
red and gold good-luck signs stuck on their windscreens. In
the first taxi, a wheezy band is playing the " Colonel Bogey
March "; in the first taxi of the second procession an equally
wheezy band is playing " Blaze Away." Pink ribbons all
a-flutter from the door handles ; the happy pairs in fine new

western clothes, the brides carrying sheaves of gladioli and gypsophila. They are on their way to an expensive reception.

Outside the temple in High Street there are vendors of tropical fish in big green-glass tanks. Black, gold, silver and red fish swim desultorily round the drowned stone effigies of Chinese sages or float in and out of miniature submerged landscapes of mountains, temples, vermilion bridges set with tiny figures fishing. Small golden and spotted carp idly ease their fat shoulders through red-lacquered moon-gates set in tiny underwater gardens of rocks, sand and weed.

On the other side of the main door, a flower and plant shop sprawls its wares over the crowded entrance and over the pavement. Potted palms, forests of castor-oil plants, tubs of ferns, small fruit trees, Japanese bonsai.

I wished there had been a bird-shop so that I might buy and release a captive soul, thus performing a meritorious deed that would stand me in good stead in the future life. But all I could do was not step on an ant that crawled out of a decayed magnolia.

A visit to Penang for Chap Goh Meh, the Lantern Festival on the 15th night of the first moon of the Chinese New Year ; it is also called Teng Chieh or Shang Yuan. (Chap Goh Meh is Hokkien dialect, widely spoken in Penang.) It is a festival which has almost died out in countries outside China proper, though it is still observed with some ceremony in Penang and in Chiengmai in northern Thailand. In the old days, children used to go round carrying lighted lanterns made into all kinds of ingenious and fantastic shapes, levying " tolls " on householders : they were rewarded with " hung pao " or red candles, but this practice has long since vanished.

To-day in Penang and to a much lesser extent in K.L. and Singapore young unmarried ladies, and others not so young, array themselves in all their finery and stroll under the lustrous rays of the full moon, parading their charms before the young men of the town. The Esplanade and Gurney Drive in Penang and Queen Elizabeth's Walk along the seafront in Singapore are popular rendezvous. It is said that here and there along the seafront on this night of all nights for anxious spinsters, unmarried girls—and not always just Chinese girls either—desirous of finding a handsome hubby may be seen casting oranges, groundnuts (kachang) and pebbles into the waves as they breathe out wishes for their heart's desire.

According to Mr. Ng Seow Buck of Kuala Lumpur, who for many years has made a study of Chinese mythology, the tradition of Chap Goh Meh began thousands of years ago when an emperor decreed that there should be a lantern procession on the night of the first full moon.

On this special night, girls who were usually kept locked behind latticed windows and never allowed to walk the streets unless accompanied by chaperones were permitted to join in the festivities : even the Emperor's many wives were allowed out, and some of them chose this night on which to elope with handsome young swains.

The Chap Goh Meh celebrations always centred round a huge dragon made from bamboo framework and tinted paper and lighted from within. Women without children thought that if they could snatch a piece of the dragon they would be able to have children. As the procession passed through the town, therefore, the dragon would slowly be torn to pieces. Some of the women would eat the paper in a ball of rice after three days' fasting : this was said to produce male offspring.

Once again I lodged in the charming Annexe of the E. & O. Hotel in Penang. I was suffering from heat exhaustion and severe colic : it is so difficult to swallow those large enterovioform tablets with iced water ! So I decided to spend the day riding round the town and the island of Penang in a hired car. It was a marvellous drive, lasting nearly six hours, and covering the whole island. It cost only thirty-five Malay dollars (about seventy shillings). No tip.

My driver was an extremely ancient and decrepit Chinese gentleman with an open blue shirt showing a chest like an ivory wash-board. I felt rather annoyed and anxious at being entrusted to someone who would very soon be entering the Celestial Gates and I was determined to be bored and horrid. But he was so sweet, and eager, in a quiet way, to tell me all he knew that, as usual, I found I simply couldn't be nasty if I tried.

Before we set out I told him about my enteritis and he quite understood, agreeing to stop immediately if I clapped my hands three times. I was going to swallow two entero-vioform tablets —I, too, had been fasting for three days—but he dissuaded me and took me to a Chinese homeopathic pharmacy where, after a long chat with the smiling and friendly proprietor during which I thought several times I was going to be taken short, I was given a black pill and a blue pill which I was told contained powdered tortoise-shell and various healing herbs. I swallowed them with a thimbleful of thickish brown liquid and all I can say is that during my six-hour ride I never had to clap my hands once.

We drove round the town first, past the Chinese Football Ground and the very lifelike statue of Queen Victoria, past the Polo Ground and the Governor's House, along Scotland Road and by the Race Course to Ayer Itam (Black Water) Temple. It is also known as Kek Lok Si and is a monastery for Buddhist monks. It is the most gorgeous of Chinese temples in all the Peninsula. It was founded in 1891, the funds for its erection being donated by Buddhists in Malaya, Burma, Siam and Indonesia. The resplendent seven-storey pagoda which dominates the temple on its lush hillside was built in 1915 and contains Buddha images from many countries.

There is an extraordinary wealth of enormous metal statues in various parts of the temple buildings. One structure houses the statues of the Four Heavenly Kings, gigantic effigies representing the four points of the compass; each figure is trampling underfoot two malefactors—the gambler, the cannibal, the drunkard, the false pretender, the liar, the thief, the opium smoker and the murderer. There was no figure representing a condemnation of sexual licence.

Many large rocks in the stepped gardens were inscribed with the names of donors, and one inscription was in English : " The stand-pipes in this temple were erected and presented by Mr. Lim Leng Cheak, 1st January, 1894." In the seven-story pagoda was a notice prominently displayed giving in three languages the information that Madame X had acquired virtue and merit by donating all the cement used in its building. I felt too weak and shaky to climb to the top.

The oldest part of the temple, built in 1895, houses the colossal statues of the Yin Phor Sat or Goddess of Mercy, whose image is surrounded by twenty-four heavenly kings and eighteen Arahans.

Behind this section there lie two beautiful lotus-flowered pools, one containing tortoises and the other white carp. I fed them one entero-vioform tablet and some violet cachous which they seemed to like. (On my next visit to the temple I fed them with ants' eggs from Chiengmai.)

There was a wonderful view of curving tiled roofs from the garden ; farther up the slopes stood the crematorium with its white dome ; in one building there were monks' coffins, stencilled with silver paint.

I was asked to sign the Visitors' Book and make a " small contribution " to this already very rich temple. I signed, intending to give fifty cents only, then was horrified to see that previous signatories (the one before me was a Japanese) had given sums of five, six and ten dollars. A bit bamboozled by the heat and the herb pills, I coughed up five dollars and in return received from an enviably healthy-looking young priest in rather dingy saffron robes a lovely smile and two very warm, grubby postcards which he produced from his bosom, so it was worth it. I did not enter the amount of my donation ; I felt it would be immodest and might prevent me from gaining merit. But I had the vaguest suspicion that perhaps those artful young priests were putting down large sums of money in the book in order to persuade other visitors to donate generously. If I'd paid another five dollars I could have had my name painted up on an enormous panel containing the names, in miniscule script, of all who had donated as little as ten dollars to the building of the temple. Lower down, in larger characters, were names of those who had donated twenty-five dollars.

The guide-boy who showed me round was quite efficient so I offered him one dollar which I thought was quite enough as I had not asked for his services—he had simply attached himself to me at the gate and started reeling off statistics. " Oh, sir," he said, " it is usual to give two dollars. I am very hungry, no food three days." Same as myself, I thought, but he's still only a growing boy, so I gave him another dollar. It was worth it for the delighted dazzle of the bewitching smile he allowed to play upon me for a set period.

Outside, in the covered arcade steps leading down from the pagoda, there were several beggars. One of them, a very old lady, was squatting on the ground outside a souvenir shop : her bowl was politely and suggestively lined with red " ang pow " or New Year Present paper. There was nothing in it. I put in a raspberry-pink ten-dollar note in order to satisfy my new æstheticism : its colour shimmered wonderfully for a moment against the crude red paper in the begging-bowl before being snatched away and placed under the old lady's silver-painted solar topee.

Penang Hill is 2,722 feet high and fortunately can be ascended by cable railway (1st and 3rd class—go up in 3rd and down in 1st). It is also called Mount Hygeia because of its cool and healthy climate, " the healthiest in the East " as Captain Robert Smith, of the Royal Engineers, architect of Penang's St. George's Church, declared at the beginning of the nineteenth century. The central peak is known as the Great Hill and a little lower down is Strawberry Hill, which is only a few minutes' walk from the Upper Station ; from these points of vantage or from Summit Road or Tunnel Road one has splendid views of the green mainland mountains and of Penang and its harbour busy with all kinds of craft—the tiny perahus of the local traders, so like the sharp-prowed boats of Portuguese *pescadores*, the picturesque Bugis vessels, the Chinese junks, the steam launches, the white ferries chugging across to Prai railway station on the mainland, the oil tankers and the luxury liners.

The breeze up here is fresh and invigorating after the clammy damps of sea-level. There is a lovely cool tearoom where Malay songs are being played over the wireless. Beyond the harbour, various small islands seem to float on misty waves towards the mainland's dark coastline of mangrove and palm.

Coming up, one's ears pop at the 1,000-foot mark ; the gradient at 2,300 feet above sea-level is one in ninety-three. One can walk up to the top of Penang Hill by passing through the Moon Gate near the Waterfall Gardens and taking a road that was made by convict labour at the beginning of the last century, and this takes about three hours. Tall walking-sticks of stout wood, like pilgrims' staffs, may be hired at the bottom for this strenuous ascent through sub-jungle and some bits of almost primeval forest. The sight of this rankly luxuriant vegetation covering deep chasms and valleys underneath the cable-car is thrilling and not a little frightening ; if one loses one's nerve on the ride up, one can get out at one of the intermediate stations and climb the rest of the way to the top. On the day when I made my cable-car ascent, a party of three Britishers, two women and a man, could be seen plodding slowly upwards on foot: they received cheers and shouts of encouragement from the Malayans in the cable-car with me.

One of these was a Chinese girl in flowered samfu. Near the top we had to pass through a fairly long, white-painted tunnel; the girl just let the back of her hand stroke mine as we passed through the white darkness. I was not surprised at this unusual display of affection because it was Chap Goh Meh, when anything may happen. Last night on the padang there were scores of couples passionately embracing in public—a most extraordinary sight in Malaya, where the affections are rarely displayed in public: they were being watched by scores of lonely men and boys who were perhaps hoping that later the Lantern Festival would bring them the girl of their dreams.

The ride downhill was uneventful. My driver took me on to the Botanical Gardens which we entered in a small cloud of yellow, white, black and blue-winged butterflies. There is a gracious waterfall here which reminded me of a passage in that best of all novels by a Westerner about medieval Japan, David Stacton's *Segaki* (meaning the season of hungry ghosts): "Over it all, quite visible now, the waterfall poured serenely down to freshen the air. . . . Though Micho waterfall is only a waterfall, at the same time it is one of the great Buddhist texts of Japan, a Koan in itself, and also a commentary on that passage in Tao Te Ching which claims that the highest excellence is like that of water, which benefits all things, and which, without deliberate effort or destructive force, also shapes all things. It is not only the source of life; it is also patience, for he who has true wisdom shapes things merely by seeking his own level. The Japanese, however, never having forgotten that they are primitive, are more subtle than that. They realise that the absence of effort is a characteristic only of great vigour. . . .

". . . There is only one Micho waterfall. Yet who is to say how it differs from any other waterfall? The surroundings make it seem unique, but are not unique in themselves. In nature nothing is unique and everything is particular. Thus one sees the world from two sides at once merely by looking at it in one way. . . ."

The waterfall in the Botanical Gardens of Penang was like any other, yet it was " particular." Its water was so white and constant in its downpouring flow that it was like a vibrant stone, one of those long, narrow stones which I once saw in a remote Kyoto temple, the Mansyu-in Temple, set in an ancient lawn, to be viewed against a screen of dark foliage. The waterfall in Penang hung, moving yet moveless, like that stone.

An amusing little notice warned : " Beware of Monkeys." I wondered what they would do to me if they caught me. Outside the Gardens, with its ornamental moon-viewing pools, lily ponds, shady walks and avenues of tree ferns, tropical foliage and creepers, a small crowd of Chinese schoolgirls at the gates of a big modern high school were diligently chopsticking hot noodles from bowls bought at the kerbside. It was lunch-time, and my driver was taking me for my own collation to a small hotel on the northern seashore. After that we were to drive round the whole island.

We passed two swimming clubs—one for Chinese, and one for Europeans, under the slopes of Mount Erskine, and reached a charming little fishing village called Tanyung Bunga, where boys were mending their fishing-nets that were slung up to dry like great airy tents on ropes suspended from bamboo poles. The fisherboys were most friendly and allowed me to take a number of photographs : apart from those I met on the East Coast, these Malays were the nicest and most natural of all those I encountered in the Peninsula or on its islands.

When we reached the hotel where I was to have lunch my old driver made the waiter lay a table for me right at the edge of a lovely stretch of sand that lay beyond the hotel garden's embankment. There was only one small Chinese boy bathing in the warm shallows, and I quickly stripped and plunged in. I am not able to swim without skin-diving apparatus so here I had to content myself with floating.

Despite my three days' fast, I was not hungry. I wanted my driver to eat something, as it was Chinese food that was offered, but he declined, probably out of politeness, when he learnt that I would not be eating.

We drove on along that scintillating coast of golden, empty beaches and sparkling blue bays with rocky, palm-tufted head-lands, to Batu Ferringi and Telok Bahang where we turned inland and drove along steep hill roads that dropped away in jungle slopes or terraced rice-fields. At the summit of a high hill we stopped for some moments and looked westwards over vast rice-plains that stretched in almost enamelled-looking plaques of watery green, to the sea beyond Pantai Acheh. We could see Kedah Peak on the mainland, and, to the north, the misted outlines of the Langkawi Islands, famed for their giant monitor lizards.

There were some strange tropical trees growing round the bridge at Titi Kerawang ; I asked the driver what they were and I thought he answered " crow " ; then I realised he meant " clove " trees, for which Penang is world famous. Other plants were nutmeg and cinnobar. There are many pools just beyond the bridge and these provide delightful bathing : I could have bathed here in the nude, as the pools and the slopes around were completely deserted, but I thought it better not to, as the Malays, though not exactly prudish, are easily shocked —or pretend to be—by total nakedness.

The road began to run downhill now, and like all the roads we had travelled it was very well maintained, with a perfectly metalled surface. We ran down into Balik Palau, a straggling but very lovely Malay kampong with neat little attap-roofed houses. As we rode on eastwards the sea again became visible, and the outline of an island called Jerejak, where there are two T.B. camps and a leper settlement. On the plain, we were surrounded by coconut plantations and rice-fields. At Sungei Kwang we stopped at the Snake Temple, dedicated to Chor Soo Kong. Here there were many ivory and black vipers, doped by the fumes of incense, coiled and curled on the altar, on trees, ladders and mirrors. The young snakes were bright green, and they too seemed to be doped. There were also two enormous, somnolent, beer-brown pythons.

The boy who took charge of me to show me round had snakes wreathed round his neck and arms, and draped a few round my shoulders : I liked their cool, dry skin on my flesh. One of them, after it had been placed on my arm, came to life a little and pushed its head under the short sleeve of my sports shirt ; after a while it emerged above my open-neck collar and began either sniffing or hissing at my left ear in an exploratory way. I requested the boy to remove the reptile ; he did so quite fearlessly, saying cheerfully that he had been bitten many times.

We proceeded to Sungei Nibong, another Malay kampong,

and at Glugor Hill took the right-hand fork of the road which again runs along the seashore to George Town, which is the name of the port on Penang Island. Though my drive had lasted well beyond the stipulated time, my kind driver, of whom I had become very fond, drove me round the other parts of the town so that I saw the Hindu Nattukottai Chettiar Temple in Waterfall Road, the Sri Mariamman Temple in Queen Street and the fine Kapitan Kling Mosque in Pitt Street. Just before depositing me at my hotel, he took me to the old Christian cemetery, fragrant with ancient frangipani trees and shady with casuarinas sheltering the worn tombs of the original East India Company settlers of Penang; among them he pointed out to me the gravestone of Captain Francis Light who took possession of the island for the British in 1786.

I had had a wonderful drive, a drive which I would recommend to all who have the chance to visit Penang : many ocean-going liners call there and stay for a day or so. Do not miss this superb scenic drive. It is unforgettable.

All the flags in Penang were at half-mast for the death of some minor royalty. Funerals here, owing to the rapid decomposition of the body in the humid heat, take place with almost indecent rapidity, sometimes on the very day of death.

Passing the Roman Catholic Cathedral of the Assumption I saw the departure of a long funeral procession. In a capacious motor-hearse whose scrolled and twisted ornamental ironwork was painted with dull silver duragilt enamel there was a coffin all white and silver, covered with already-browning wreaths of white magnolia and frangipani. The hooded nuns were all in spotless white : they followed the hearse in a hired omnibus.

Some curious traditions surrounded the arrival home of the body of a prominent Penang gentleman who had died in London. When the chartered plane bearing his mortal remains landed at Bayan Lepas airport in the southern part of the island, he was welcomed home by members of his family as if he were still alive. No mourning was worn at the airport and there was no weeping. Only when the coffin arrived at the dead man's home would a member of the family announce the gentleman's death, and then a sackcloth scroll would be hung up to indicate a house of mourning.

According to Chinese custom, the body of a person who dies

outside his home cannot be taken into the house. (This is one of the reasons for the death-houses.) Because of this custom, the dead gentleman was not proclaimed officially dead until after his body had been brought into the house.

A clouded moon for Chap Goh Meh greeted the endless procession of girls in twos, threes and larger groups walking along the Esplanade and Gurney Drive, wearing their best new clothes. Some more fortunate drive along in lantern-lit cars and trishaws. Very young girls are chaperoned by mothers. There were some Indian belles with an enormously fat lady in a purple and gold sari who had tiny diamond studs winking in her ears. Although this is a Chinese festival, Indian and Malay girls are also present, as might be expected when it's a question of competing for a prospective marriage partner. There are processions of small, decorated floats hung with small dragon-lanterns; riding on them are bands and choirs.

There is even a float afloat—a motor-launch with a large illuminated model of a packet of " Rex " cigarettes chugs backwards and forwards over the harbour. The young men in thousands throng the pavements and the low sea-wall where the eating-stalls are packed. The men are not very dashing : they stand about in guffawing groups watching the young ladies demurely parade their charms.

I saw no other European, either male or female. As usual on such occasions, I felt only the melancholy of someone who cannot participate ; but at Chap Goh Meh in particular I felt rather silly and out of place in all the heterosexual conviviality. Nevertheless, I did in the end find a partner, but not for marriage.

Next evening, a lovely view of palms and sunset from the broad balcony outside my hotel room. A fisherman was rowing across the rosy clouds of water, standing in the stern of his pointed boat's curving prow, rowing with two long, crossed oars.

A group of Malay boys, half-naked, and an English schoolboy were fishing against the afterglow. They began chasing each other and then they started moving their bodies in a strange way; I thought they were beginning to do " improper " things. However, they were just trying to show each other how to do the Twist which has hit Penang like a tornado. Everybody's doing it, including me.

For the pills have cured me.

19. Processions and Penitents

One Sunday evening in Singapore I walked up Fort Canning Road, through King George Park and across to Tank Road, where there was the most enchanting Hindu temple I'd so far seen.

There were interesting paintings of Indian gods and cherubs on the walls of the outer courtyard, facing the street. Saracenic arches rimmed with naked electric light bulbs gave the entrance a fairground aspect.

A number of Indians were sitting outside the main door and when they saw my interest in their temple they invited me to step inside. They said it didn't matter removing my shoes but this was just politeness and of course I did take them off.

Inside, a ceremony was going on, attended by a small group of people who were clustered in sari and sarong round the main central shrine. They smiled at me and made room so that I could stand beside them.

An exquisitely-gilded and barbaric image of the god was enshrined in the depths of a grotto of electric light bulbs, glittering tiles, Christmas-tree tinsel baubles and coloured glass balls. From the art-nouveau tiles of the roof hung scores of oil-lamps like goblets of coloured drinks inside inverted crystal domes. Plain and coloured glass globes by the score were also hanging from the ceilings of the side-chapels.

Chandeliers of glittering crystal, old-fashioned gasoliers of art-nouveau metal and glass, adapted to electric light, the bulbs fitted into fluted white shades and lily-shaped bowls. It was a perfect museum of absolutely authentic art-nouveau fittings.

A vast, dowdy mirror leaned at an alarming angle from an end wall, making me look like a sad dwarf.

The worshippers formed two long lines, the men in white robes, the women in saris. Children in smart Western clothes tried to attend to the service but kept running about, exploring and playing games in a very natural way that no one objected to. A priest with half-shaven head was playing a small instrument like a harmonium or like the " organ of the angels " which one sees sometimes in tapestries of the Virgin and the Unicorn. Only one note was endlessly droned out as an accompaniment to the priest's chanting.

An ancient mystic, his forehead and arms and chest ash-smeared, was doing push-ups near the door : these were rever-ential motions. The priest seemed to be telling a story. When it was finished he took up a dish of flames and moved it up and down and across the golden image while the two long rows of worshippers stretching away from the shrine leaned forward to catch a glimpse of what seemed to be a significant moment. As the priest moved the flames across the image a salvo of crackers went off outside.

This was at Chinese New Year, so I do not know whether the crackers were part of the Chinese celebrations or part of the Hindu ceremony.

I who, to my shame, had never liked Indians very much, found that here, in their own place, the temple of their true homeland as it were, they were kindly and relaxed and good. I was to find this in all Indian temples I visited. After long months in Malaya, my initial prejudice against the Indians was gradually overcome by frequent visits to their homes and religious ceremonies and festivals. In those places and on those occasions the true quality of the Indian seemed to come out in a way that I could recognise and appreciate.

And in all their temples, there was this atmosphere of reverent informality, mixed with a rather sombre gaiety ; the atmosphere of a mighty and profoundly fervent religion.

Early on the morning of 14th January, when Hindus celebrate their harvest festival known as Thai Ponggal, I went out into the countryside with a Ceylonese I had met in the street ; one of his names, surprisingly enough, was Lingam. We went to visit some of his relatives.

The ground outside their house was decorated with formal coloured patterns, mostly geometrical ones of interlocking triangles and circles. Some of the patterns were severe white representations of fish and pineapples, drawn with slaked lime.

The designs used to be made with rice flour, but to-day chunam or calcium hydroxide is used : this is deplored by the older generation, because originally the rice grains were intended as food for ants.

This art of drawing on the ground, or sometimes inside a big circular, shallow dish or pan, for decoration in the house, is known as kolam, and comes from India where it is widely practised by girls and women in Gujarath, Maharashtra and Bengal. The Telugus and Parsis are also experts at this kind of domestic art.

There are special designs for certain festivals : for example, the birthday of Lord Krishna calls, in Southern India, for drawings of a child's feet symbolising the god's entry into the house. A sun chariot is often drawn on harvest festival days, usually in the open courtyard of the house.

The original purpose of these drawings was to let strangers know that there was no disease, infection or death in the houses before which they were composed ; and in houses where a birth is being celebrated, no kolams are designed. Women compete with each other in the decoration of the beaten earth in front of their doors, and a girl's marriage chances are increased in the eyes of her own and her suitor's parents if she can draw her kolams well and in a good variety.

An exhibition of this truly popular art was held recently in Madras, and drew thousands of people of all classes and from a very wide area.

Around the decorated floor on Ponggal Day the housewives place sugar-cane, pumpkins and other field crops. A small stove is made of baked clay or dry cow-dung and this is placed in the middle ; then a new clay pot is decorated with various pretty figures and round the neck of the pot a bunch of turmeric roots and leaves is tied with a piece of new white thread.

Various grains—but chiefly rice—are placed in the pot with sugar and milk and are cooked over the new stove. The women sing " Ponggal Ponggal," a traditional song which describes the bubbling of the pot's contents. Lingam told me that one of his friends had boiled sweet rice and peas in the new pot at sunrise ; the pot had been allowed to boil over : the pot had boiled over in the direction of the rising sun, and this was felt to be a sign of great good fortune for the family's crops during the coming year.

We were served with this sweet porridge-like substance : it reminded me somewhat of the *amazake* or sweet rice I was served in a little snow-house in Northern Japan.

The men bathed and decorated their bullocks, wreathing their horns and necks with flowers and feeding them well. In the evening some of the young men tied the bullocks to small wagons and had racing contests. The winners were presented with " Angavasthiram," a piece of silk covered with embroidered patterns ; these cloths were worn by the winners for that evening only, then stored away in the family cedarwood chest. These country Indians were entrancingly gay and intelligent, graceful and devout, and they were fine musicians, singers and dancers. They treated me as an equal, and I shall never forget their kindness—the natural way they shared with me everything they possessed, though I was a stranger, a foreigner, and indeed a member of that race which had so long oppressed them. It was a happy day.

Out walking one night, near Wearne's Motor Showroom in the Pudu Road I turned down a darkish side-street, attracted by a display of fairy-lights and a tower crocketed with naked electric-light bulbs. I thought it might be another Indian celebration. But I discovered that the lights were illuminating the white façade—rather good colonial Gothic—of the Roman Catholic church which also had bunting and ropes of coloured pennants flying in honour of Christmas. The Malays pronounce Christmas " Keris-mas."

But in Kuala Lumpur the year's greatest Indian festival is Thaipusam. The " Nine Nights " or Navarathiri in October is also an important festival but Thaipusam is the most splendid and popular of all. It is the Hindu festival of penance, when hundreds of men and boys, the flesh of their backs and shoulders pierced with silver and steel skewers, carry on these skewers wooden frames called kavadi, decorated with peacock feathers and coconut leaves, in fulfilment of solemn vows.

On 20th January I went to the Sri Maha Mariaman Temple in Kuala Lumpur's High Street just after 6 a.m. The cool of early morning was unusual and delicious, after all the rain that had fallen during the past days. Walking was quite pleasant.

The sun rose, but the light was still greyish, veiled by wadded cloud. The streets were already thronged with workers and housewives. The market was a vast hubbub of noise and scents and stinks—particularly of dried fish. Bullocks pulling decorated carts from nearby kampongs had their horns painted red, and some had one red and one green horn.

So far there were only about two dozen worshippers at the temple, which is a pretty, open, lime-green structure with a very brilliantly-coloured altar and lots of bright naked light-bulbs. The shrine, an enormous, lovely peacock, incredible in its complexity of colours and ornaments and swagged with ropes of flowers, stood in a wide arcade next to the deep-set altar. Four creamy bullocks, their horns decorated, and two of them also with red ceremonial cloths on their backs, were standing at one side of the courtyard, near an altar centred in a huge, ancient, overhanging banyan.

Musicians stood near the main altar, wearing white robes and accompanying the preparations for the long procession to the Subrahmanya Temple at the top of the steep flight of steps leading to the Batu Caves. A drummer, his fingers sheathed in bamboo, was creating an ear-cracking noise with slim but powerful fingers. Two men were blowing long trumpets that sounded like enormous kazoos. There was another man in charge of cymbals and a pair of small metal hemispheres which he kept clinking one against the other.

Outside the big temple gateway whose lintel was wreathed in banana-leaves and adorned with stems of finger-size green bananas stood two large red wagons which perhaps ought to be called juggernauts or jagganaths. On the first and larger one was a massive domed canopy with eight polychrome pillars adorned with prancing lions and hovering cherubim; there were two white, almost heraldic horses rearing in front beside wooden images of two women—goddesses ?—in flowing robes. The whole thing was quivering with those coloured, metallic Christmas-tree globes, with little round mirrors and fairy-lights. It all looked absolutely gorgeous in its all-inclusive wealth of detail, like an old-fashioned merry-go-round. The shrine and the image of Lord Subrahmanya will be placed underneath the canopy.

As seven o'clock approached, men who appeared to be beggars or holy men or both brought out pennants and flags of scarlet and white cloth with a star and crescent device on them.

They also carried, at the end of long poles, two large, heart-shaped padded things like cushions in the centre of which a lovely formal golden sun with very twisty rays was embroidered.

The majority of people in the courtyard round the temple are bare-foot—such dark, almost black skins some of these southern Indians have, yet such pale soles and palms!

Some wash their feet at a trough by the inside of the gate before walking across the courtyard to the shrine. I feel I don't want to take off my shoes because then I would have to take off my stockings also—after all, if they go bare-foot, I must too—so I stay by the gate. But I notice some Indians are wearing sandals in the courtyard. An elderly Indian smiles and invites me to walk round the yard with him. I keep on my shoes, but do not enter the temple itself.

The music round the lighted, scented altar is rising to a crescendo of bangs and hoots and clinkings. The little group of worshippers is turned sideways from the altar; they raise their joined hands beautifully above their heads, lowering them then to their breasts in adoration of Lord Subrahmanya, whose birthday this is.

Suddenly a worshipper standing beside me makes me jump by casting a coconut down on the outer step of the temple; it detonates dully, like a smashed skull, showering us both with coconut water and fragments of shell and pith.

A priest with a half-shaven head of grey hair, lightly marcelled, carries round a tray of fire; the worshippers stroke the flames with both hands, at first timidly, then more boldly, and raise their purified fingers to their brows—a lovely, quick, playing yet reverent gesture. (There is surely some trace of Persian Zoroastrianism in this religion.)

The priest bearing fire is followed by another bearing what seems to be scent or perhaps a bowl of rosewater. The worshippers take a little and smooth it on their face and hair. Drums, horns, clappers. A great din.

It is getting much lighter now. A whole troop of young Malay auxiliary policemen arrives, in khaki shirts and shorts, on their heads black berets with a scarlet flash.

Some of the Indians now have what appear to be streaks of whitish ash across their foreheads, and in the centre, between the eyebrows, a large, rough, glistering crimson mark that looks like a round, festering sore. A priest is carrying round a big tray loaded with sacred ash. Some also daub their breasts and arms with it. Another priest is putting the crimson marks on the worshippers' foreheads.

A long, narrow banner on two long poles is brought out. This will be carried at the front of the procession. Behind its bearers the flag and cushion-bearers range themselves. After these come two torch-bearers with orange-flaring torches.

Then, amid great musical agitation, the glittering, shivering shrine with its three tiny golden figures degged and tagged with jewels, dappled with charms and swathed in flowers, a miracle of gold and silver and crystal dangling dewdrops and ribbons of embroidered cloth with a large panel of flowered lemon silk billowing behind, is lifted on to two stout, long poles and borne on a dozen young men's naked shoulders. There is a man holding a fringed, salmon-pink umbrella on a six-foot handle high over the sacred image. He walks immediately behind it.

The procession moves forward, with the band in front, and proceeds in a stately way round the courtyard and out of the gate, where the shrine is transferred to the larger of the juggernauts.

The entranced worshippers rush out into the street and suddenly start throwing dozens of fresh coconuts on the ground in front of the first wagon, where the bullocks already stand, mild and patient, and, as always, so contented looking, yoked to the shrine they and a host of devotees will pull for seven miles to the Batu Caves. The scores of coconuts make a tremendous smashing sound as they are cast upon the roadway. The Indian women's thin, silk-clad arms raised high above their heads as they ferociously dash the coconuts to the ground with wild shouts look like the arms of dark Maenads and seem to be possessed of a sinister and rapturous energy; they make the juice and the fragments of nut and shell fly all over the place. If one of the coconuts happens not to burst, the woman who has thrown it runs after it as it rolls down the road, and her second attempt to smash it seems the act of a wanton fury. Soon the women's breasts are heaving, their hair is uncoiled and their eyes flashing as they cry and pant with their exertions. The watching crowd is driven back, smiling in awe at the women's frenzied vigour. They look as if they are killing invisible snakes, so maniac is their concentrated ferocity.

Soon the whole road in front of the indifferent and un-alarmed bullocks is littered with broken segments of coconut shell and wet with juice that smells exquisitely fresh and sweet in the cool air, scenting the whole street with that intoxicating, nutty, spicy aroma of volatile oils that pervades the hair and skin of Orientals.

After all the coconuts had been ceremoniously smashed, the music struck up a march and the juggernaut tottered and shud-dered and glittered as it slowly moved off. A police officer walked at the front; behind him came a long line of young devotees hauling the thick rope attached to the front of the first wagon. The other young policemen were spaced out round the shrine and the worshippers : they would accompany it to the Caves and be responsible for its safe keeping until it returned to the temple.

One of the young policemen had spoken to me and invited me to go with them to the Batu Caves : he said he would give me a lift in a police van. I was dying to accept, but I had to attend my students' viva at 8.30 a.m. I explained this and he suggested that I meet him at the Batu Caves that evening at seven-thirty, and he would show me round. I eagerly accepted the invitation, and ran all the way back to my hotel in a state of gentle elation : I had spoken to a new person, and made a friend ! I hardly knew myself.

But how was I to get to the Caves ? The buses and trains were jam-packed, and long queues were waiting. I could have walked or thumbed a lift but I was afraid to be late so I hailed a taxi and haggled with the driver : he agreed to take me for only three dollars, even though it was a very busy night.

On the road to the Caves, there were candles burning outside and inside many Indian and Malay dwellings, and the little wayside shrines were ablaze with illuminations. The mosques, too, not to be outdone, are full of lights and worshippers.

As we drove past the little kampongs, the dark, enormous, animal-like humps of the great limestone outcrops began to appear sombrely against the tropic sky. But those darksome heights, so isolated, odd and uncanny, that at night have a blackness blacker than all blacknesses, were on this occasion softly irradiated from below.

Then I caught the first distant glimpse of the hundreds of

steps leading up to the main caves, steps now garlanded with ropes and loops of coloured lights.

All round the bottom of the steps, covering at least five acres, was a vast fairground, brilliantly illuminated, spread out over the whole area between the main road and the caves. There were two principal lanes dividing the fairground, both dazzlingly lit. At the fairy-lit entrance arch was a battalion of flag-sellers who pursued me as I strolled along trying to light a cigarette. I put twenty cents in a tin marked simply " 5 " and had a serrated flag of green cardboard affixed to the pocket of my peacock-blue silk shirt with a large no-tear paperclip. The flag's superscription, in Tamil and English, informed me that contributions were to be devoted to a building fund; "Muthami" was the one word I could read in the name. Other men were selling what at first I thought were cubes of sugar, but these were paper-wrapped blocks of pure camphor for burning at the shrines and before the holy men and penitents carrying kavadis.

The place was milling with people and bursting with noise. Along either side of the two main lanes were the chief booths and shops, sizzling with acetylene flares and lamps and strips of neon. They were selling soft drinks, food and sweets, coconuts, flaked ice topped with fluorescent flavourings, balls and floral garlands of jasmine buds, coconut juice with shredded ice and all kinds of cakes and puzzling delicacies. There were sellers of betel leaf and nut parings (these are actually from the areca-nut); many low-caste Indians were chewing it, their teeth and lips a repulsive red. It seems to promote excessive functioning of the salivary glands, for many of the chewers had red dribbles running from either corner of their mouths and they were constantly spitting out gobbets of the stuff they were masticating. I began to feel that I would rather see gum-chewers than betel-leaf chewers; even bubblegum blowers might possibly be a little less disgusting.

Screwing up my courage, I tried a chew of it myself. I didn't know that slaked lime was also used in the composition of a betel chew : my mouth seemed to fizz with heat and my tongue shrivelled as if I had applied astringent skin tonic to it. At once I spat out my wad, and dowsed my gullet's seemingly unending recalescence with bottle after bottle of Green Spot.

There was a row of open stalls all a-glitter with every conceivable kind of brass and copper ware—pots, pans, vases, bowls, lamps, ornaments, cobra candlesticks, slipper ash-trays, brooches, charms, bangles, incense burners, inkwells, trays, trinkets, dishes, images—all sparkling under a bleaching battery of white lamps. There was a stall selling thin, coloured metal bangles : at first I thought these were rolls of shot silk, but on looking closer I saw they were cardboard tubes covered with hundreds of these bangles pressed tightly together. Indian girls often wear as many as a dozen of these bangles on a long, thin, brown wrist where their glittering facets of brilliant enamel look enchantingly pretty. They jingle softly and coolly on a hot tropic night : I bought a dozen then found I couldn't get them on.

There were stalls selling pictures of gods and goddesses and lesser divinities, all the pantheon of the bewildering Hindu mythology encrusted with gold and silver and rainbow-coloured glitter-frost, the tones all violent and clashing in a hideous bariolation, the faces sentimental, idealised, almost simpering, even when a handsome prince was disconcertingly seen to have a nose in the form of an elephant's trunk.

In the darker spaces behind the main avenues there were all kinds of amusements and carousels. Some of them were blindingly lit, like the miniature " Wall of Death " (with an ordinary racing-cyclist riding round it instead of a motor-cyclist) and a roaring roundabout called " The Flying Man." These two attractions sent out a constant, deafening blare of music and comment from the amplifiers—barbaric music alternating with shouted appeals for the patronage of the public.

A little distance away a couple of small, unilluminated, creaking Ferris Wheels, operated by hand and carrying only four little Indian passengers, were turning with melancholy and solemn slowness in the dark. Remote, silent, only on the fringe of light and life, these contraptions with their silent children placidly revolving were like dream-abstracts, the shadow-visions one sees when turning the eyes away suddenly from something too blatantly bright.

There were long huts whose walls were composed mainly of large-meshed wire—I believe they were schools—in which families were camping or squatting, having booked for a small sum a resting-place for the night. I wondered how much rest they would get, for the fair keeps going until well into the small hours. Buses are running until only 1 a.m.

How on earth was I going to find my new friend among all these thousands of people ? I went to one of the police posts but he was not there.

In the distance, illuminated by immense arc-lamps, thousands of Indians were slowly ascending and descending the hundreds of steps to the Batu Caves. It was like a long white waterfall : hundreds of people had collapsed in the long climb up to the caves to fulfil their Thaipusam vows. Hundreds of children were lost, only some of whom were restored to their parents. Over four hundred Indian men, women and children, their bodies skewered with spikes, some of them with silver needles stuck through their lips and tongue, took part in the penance of carrying kavadis ; they climbed, bearing those heavy burdens on the spikes that rested in their own flesh, to the Subrahmanya Temple, there to keep vows they had made to the Hindu god on their recovery from illnesses. The carrying of a kavadi is also a self-purifying act : those who wish to undertake this penance must for a long time eat only one meal a day in pre-paration for the trial, which is a test of the spirit as much as of the body. All meat, fish and eggs must be excluded from their diet.

Children carry a smaller form of kavadi which is called a " pal kavadi." " Pal " is the Tamil word for milk. A " pal kavadi " means a small kavadi. There are also " fish " and " fruit " and " snake " kavadis, but these are too heavy to be borne by children, and women are not allowed to carry these kinds. The milk, fish, fruit, snake or whatever it is that is being carried is contained in two new earthenware jars which are placed inside the kavadi or paper-decorated shrine. There were a number of these shrines in an enclosure at the foot of the steps, and some of them were splendidly decorated with garlands of flowers and coloured paper streamers : they were being guarded by half-naked holy men who still seemed to be in a trance. One of them, as I was watching, pierced both cheeks with a skewer like some old dame impaling her bonnet with a hatpin. He protruded a tongue and a friend stuck a silver needle through it : the skewer and the needle would be the basic supports for the kavadi, which, as he was a man, would be a heavy one. Some of the weight would be taken by spikes pressed into the back and shoulders and chest. There were one or two kavadis in the shape of floral chariots. These would be dragged along by penitents with ropes attached to large hooks dug into the flesh of their backs.

I wandered aimlessly round the booths, looking in vain for my friend. Suddenly I found myself in front of the shrine from the Sri Maha Mariaman Temple, on the back of the big, decorated peacock. Two lamps, in the form of bronze peacocks, were burning on either side of it. It was standing in a large, open-ended marquee made of what looked like white butter-muslin or common mosquito-netting. Worshippers kept coming and going, the frail, gauzy scarves of the sari-clad women floating like the mists of incense. The head priest and his assistants from the temple were there ; they recognised me and one gravely bowed. I think they were pleased to see me, and I was glad to be there because once more I felt very strongly that here, in a religious setting, I was seeing Indians at their best : in the fairground, surrounded by commerce and material-ism, they did not seem nearly as attractive as here, in this simple tent containing the essence of their faith. It was a faith I simply could not make head nor tail of, but which I knew to be real because of the transformation it worked upon its devotees ; and because of the bloodless, painless wounds, wounds that were not wounds, suffered by those extraordinary kavadi-bearers. This was indeed justification by deeds : only a few Christian saints have reached the sublime heights of faith attained by hundreds of ordinary Indians.

There were a number of tiny, near-naked children lying along the sides of the marquee on straw mats. They had obviously been put there to sleep, but how could they, poor little devils, in all that din and dazzlement ? One rolled his weary head round to look at me, and was not too tired to smile, with perfect sweetness, showing his tiny white teeth.

I laid my bangles before the shrine of Lord Subrahmanya, put my hands together, raised them to my forehead and bowed. A priest brought a tray of ash : I took a pinch and smeared my forehead with it. I dropped coins into the bowls of many beggars who were squatting near the sacred tent, and burned a cube of camphor, holding it in my fingertips, not even surprised to feel no heat from those volatile flames. If I had had a skewer, I would have transfixed my tongue, I felt so rapt out of myself.

The head priest gave me an incense-stick which he lit himself at the peacock-flame, and I carried it all evening like a living rose of scented smoke.

In a makeshift shed there stood the domed canopy in all its gorgeous glitter of rococo radiance, and beside it squatted more beggars. I recognised the torch-bearers and banner-bearers I had seen that morning, and they recognised me. One offered me a little roll of betel, which I accepted and chewed ; this time it had, it seemed, a refreshing acid sweetness, an only faintly-stinging tartness. (Betel is a Portuguese corruption of Malayalam or Malabar " vettila.")

The immense crowd is of course mainly composed of Indians and Ceylonese, with a fair number of Malays gazing at all the religious paraphernalia of these " infidels " with smiling incomprehension, as if observing the inscrutable games of foreign children. There are also a few Chinese about, obviously interested in all the money that is changing hands.

I strolled back to the towering flight of steep, fairy-lit steps where the white-robed throngs are still moving like slowly-falling, slowly-rising water. High above them, the hanging roofs and entrances of the caves: the lower cliffs are bathed in a roseate glow that dwindles as the soaring, fantastically-moulded rock-face rises into darkness.

The penitents were still there in the enclosure at the bottom of the steps, preparing themselves for the next day's pleasant passion. Though they were all Indians, it is not only people of this nationality who skewer their flesh and perform prodigies of delicious smart. Certain Buddhists are experts at this kind of self-forgetting. For example, at the Festival of the Nine Emperor Gods (Kew Ong Yeah) there are skewer men, tranced acrobats who carry thirty-foot poles on foreheads and chins and men who walk barefoot over red-hot coals. These witnesses to a powerful faith are Chinese and are known as " mediums " in Malaya. At the Kew Ong Yeah festival in Ampang New Village, about six miles from K.L., mediums with iron skewers pierced through both cheeks walked across a pit of burning charcoal twenty-five yards wide. Devotees also carried sedan chairs bearing the images of the Nine Emperor Gods across the pit. There was a crowd of nearly ten thousand spectators, forced well away from the pit by the heat and smoke, watching in fascinated silence as mediums walked or danced across the pit in their trial of fire, a final act of thanksgiving to the gods.

I watched the mediums carefully to see if there was any trickery, but they rubbed no special preparations on their feet and legs ; some carried charcoal embers in their mouths. They walked or danced rapidly and light-footedly across the pit, but even so it took them several seconds to get across, and both feet trod the glowing ashes many times. Gold and silver papers were continuously strewn across the lengthily-prepared pit to feed the embers as the gaily-decorated sedans were carried briskly but reverently back and forth. It was all done by absolute faith. And the mediums were ordinary people who chose this way to fulfil vows and give thanks to the gods. Some of the mediums were small boys.

Another type of medium, bare to the waist, flayed himself with spiked iron balls while another man in a trance rolled a red-hot iron ball along the street with his feet and hands. Another slashed his back with a large sword in a kind of ritual dance : this was similar to the self-woundings, which cause no pain and heal quickly, of Siamese worshippers. In Teluk Anson a devotee seated in a chair of razor-sharp nails was carried in procession through the main streets of the town.

This kind of demonstration is not masochistic, for the men who do these things feel no pain and sustain no injuries. Nor is there anything " fanatical " about such acts of faith : they seem to spring from profound religious exhilaration only, and cannot be faked without serious bodily damage to the faker. What was surprising was the atmosphere of gaiety as well as reverence. Both performers and spectators seemed to be released from petty earthly problems and transported into a realm where there are no longer any arbitrary divisions between body and spirit. I can only describe my own sensations as I watched as partaking of an ethereal earthiness : I felt I was for a while one with the mediums and with myself.

And for once I did not feel apart, but at one with the rest of the crowd, and with the world.

As I stood pondering these things at the Batu Caves I felt a warm hand slip inside my left arm : I turned and saw Mohammed my policeman friend standing beside me. I told him I was going to ascend the steps to the caves, and he at once nodded and said: " Come." We mounted the packed steps, with a pause half-way for breath and to mop our faces: as we stood at that half-way point among the ascending and descending crowds we enjoyed the scintillating and spectacular spread of fairground illumination at our feet. In the distance, the lights of K.L. cast a faint glow on the low cloud or mist over the city.

The authority of Mohammed's khaki uniform and his well-built bulk helped to clear a path for us among the swarms of worshippers, but even so the going was difficult. A young man had collapsed on the way up and was being carried down on a stretcher; two small Indian girls were lost and were being escorted back to the police post; an old lady in an opulent sari was being carried up the last few steps by two strapping young men.

My companion asked me, as we climbed, if I knew any stories about the caves. I replied that I didn't, and he told me he didn't know any either, but added that many people believe that the big, high main cave, which is so long and narrow, was originally a ship. I could well understand that simple and imaginative people in the past might have entertained this poetic concept. Mohammed also told me the Malay name for the fruit-eating bat: kalong. He said there were a few white bats in the smaller caves, which it was impossible to reach because they were unlighted.

We reached the top of the steps at last: there are over seven hundred of them. I was lathered in sweat and greeted gratefully the cool gust of air at the entrance to the cave. We went in. At night, by the light of candles and torches and electric lamps, it seemed even more impressive than by day. It was high and grey and ancient, mysterious and venerable. One is simply awed by its immensity, by those beetling, overhanging cliffs and folds of rock above the cave's entrance, by the massive, contorted crags and tattered-looking draperies of stone on either side. It is a terrifying and awful sight. Human beings are so small and insignificant in such a setting. The whole terrible mass of rock, its grim, vertical flanks proudly isolated in the lush tropical plain, is impersonal and grand and inscrutable, like the great god of some utterly foreign religion whose rites and mysteries are for ever closed to us and are beyond the comprehension even of its adepts.

Holy men outside the cave shrines hold out dishes of greyish ash for me to daub on my forehead and arms. Mohammed naturally does not follow my example. The feeling of the soft, warm ash on my skin fills me with ecstasy : Mohammed smiles broadly at me ; I must look a real sight by now, for some of the ash has got on my hair. He tries to brush it off but I stop him.

We see a group of three policemen wearing blue flashes on their berets. Mohammed tells me they are Jungle Police. Apart from the blue flash, Mohammed is dressed exactly as they are ; he is wearing a pistol in a blancoed holster on his left hip, and a long rosewood baton dangles from his heavy belt over his bare right thigh, extending down to a knee brown as nutmegs. Occasionally in the press my hand knocks against the revolver or the dangling baton : they are vibrant with life.

Some Indians in white robes are smashing dozens of fresh coconuts on two small rocks just rising out of the level, trampled earth of the cave's floor. The juice streams down a slight slope at the bottom of which sits a row of beggars, their backs turned indifferently to the spectacle of the coconut-smashers, who are watched by a large crowd. We leave the cave, walking between a double row of pleading beggars—how rhetorical the gestures of their thin, outstretched arms, their skinny fingers !

We slowly descend the steps ; by the time I get to the bottom my knees feel weak as water. Mohammed and I exchange addresses, shake hands and say good night : he is on duty until twelve o'clock.

January 23rd: Last night, at midnight, I witnessed the return of Lord Subrahmanya to the Sri Maha Mariaman Temple. He came back, the blessed idol, in his glittering chariot ablaze with mirrors and lights and enthusiasm. On the very top of the canopy was a brilliant blue light representing his holy star.

The dozen bearers lifted the shrine carefully from the chariot and placed it on the waiting trestles on the pavement before carrying it, very slowly, with a rhythmical swaying of their bodies, into the temple courtyard that was lit with ropes of lights.

This time I had come out without socks, in a pair of heel-less sandals. I slipped them off and walked barefoot behind the shrine.

There was a frantic crescendo of drumming and fluting and cymbal-clashing as the image was borne into the little lime-green temple. Its multi-coloured garlands still looked as fresh as ever, its jasmine buds still smelt almost as overpoweringly sweet as the day of its departure. Some of the thicker outer garlands were encased in tubes of cellophane.

As the shrine was set in place, there were shouts of acclamation and wild huzzas of adoration, ecstatic liftings of joined hands in lovely thin-armed arches above gleaming black or white-haired heads. The man who on Saturday morning had caused such a startling detonation by casting down the first coconut on the temple step now cast down another, the last, in exactly the same place.

There were great baskets full of broken coconut and bananas that had been offered to the god; occasionally a beggar would pick over the contents of the baskets and select a few slightly bruised bananas.

Worshippers were being given handfuls of rice, wrapped in banana leaves, and a few blossoms of jasmine along with a couple of bananas all taken from the main central altar by the chief priest, a jovial, plump, elderly man with grey stubble on his chin and the front half of his head shaven. The rest of his yellow-grey hair, which had been allowed to grow long, was arranged in careful waves and gathered into a greasy bun on the nape of his neck.

The band kept up its playing for an hour or so. It was joined by an extra drummer and two more horn players who improvised endlessly to rhythms suggested by a fervent young drummer wearing a simple loincloth and who at times, bending over backwards, seemed almost in a trance as he jerked and twisted and writhed, intoxicated by his own inventions. One of the horn players would beat time by opening and closing his right fist, giving directions to the man clashing the small brass cymbals, obviously a very important member of the small orchestra, though at first I thought his job seemed easy and monotonous. But listening intently I began to realise that the already-complicated and quite inscrutable rhythms of the drums and horns were being commented on by the cymbal-clasher in an even more subtle and incomprehensible rhythm. It was quite impossible for me to analyse it; I was quite unable to detect any pattern or system, though there must have been one, in the cymbal-clashes. I stood listening to them, utterly spellbound by the noises they made. Long before coming to Malaya I had lost all my former deep passion for music, and after listening to these oriental rhythms and sounds I could not imagine myself ever wanting to listen again to Beethoven or Bach.

The musicians were surrounded by an appreciative crowd, and in the end even I could enjoy the fascination of the sound though not understanding it and sometimes disliking the notes emerging from the long black horn which often sounded like the honking of a klaxon.

The chief priest and his assistants now carried round a bowl of flames in which worshippers dipped their hands. Bowls of ash and oil were next handed round. Many put a little ash and oil in their mouths before smearing forehead and forearms with ash and wiping the glistening oil on their hair. The priests now automatically offered me everything they offered the Indian worshippers. I bathed my hands in the flames and raised my purified fingers to my bowed forehead in front of the golden image of the god. I took ash and oil, put some in my mouth and smeared my forehead and arms and hair with them: my participation in these rites, though I barely understood what I was doing, gave me a strange feeling of elation and filled me with a warm love for my fellow-worshippers. There was joy in my heart because where once I had disliked them I had now come to love the Indians, to begin to understand their sombre charm and gentle wildness. Worshipping with me here, they were at ease, gay, reverent. I had the sudden vision that all religions belong to one another, and that there is something in all of them which we can all comprehend and learn from. No religion, I knew, and no sect should exclude any other: exclusion could only mean weakening and diffusion of faith, the undoubted faith that does exist within and beyond all religions and is common to all. It is available to all men, if they will take it where they find it, irrespective of creed and dogma. Faith is something beyond religion, but not beyond man.

Exalted by my new-found knowledge, which I prayed might help me to love my fellow-men with ever-clearer eyes, I walked round the back of the temple, looked up at the full moon swimming in lime-white clouds above the white, red and green tower where doves were treading the narrow cornices between the small painted images that thronged every ledge. Behind this was another, small, walled courtyard where the lavatories are. The men's lavatory is designated by a large, crude painting of a man's head, the women's by a woman's broadly-smiling face.

On my return to the main courtyard there came the ceremony of taking the jewels and golden decorations from the image of our dear Lord Subrahmanya. The chief priest sat with a large, plain jewel-box before him: it had a cheap mirror inside the lid. Two young assistant priests cut the threads holding the ornaments among the great ropes of flowers with nail-scissors and handed the treasures to the priest. An old, grey-haired Indian woman among the worshippers prostrated herself before the image as the first ornament was taken off, kissing the ground lightly with her lips, then turning her head to touch the ground lightly with each cheek. It was a joyous abasement or rather obeisance, and was done so neatly and undemonstratively that it was a truly joyous sight. One by one the young priests removed the ornaments and laid them in the chief priest's hands: he examined each one carefully before putting it in the jewel-casket—chains, bangles, diadems, necklaces set with hundreds of tiny rubies, sapphires and emeralds; and a large golden spear, on the blade of which a big crimson mark similar to that made on the forehead of worshippers had been neatly daubed. When all the ornaments had been taken off, the chief priest sat carefully counting and examining them again. There must have been at least fifty pieces.

Then all the men and boys who had taken it in turns to carry the image to and from the Batu Caves sat in two long lines on one side of the temple courtyard. An old man carrying a large pail of milky coffee and an enamel mug ladled the beverage into glasses which the men, their festival fervour preserved within their flesh and bones, sipped slowly as they quietly chatted about ordinary things.

I made a final obeisance to Lord Subrahmanya, slipped on my sandals and wandered back to my hotel room just as dawn was beginning to break. I did not feel transformed, but I felt I was a little better; a very little better; but at least I was no worse.

20. *The Champak Odours Fail*

An Italian writer with whom I feel much sympathy, Cesare Pavese, writes, in *This Business of Living*, an hallucinating journal (a form of letters so popular on the Continent, so unjustly ignored to-day in England): "When I arrive in a fresh place, a new locality with different natural surroundings, different customs, houses, faces, I notice many things that, if I had always lived there, would now be childhood memories."

Perhaps in my persistent urge to travel, to be always on the move in new places, it is my childhood and the evergreen freshness of its memories that I am pursuing. As soon as I leave Europe, I become a child of wonder once again. I have no wish to grow up then, no officious urge to "cope with life" as people are always telling me I must, no desire to compete, to "make my mark." And like a child, I take up countries, play with them for a while as if with dolls, then cast them aside. A human being's relationship with a doll is very profound, as can be seen in the art of the ventriloquist and in many of the great puppet theatres of the East. The Japanese play with dolls, and taught me how to play with them, but not in the infantile way we in Europe think of when we think of a grown person playing with dolls. In the East one learns to play with dolls as if they were humans and superhumans, in ritual acts of affection, adoration and fun.

So though I cast many of my doll countries aside, there are some with which my relationship is so deep that I always keep returning to them: those countries are Thailand, Formosa, the Philippines and Japan. My idea of perfect happiness would be to have a small boat and to voyage from one of those countries to another for the rest of my days.

A childish and irresponsible attitude towards life, some people may think, forgetting that we are all children, that we all have childish streaks. And life is itself irresponsible, yet it gets along. I see no virtue in having a sense of responsibility : people who pride themselves on having such a sense have, I notice, nothing else. Certainly I feel no sense of duty or responsibility towards my native land, or towards what is left of my family. I do not see why, just because one happens to be born in a certain place, and into a certain family, one should be bound to them for life.

Here, again, a marvellous passage from Rose Macaulay's *The Towers of Trebizond* speaks to my need:

... " Still, a man or a woman may love his country, her country, even if they enjoy travelling. We Turks love our country very deeply. We see its faults, but we love it. Don't the English do the same ? "

" Some do, I suppose. And lots of us quite like it, for one thing or another."

" Everyone should love his country," Halide looked handsome and firm and patriotic, and as if she would fight for Turkey to the death.

I asked, " Why should they ? Is it a merit to love where one happens to live, or to have been born ? Should one love Birmingham, if one was born there ? Or Leeds ? Or Kent or Surrey ? " For I had never been able to see why, except that I suppose it is better to love every place and person. " Or Moscow ? " I added, to vex Halide.

" Moscow ! " She said it like a curse. " Still, I suppose Russians love it. I cannot reason," she said, " about loving one's country. It is just a thing one does. As one loves one's mother."

.... We mused for a while about parents. Then I went on musing about why it was thought better and higher to love one's country than one's county, or town, or village, or house. Perhaps because it was larger. But then it would be better to love one's continent, and best of all to love one's planet. ...

I would say it is best to love the universe, and space, and infinity ; not the infinite. However, I am happy to content myself with those four countries of the East which I have mentioned.

Alas, though I tried hard, and though she gave me some

wonderful moments, I could not love Malaya. Oh, my hyper-æsthesia !

Malaya : a peninsula of cloud, curried with storms. Livid heat. The rain's whole water, white as lumps of boiled rice. The dark green sweat of jungle staining the armpits of the mountains. The rubber plantations as grey as elephants, with brown-chevroned trunks, their young leaves' orderly, despairing hang of hands. The monsoon drains in bamboo bays. The scented stink of mangroves, of fruit rotting-ripe. The phantasmagoria of clouded limestone crags, caverns like fallen faces. Beggars, bundles of rags. Massing clouds like great bundles of filthy rags. And here and there, in man-made clearings in the dull, ferocious, lethargic, untameable jungle, attempts at respectability, the worst sin of all.

But if I had to live in Malaya, and could choose where I wanted to be, it would be on the East Coast, that heavenly white fringe of turtle-haunted beaches stretching from Tampat to Kota Tinggi. And in particular the little-known northern part of the East Coast—Kota Bahru, Kuala Trengganu, Jambu Bongkok, Rantau Abang, Geliga, Telok Chempedak, Chukai, Kuantan. Near Kota Bahru is a little place called The Beach of Passionate Love known in Malay as Pantai Chinta Berahi. But the love one finds there is no more passionate than the love one finds at any of these small towns and fishing villages with their en-chanting inhabitants, creatures of grace and beauty and simple kindliness, the loveliest natures in all Malaya.

The express train from Kuala Lumpur to the East Coast has an exotic name : The Golden Blowpipe. Or one can fly or go by bus to Kuantan, a seven-hour journey through superb mountain scenery. It costs just about a pound sterling to go by bus.

I should like to go back to the East Coast one day, to see the fisher-boys hauling in, in the sunrise, their shimmering nets. To see their brown bodies pearled with scales or gleaming with phosphorescence in the starlit waters of a palmy bay.

I should like to go back again and see the men flying their great kites, those noble, brilliantly-painted bamboo birds that fight to cut each other's strings. Forest gum and powdered glass are applied to the upper sections of the guiding twine; this, when it rubs against an enemy kite, caused its cord to snap. There are many different shapes of kite: the Moon, the Peacock, the Fish, the Man, the Frog, the Cat, the Swallow, and the Parakeet. There is also the Western kite which is of Siamese origin; and the most popular form, the Moon kite or Wau Bulan, which has a representation of a sickle moon for its tail, is a shape I have also seen in Thailand.

The framework of these Malay kites is constructed of a particular species of bamboo called buloh duri, and the length and wing-span are about six feet. Making a good kite is a very fine art, and may take weeks of patient labour. Many kites have a bow-like attachment called a busur which makes a pleasant humming sound when the kite is in the air. The bow is made of a bamboo called buloh betong, and the vibrating string is cut from a leaf called daun mulon. This humming sound is very thrilling to hear, and many Malays when they hear it believe that the kite has become alive and is singing its pleasure at being once more released among the birds and the stars.

How sweet and soothing is this rapt, humming sound at night, high above the moonlit bay of a Kelantan village! It is mysteriously lovely, and some kite-flyers are said to have been so spellbound by the sound of their own kites that they have fallen into deep trances from which they can only be roused by the cutting or snapping of the string.

There is an aboriginal legend that says the lightning is the flashing of top cords in the hands of giant top-spinners in the spirit world. Top-spinning is another popular and rather mysterious East Coast pastime which anyone may practise: but it takes a long time to learn the knack. There is no other top quite like the Malay top, called a gasing, as wide as a dinner-plate, about two inches thick and sometimes weighing as much as twelve pounds.

Top masters cast their tops with a rope, and can make them spin on a sheet of thick glass for hours on end. Experts compete to see whose top will spin longest, and sometimes a whole village will wager on its champion. Tricks include scooping up a spinning top on a wooden bat and tossing it to an assistant who catches it on a similar bat. Brilliant designs painted on the tops rotate into still-centred circular rainbows of colour as the spectators stare fascinated, waiting to detect the first faint wavering.

Among the rice-farmers, rubber-planters and fishermen of the East Coast one still can find some of the old village craftsmen —weavers, padanus-leaf basketwork makers and silversmiths. Some of the kampong houses have ancient hand-looms on which the women weave the kain songket sarong material interwoven with silver and gold thread which is used to make Malay ceremonial garments. They now produce this beautiful material in five-yard lengths for Western-style evening gowns and stoles. In Kuala Lumpur there is a top-flight couturier, Arthur Dorsey, who is very skilful at transforming these and all kinds of native materials into glittering evening wear. Kelantan silversmiths produce everything from Malay regalia for Sultans and heads of state to practical things like vases and tea-sets and costume jewellery of great delicacy. Pewter ware is also made on the East Coast, though not to such a great extent as in Kuala Lumpur, where objects made of Selangor Pewter are often exquisitely designed. The pewter trade began in 1885 when Yong Koon, a young Chinese pewterer, arrived in Kuala Lumpur from Swatow. He made incense-burners, joss-stick holders and candlesticks for the Chinese tin-mining community living in the village at the confluence of muddy rivers that was to become the capital, Kuala Lumpur.

From Kelantan in the north to Johore in the south the lovely beaches and fishing villages have many treasures to reveal. Not least of these are the fishing-boats adorned with the bangau. This is the curving arm at bow and stern, painted in many colours, which cradles the boat's spars and mast when this is unstepped. Bangau means egret in Malay ; because the curve of this arm resembles an egret's neck, many of them terminate in the head and beak of the bird, or of a kingfisher or hornbill ; or they carry the grotesque heads of characters from the Ramayana or the Mahabharata.

Another of the treasures of these beaches are turtle's eggs, which, like battered ping-pong balls, can sometimes be seen on sale in the shops during the turtle's egg-laying season. This is from May to September, and unfortunately I was never able to get to the East Coast at this period to watch the mother turtles dig their holes in the sand in which to lay their store of eggs.

The " leathery turtles " are among the world's largest and in Malaya they haunt the beaches of Trengganu ; they come from Sumatra and Borneo, and as many as a hundred of these giant turtles have been seen in one night on the " laying beach " at Jumbon Bunglok. They lay an average of 120 eggs each. The contents of the eggs resemble those of hen's eggs, excepting that the white will not boil.

Malays warm the eggs in water and suck them; if they soak the eggs in salt water for three days, they can hard-boil them, but only after an hour's cooking.

Tigers regard these eggs as great delicacies, and those who go to watch the turtles spawn have to be on the lookout for tigers marauding from the jungle, which in places comes right down to the beach.

The turtle lays her eggs at about the rate of one a second ; the first are round and big as ping-pong balls, but later they grow elliptical and finally the last eggs are no bigger than moth-balls. When she has laid her eggs, she quickly and deftly covers them over with sand that she digs up with her heavy flippers. Then, slowly, mournfully, she moves back to the sea. The eggs hatch in the warmth of the Malay sun and then the baby turtles may be seen struggling pathetically down the sands to reach the ocean.

But most eggs are taken by watchers as soon as the mother turtle has left them. Now the Ministry of Agriculture has set up protected hatcheries for them, so that the species does not die out in Malaya.

A fish-drive in Pahang : it is the Sultan's birthday celebration. The juice of tuberoses is poured into the river. This upsets the fish, that rise to the surface. Everyone is out in decorated boats, and there is great excitement. The Sultan, in his State Barge, has to spear the first fish. Then everyone can have a go, and the fun waxes fast and furious with many youths falling gaily into the water and pulling each other in. They get up to all kinds of larks.

Then there is ronggeng dancing, feasting on baked fish and singing throughout the night.

I am told that there are " flower girls," some of them aborigines, living on rafts with small houses built on them along the river bank at Kuala Lipis. I must go and see for myself.

An interesting court case reported from Singapore : a father offered in court to compound a case involving his teenage daughter if a man accused of outraging her modesty would compensate him with 2,000 packets of fire-crackers.

Tong Cheong Lam, of Ponggol, said: " I want to let off the fire-crackers to proclaim to my neighbours that the court case has ended in my favour. I also want to expel the demons of ill-fortune."

When told that a police permit would not be granted for such a purpose, Tong suggested that the accused, Ang Chin Chuan, should defray the cost of a four-table dinner to mark the end of the case. Tong said that his suggestion was made according to the demands of Chinese custom.

In another case, it was stated that a man was challenged to cut off the head of a white cockerel to prove his innocence. He successfully bit of the cockerel's head at a Hindu temple and thus proved his innocence.

The Malayan National Anthem is a well-known popular song that was once known as " Terang Bulan." I can't understand how it became so popular, as it seems to me utterly tuneless.

I spent over two months travelling to Hong Kong, Macao, the Philippines, Japan, Formosa, Vietnam, Laos, Cambodia, Thailand and back to Malaya.

I returned to my own house, newly decorated, and which I industriously supplied with pots and pans and lamps, a gas cooker and an " electric ice-box " as my Japanese friend calls the refrigerator.

I also had my own car, the M.G. Magnette, which I was driven in for about a fortnight by a succession of unsatisfactory drivers. I didn't dare learn to drive : I had once, during the war, tried to drive a tractor, and had sent it hurtling straight into a stone wall. Now I had my first car, and it bored me to extinction.

Tropic Temper

The Malay house was pretty, but not very quiet and not very cool. Some days I tried scattering bits of cotton-wool all over the floors and furniture, to give an impression of snow, but it didn't work.

I had to engage a cook, a dear old Chinese gentleman called Kwong. He had a little house at the back of mine. I had to provide him with furniture, two uniforms and an electric fan, because if my house was hot, his little cabin was an oven. He also had to have a dog because he was afraid of burglars. One day he brought the strangest brown puppy I have ever seen. He is not like a dog at all, but more like a piglet covered with smooth bright-ginger hair. Two tiny, vivid green-blue eyes, a rose-red tongue and a slightly duskier nose, two pointy ears and a six-inch, thin, limp-looking tail that wags well. He has an almost naked, lavender-pink belly. I have a vague suspicion that Kwong is going to eat him. Kwong, so sweet, so devoted to me, hears me calling to the puppy: " Doggy, doggy, doggy! " He knows I didn't want the dog. So in deference to me he calls the puppy Doggy-doggy, which is quite a good name for him.

Kwong was a gentle old man and a very good cook, but the money he spent at market was really exorbitant. He goes shopping with another cook-boy, a friend of his, and they meet other cook-boys at the market. They are all prestige-seeking ; they all want to know what the others are buying for their masters, and all want to be buying the most expensive things in the largest quantities. They all want to give the impression they are working for a " big boss." Kwong would lose face if he had less than ten dollars a day to dispose of.

My jungle garden : the casuarina's rusty-green foliage, the frangipani's clusters of dead-white flowers, the rain-tree, the one bedraggled palm that droops over my roof, the hibiscus and the magnolia, the banyan, the papaya like a farmyard toy, the rambutan and the round-topped mango tree. Various leguminaceous shrubs. The " poison-tapioca " tree.

Behind the house, waist-high grass sloping down to a dried river-bed and a disused tin-working. Wandering among the insect-haunted undergrowth I frequently get lost and have to be rescued by the local fire-brigade, who are always perfect to me.

Fumio Ano sends me from Japan a delightful picture by

Taikan Yokoyama, the title of which he translates as " Self-Effacement." It is a picture of a stout child—or is he a monk ?—in a very floppy brown kimono whose long, wide sleeves almost completely cover his hands. His straggly hair is tied in a top-knot with a bit of white rag. Behind him, the suggestion of a river and some pussy-willow. Four little Düreresque violet plants, two behind him and two in front. I wonder why Ano-san sent me this particular picture ? Self-effacement is something I know all about but have no desire to practise any more.

My relations with servants : only Kwong, gentle old thing, has been really satisfactory. He conceals well his constant puzzlement at my goings and comings, abrupt changes of plan and mood. He brings his family, in little separate groups of three and four, to meet the foreign devil and gaze for a moment upon his mad, unpredictable, disordered life. (But then *their* life seems totally disordered to me : I could never live like that, surrounded by din and people all the time.)

Relations with my drivers have been bad. These young Malays are just like puppies. They want everything their own way, and are sulky when crossed. But they soon come round again, for they have no badness in them. They will sometimes, after I have been " severe " with them, sit quietly looking at me as I write, with the puzzlement of thwarted pets. They don't like my long silences and the emptiness of my abode, and mope the hours away which they have been used to spend in convivial company. They cannot bear stillness and loneliness, because all their lives they have been accustomed to big families, small houses, and in the streets one rarely sees a Malay walking alone.

They love sleep, love lounging about in smart clothes giving a false impression of leisured ease. Everywhere in town one sees them hanging about in languorous gangs ; the drivers, some of them in smart white uniform and black velvet songkok, have much free time and spend it gossiping and having their makan or food. They seem to spend hours gracefully, drowsily doing nothing, waiting for their masters to finish business. Occasionally one sees them washing and polishing their cars, which they keep smart and spotless, as extensions of their own deep desire to have a spruce and opulent exterior.

They love to seem to be doing things with ease and nonchalant grace, and usually the illusion is complete : their neat bodies and fine heads, their swaying, unhurried walk and their natural skill as dancers contribute to this. Beside them, even the handsomest Europeans look blowsy, fussed, ill-dressed, ratty, mean.

" What do they think about ? " people ask. I'm fairly sure they don't think about things as we do : their thoughts are of a vegetable nature, which perhaps accounts for that sulky, indifferent charm.

After owning it for a month, I have sent my M.G. back to the sale-room. I have never been so wretched and unhappy as I am now, with all my possessions, responsibilities, and consumer goods.

To make things worse, I bumped my head on the steering-wheel when the driver suddenly braked, and cut my eyebrow. Then I developed agonising shingles, such a mundane disease. I also had an ear infection. Someone stole my watch. I was visited by the Chinese Ladder Gang, who in the middle of the night erected a ladder against my open bedroom window and fished out my coat and trousers by means of a fishing-rod, stealing untold treasures. Kwong's little puppy suddenly moped and died.

It was all too much. On 30th June, 1962, I got on a plane and flew straight to Tokyo, after providing adequately for Kwong. I told no one of my departure. I just up and left, leaving behind nearly all my worldly goods—car, cooker, refrigerator, books, clothes, pots and pans. I always like to make as clean a break as possible.

Bath, September-October, 1962.

Bibliography

Bibliography

ALLEN, BETTY MOLESWORTH: *Some Common Trees of Malaya.* (Singapore, Eastern Universities Press, 1961.)

ANDERSON, PATRICK: *Snake Wine.* (Chatto and Windus, 1955.)

DOBBY, E. H. G.: *Southeast Asia.* (University of London Press, 1950.)

EAST and SPATE: *The Changing Map of Asia.* (Methuen, 1958.)

EDINGER, GEORGE: *The Twain Shall Meet.* (Thomas Yoseloff, New York & London, 1960.)

FAUCONNIER, HENRI: *Malaysie.* (Paris, Stock, 1930.)
    The Soul of Malaya. (Trans. Eric Sutton.) (Matthews and Marrot, 1931.)

FISHER, C. A.: *The Problem of Malayan Unity in its Geographical Setting.* (In " Geographical Essays on British Tropical Lands.") (George Philip and Son Ltd., 1956.)

Fodor's Guide to Japan and Southeast Asia.

GINSBURG, NORTON and ROBERTS, CHESTER F. JNR.: *Malaya.* (University of Washington Press, Seattle, 1958.) (American Ethnological Society.)

HAHN, EMILY: *Raffles of Singapore.* (1948.)

HALL, D. G. E.: *A History of Southeast Asia.* (Macmillan, 1955.)

HENDERSON, M. R.: *Common Malayan Wildflowers.* (Longmans, 1961.)

KING, EDWARD S.: *Speak Malay!* (University of London Press, 1960.)

Modern Malay Verse, 1946–61. Introduction and translations by James Kirkup. (O.U.P., Kuala Lumpur, 1963.)

MOORE, DONALD: *The Young Traveller in Malaya and the China Sea.* (Phœnix House, 1956.)

MORAN, J. W. G.: *Spearhead in Malaya.*

MORELL, R.: *Common Malayan Butterflies.* (Longmans, 1961.)

OMMANEY, F. D.: *Eastern Windows.* (Longmans, 1960.)

RAU, SANTHA RAMA: *View to the Southeast.* (Gollancz, 1958.)

ROBEQUAIN, CHARLES: *Malaya, Indonesia, Borneo and the Philippines.* (Longmans, 1954.)

SCHEBESTA, P.: *Bei den Urwaldzwergen von Malaya.* (Leipzig, 1927.)

SCRIVENOR, J. B.: *The Geology of Malaya.* (1931.)

SLIMMING, JOHN: *Temiar Jungle.* (Murray, 1958.)

Bibliography

STACEY, TOM: *The Hostile Sun.* (Duckworth, 1953.)

STAMP, L. DUDLEY: *Asia.* (Methuen, 1959.)

SWETTENHAM, SIR FRANK: *British Malaya.* (Allen and Unwin, 1948.)

Teach Yourself Chinese. (English Universities Press.)

Teach Yourself Malay. (English Universities Press.)

THOMSON, IAN: *The Rise of Modern Asia.* (Murray, 1957.)
    Changing Patterns in South Asia. (Barrie and Rockliffe, 1961.)

TUCCI, GIUSEPPE: *Nepal: alla Scoperta dei Malla.* (Leonardo da Vinci Editrice, Bari, 1960.)
    Nepal: The Discovery of the Malla. (Allen and Unwin, 1962.)

TWEEDIE, M. W. F.: *Common Malayan Birds.* (Longmans, 1960.)

WAVELL, STEWART: *The Lost World of the East.* (Souvenir Press, 1958.)

WINSTEDT, R. O.: *Malaya and its History.* (1949.)

Novels and Short Stories set in Malaya

AMBLER, ERIC: *Passage of Arms.*

BOULLE, PIERRE: *Sacrilege in Malaya.*

BURGESS, ANTHONY: *Time for a Tiger.*
    The Enemy in the Blanket.
    Beds in the East.

CONRAD, JOSEPH: *The Shadow Line.*

MAUGHAM, W. SOMERSET: *The Force of Circumstance. Neil Macadam. The Yellow Streak. Footprints in the Jungle. The Outstation. The Yellow Streak.*

MCMINNIES, MARY: *The Flying Fox.*

OSARAGI, JIRO: *Homecoming.*

SUYIN, HAN: *And the Rain my Drink.*

Index

Index

Index

Index

Index

Index